Chiapa de Corzo, Mound 17: Comparative Analysis of a Salvage Excavation

Mound 17, Chiapa de Corzo, Mexico, at the time the archaeological salvage project began.

PAPERS

*of the*

NEW WORLD ARCHAEOLOGICAL FOUNDATION

NUMBER EIGHTY

# Chiapa de Corzo, Mound 17:
# Comparative Analysis of a Salvage Excavation

*by*

Thomas A. Lee Jr. and John E. Clark

*with contributions by*

Phillip Walker, Andrew J. McDonald, and Victor Manuel Esponda Jimeno

VOLUME EDITOR

Mary E. Pye

New World Archaeological Foundation
Brigham Young University Press
Provo, Utah
2016

# FOREWORD

This publication reports 10 days of salvage excavations by Thomas A. Lee Jr. at Mound 17 at Chiapa de Corzo in 1969. The 1970s handwritten manuscript which birthed this monograph witnessed four decades of travail, the last of which brought me into the project as an accidental author. A few words are appropriate to explain my promotion from editor to junior author.

I became aware of Tom's Mound 17 excavations in the early 1980s when he let me read his manuscript in conjunction with a study of Preclassic Chiapas burials (Clark 1983), information that we used in our co-authored essay on Preclassic public economies in Chiapas (Clark and Lee 1984, 1990). My next serious encounter with the text was late October 1987, a week after I had been named NWAF director and charged with closing the institution within a year. From then on everything at the NWAF became turmoil and rescue work. Among the high priorities was getting Mound 17 published. I received a typed copy of the manuscript from Tom and recommended on 4 November 1987 a massive restructuring of the text, rewriting, and addition of introductory material. I took the photographs and drawings to the States in 1988 for publication, pending completion of a publishable text. Meanwhile, Tom opted for early retirement in 1988 and began his odyssey of staying involved with Chiapas archaeology by working with local universities and institutions (see Appendix 3). Things were extremely frenetic in both our lives in 1988 and for the ensuing decade. Mound 17 was not high on the list of emergencies that had to be attended to, hence neither Tom nor I advanced the manuscript. Sometime in that interval Tom decided to publish the manuscript in Mexico, so I returned the illustrations to Mexico to his care.

In 2010 I was relieved of NWAF administrative duties and was able to devote more time to working through the piles of unpublished manuscripts left by my NWAF colleagues from the 1987 days. In 2012 I again approached Tom about publishing the Mound 17 report since he had not published it in

Spanish. He gave me a 1998 draft in English, which became the core of this monograph. I told Tom the manuscript needed to be restructured, rewritten, and updated. At the time he wryly observed I had made the same recommendations at least three times in the previous 20 years, with the recommended changes always of a different sort. Tom was more than happy to let me tame this monograph in the manner I saw fit, part of which involved chasing down all of the illustrations, some of which had been dispersed in his personal papers as he used parts of the text and illustrations for different articles (see Cheetham and Lee 2005). After repeated searches I found most original photographic plates, ink drawings, and original field drawings. With Tom's blessing I put the text into its current form, reorganized the illustrations, reconciled cache and burial numbers, worked on stylistic matters, and identified tasks that remained. I left the pending writing assignments with Tom in August of 2012. Two lost drawings were redrawn by Carlos Hoover, but as far as I know Tom did not work on the text. His unexpected passing on 18 February of 2013 left things incomplete.

Tom's death changed the depth of my involvement with the Mound 17 report as well as its content. I had removed Tom's long section on comparative architecture from the final chapter because it was outdated and not germane to the descriptive purposes of the monograph. I thought this material, once upgraded, could be best published separately. Since this is no longer an option, I restored some of this discussion in this monograph and brought it up to date to have Tom's last work on Chiapa de Corzo represented. Because this is the last manuscript we worked on actively together, I have also added aspects to honor Tom's contribution to NWAF work by including in an appendix a bibliography of his work and a short essay by his dear friend and close colleague Victor Manuel Esponda Jimeno.

John E. Clark
18 May 2016

# PREFACE

The purchase of part of the ancient site of Chiapa de Corzo by the Compañía Nestlé, S.A. and the beginning of construction of a new multi-million dollar milk processing plant on the property in mid-February of 1969 led to a series of rapidly organized meetings between representatives of the Nestlé company, the Instituto Nacional de Antropología e Historia (INAH), and the Museo Regional del Estado de Chiapas. The New World Archaeological Foundation (NWAF) served as the latter's technical advisor. Recognizing the importance of this sector of the site of Chiapa de Corzo, all parties agreed that at least a minimal archaeological salvage program needed to be carried out immediately, since the construction schedule was trying to take advantage of the dry season.

Because Mound 17 was, by far, the largest prehistoric structure slated for removal it was decided that it should be salvaged as thoroughly as time would permit. Construction schedules and the imminent beginning of the annual rains meant that only ten days could be allotted to the salvage project. In view of the short time available, twenty laborers were contracted to accomplish the work necessary to recover a sample of the mound and its contents. The Nestlé Company provided the financial support needed to purchase picks and shovels and to pay the workmen. The NWAF, through its Field Director, Gareth W. Lowe, granted me a leave and provided support to conduct the salvage excavations. Jorge Acuña Nuricumbo, NWAF archaeological assistant, helped supervise the excavations. The NWAF also provided space to study and store the artifacts recovered and the time to study them and write up the preliminary reports (Lee 1969a, 1969b) and the first draft of this monograph.

The Compañía Constructora de Chiapas handled all the payroll funds and equipment purchases and agreed to put trucks and heavy earth-moving equipment at our disposal to remove the backdirt from the edges of the archaeological excavations. Excavation began at 6:00 a.m. on February 14, 1969 (just a few days after the meetings with Nestlé and other officials) and ended at 2:00 p.m. nine days later. Although the excavations were not conducted under optimal conditions, the results contribute significantly to our understanding of the ancient history of Chiapa de Corzo and Chiapas.

Thomas A. Lee Jr.
November, 1998

# ACKNOWLEDGMENTS

The successful archaeological salvage of Chiapa de Corzo Mound 17 and its contents can be traced directly to the spirit of collaboration and interest of many parties concerned with protecting part of the cultural heritage of Chiapas – without affecting adversely industrial and economic progress. I dedicate this small report to the institutions and individuals who made the 1969 project possible. The following individuals, most now deceased, provided key support at decisive moments in the planning, excavation, study, and publication of the Mound 17 excavations: from Nestlé, José Represas (General Manager) and Cornalis Van Dam (Administrator, Chiapa de Corzo Plant); from INAH, Dr. Ignacio Bernal (then General Director), architect Ignacio Marquina (then chief of the Departamento de Monumentos Prehispánicos), and Dr. Eduardo Matos Moctezuma (then Assistant Chief); from Departamento de Monumentos Prehispánicos, Armando Duvalier (then Director of the Museo Regional de Chiapas, INAH), Ramiro Jiménez Pozo (then Curator of the Museo Regional de Chiapas, INAH); from Constructora Chiapas, S.A., Flavio Coutiño and Gumaro Camacho Camacho; from NWAF, Howard W. Hunter (then President of the Advisory Board), Joseph T. Bentley (then Treasurer of Advisory Board), and Dr. Gareth W. Lowe (then Field Director).

Several individuals have helped in the preparation of this study and publication. John Clark read the manuscript for general archaeological content and accuracy. Ramiro Jiménez Pozo drew most of the complicated burials in the field, as well as some of the finished burial drawings for this report and all drawings of artifacts published here. Mario Vega took most of the studio photographs and did the darkroom photographic work necessary for this report. The maps, plans, and sections are all the fine ink work of José Nuñez, with a few additions by Elizabeth Ross. I also thank Lawrence Feldman for identifying the shell artifacts based on photos supplied to him.

Thomas A. Lee Jr.
November, 1998

# CONTENTS

APPENDICES

1. THE HUMAN SKELETAL REMAINS FROM MOUND 17 AT CHIAPA DE CORZO

2. MIDDLE PRECLASSIC CEREMONIAL CENTERS IN SOUTHERN CHIAPAS

**FIGURES**

## TABLES

# CHAPTER 1

# INTRODUCTION

This monograph reports the 1969 salvage of Mound 17 at Chiapa de Corzo and describes the caches, burials, and artifacts recovered in the excavations. The mound was bulldozed away to make room for a Nestle factory. The many burials and offerings found in Mound 17 have been critical for understanding the early history of Chiapa de Corzo. The mound was built and used from Middle Preclassic to Protoclassic times.

Our report pursues two objectives. The first half describes the excavations undertaken, offerings, burials, and artifacts, and in this order. The second half summarizes what we know of Chiapa de Corzo for the period represented by the construction and use of Mound 17. In the final chapter we reassess the Middle Preclassic architecture at the site in light of coeval developments in surrounding regions. A comparative analysis of Middle Preclassic burials and offerings is presented elsewhere (Clark 2016), hence, we do not include comparative material here for such things. Likewise, artifact typologies are avoided. We rely on artifact types described by Lee (1969c) and on Bruce Warren's (1978) ceramic typology for Chiapa de Corzo. As a prelude to the descriptive summaries of Mound 17 we provide a brief background on Chiapa de Corzo, site chronology, and Mound 17.

## THE CHIAPA DE CORZO SITE

Bernal Diaz del Castillo (1968, ch. 166:136) records the conquest of Chiapa de Corzo, a city of 20,000 inhabitants, by the Spanish in 1524 (probably a population overestimate, Tim Sullivan, personal communication 2007). There were still 20,000 or more people in the Chiapanec polity four decades after the Conquest (Navarrete 1966:19). The Chiapanecs were late arrivals in Chiapas. Renowned as fierce warriors, the Chiapanecs took the city from its traditional Soke residents.[1] The early history of Chiapa de Corzo concerns Sokes and Mayas rather than Chiapanecs.

Chiapa de Corzo is one of the largest archaeological sites in central Chiapas and the best known (Figure 1). It lies on the right bank of the Grijalva River just a few kilometers upstream from the mouth of the Sumidero Canyon. The Chiapa de Corzo locale corresponds to the broadest and most fertile levee lands along the whole course of this large river (Lowe and Agrinier 1960:1) and during pre-Hispanic times was an ideal place for agriculture as well as for benefitting from trade plied along the river. The site rests on a low plateau just east of the modern city from which it takes it name. At the time of the Spanish Conquest the city was known as *Chiapan*; shortly thereafter it became an administrative city known as *Chiapa de los Indios*. These names were taken from the name of the people, the Chiapanecs, who occupied the city at the time of the Conquest.

The archaeological site of Chiapa de Corzo has over 200 mounds spread over 110 ha, or just over a square kilometer. The highest mounds are about 12 m tall. These are surrounded by lower mounds. Most of these mounds were erected in the Preclassic period. Mound 17 was one of the earliest mounds constructed and was part of the original ceremonial complex at the site.

Chiapa de Corzo was first excavated in 1941 (Berlin 1946), and major excavations were undertaken there by the NWAF from 1955 to 1963 (Lowe and Mason 1965), with some later salvage operations (Glauner, Herman, and Clark in press; González and Cuevas 1998; Lee 1969b; Lowe 1995; Martínez and Lowe in press; Warren 1978), one of which we report here. It

---

[1] We follow the new recommended spelling of language names (Kaufman 1994a, 1994b; Kaufman and Justeson 2007:193) and use "Mije" and "Soke" for the traditional spellings of "Mixe" and "Zoque."

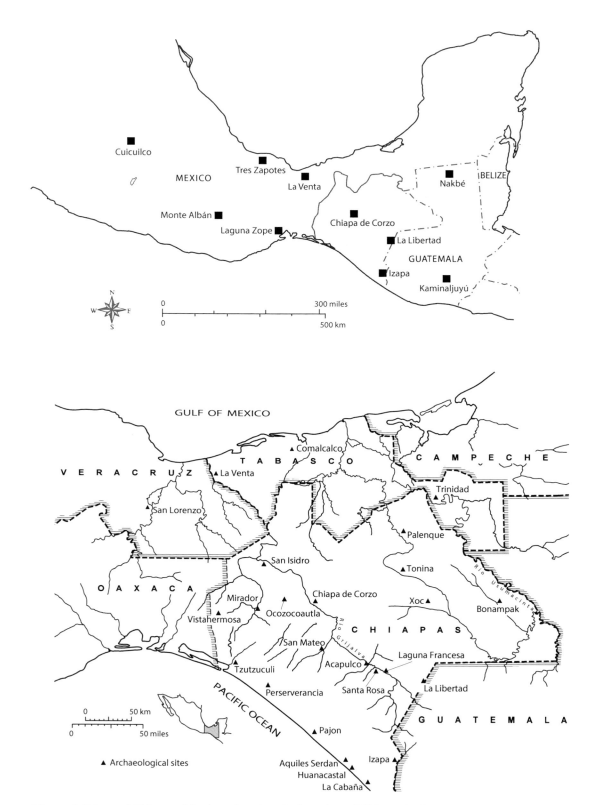

Figure 1. Maps of Chiapas, Mexico, showing the location of Chiapa de Corzo.

was most recently excavated by NWAF and UNAM archaeologists in 2008 and 2010. The major excavations carried out over a 55 year period reveal that Chiapa de Corzo was one of the earliest cities in the Chiapas interior, and it has been continuously occupied until the present day. During the Middle Preclassic, Chiapa de Corzo was one of the largest kingdoms in Chiapas, and it may have become a small state by 100 BC (Clark et al. 2000). The Middle Classic period witnessed a severe decline in population and the near abandonment of the site (Lowe 1962a; Lowe and Mason 1965:226; Sullivan 2009, 2015; Warren 1978:85), with a resurgence in the Late Classic and Postclassic periods. Mound construction on the plateau ceased by Late Classic times, but the site continued to be occupied (Lowe and Agrinier 1960:3). Later occupants (probably the invading Chiapanecs) moved the city to the foot of the plateau, in the area covered by the modern city of Chiapa de Corzo. Consequently, the latest pre-Hispanic occupation of Chiapa de Corzo is poorly known because all the mounds and buildings have been covered over by the modern city (Navarrete 1966).

## CHIAPA DE CORZO CHRONOLOGY

The first full chronology for Chiapas archaeology was based on NWAF excavations at Chiapa de Corzo in the late 1950s (Lowe 1959b, 1960a; Lowe and Mason 1965; Warren 1959, 1961b, 1978). Different phases were based on the delineation of ceramic complexes. These phases and complexes were named in numerical and alphabetical order, as evident in Figure 2, starting with the letter "C" and the Roman numeral "I." Phase names relate to individual regions. The phase sequence for each is tied, when possible, to a generic numerical sequence. For example, the Escalera phase at Chiapa de Corzo is a specific instance of the Chiapa III phase for the state of Chiapas. The Escalon phase at Izapa, the Equipac phase at San Isidro, and the Enub phase at La Libertad are also

regional manifestations of the same "E" phase or the Chiapa III phase. As a general rule, all the phases beginning with the same letter were contemporaneous. For many historical reasons, this logical sequence of alphabetical names is not consistent for the whole state because some investigators did not follow this naming practice, and some phases are not equally manifested in different regions. A greater difficulty is that some of the original phases were subsequently split into two phases, so the resulting names do not fit the original logic of naming phases. Late changes to phases of importance for the current work is that both the Chiapa I and II phases were divided by Gareth Lowe in some of his last work (see Agrinier et al. 2000). In the following discussion we will be concerned with early Chiapa II (II-A) and late Chiapa II (II-B) phases.[2] Another problem is that ceramic complexes older than the Chiapa I period were found and thus precede the numerical scheme (see Agrinier et al. 2000). In following discussion we use the Chiapa de Corzo phase names interchangeably with the generic numbered phases to which they refer.

The chronological spans for all these phases in real time (calibrated radiocarbon years) are still being refined, but the relative sequence of phases qua ceramic complexes is well established for most regions of Chiapas. Relative dating relies principally on analyses of diagnostic pottery and ceramic figurines to determine phases of architectural features, offerings, and burials. Artifacts from Mound 17 indicate that its earliest levels and constructions date to Dili or Chiapa II-A times, meaning the early half of the Middle Preclassic period. Its latest levels and constructions date to the early Protoclassic period, which ended about AD 100. As with other NWAF monographs on Chiapa de Corzo, the data presented in the following chapters are arranged chronologically by sequential phases for each class of information. We distinguish offerings from burials and accord each separate treatment.

---

[2] Bruce Bachand (2013) has proposed revisions to the Chiapa de Corzo sequence. We have not been able to evaluate the merits of his proposal based on the artifacts in question and thus do not use his sequence in this study (JEC).

| Cultural Periods | | Chiapas | Chiapa de Corzo | Middle Grijalva | Upper Grijalva | Soconusco |
|---|---|---|---|---|---|---|
| 1600 AD — | Early Colonial | | Urbina | Santiago | Ux | |
| 1500 AD — | Late Postclassic | | | Quejpomo | Tan | Late Postclassic |
| 1400 AD — | | XII | Tuxtla | | | |
| 1300 AD — | Middle Postclassic | | | | | |
| 1200 AD — | | | | | | |
| 1100 AD — | Early Postclassic | XI | Ruíz | Pecha | Nichim | Remanso |
| 1000 AD — | | | | | | |
| 900 AD — | | X-B | Paredón | | | |
| 800 AD — | Late Classic | | | Mechung | Mix | Peistal |
| 700 AD — | | X-A | Maravillas | | | Metapa |
| 600 AD — | Middle Classic | | | Kundapi | Lek | |
| 500 AD — | | IX | Laguna | | | Loros |
| 400 AD — | Early Classic | | | Juspano | Kau | Kato |
| 300 AD — | | VIII | Jiquipilas | | | Jaritas |
| 200 AD — | | | | | | |
| 100 AD — | Protoclassic | VII | Istmo | Ipsan | Ix | Itstapa |
| 0 — | | VI | Horcones | | Hun | Hato |
| 100 BC — | | | | | | |
| 200 BC — | Late Preclassic | V | Guanacaste | Guañoma | Guajil | Guillén |
| 300 BC — | | | | | | |
| 400 BC — | | IV | Francesa | Felisa | Foko | Frontera |
| 500 BC — | | | | | | |
| 600 BC — | Middle Preclassic | III | Escalera | Equipac | Enub | Escalón |
| 700 BC — | | | | | | |
| 800 BC — | | II-B | Dzemba | Dzewa | Dyosan | Duende |
| 900 BC — | | II-A | Dili | Dombi | Chacte | Conchas |
| 1000 BC — | | | | | | |
| 1100 BC — | | I-B | Jobo | B Cacahuanó A | Jocote | Jocotal |
| 1200 BC — | | | | | | |
| 1300 BC — | | I-A | Cotorra | | Chacaj | Cuadros |
| 1400 BC — | Early Preclassic | | Ocote | Bombaná | Ojalá | Cherla |
| 1500 BC — | | | | | | Ocós |
| 1600 BC — | | | | | Lato | Locona |
| 1700 BC — | | | | | | |
| 1800 BC — | | | | | | Barra |
| 1900 BC — | | | | | | |

Figure 2. Middle Preclassic chronology chart for regions in the greater Isthmian area.

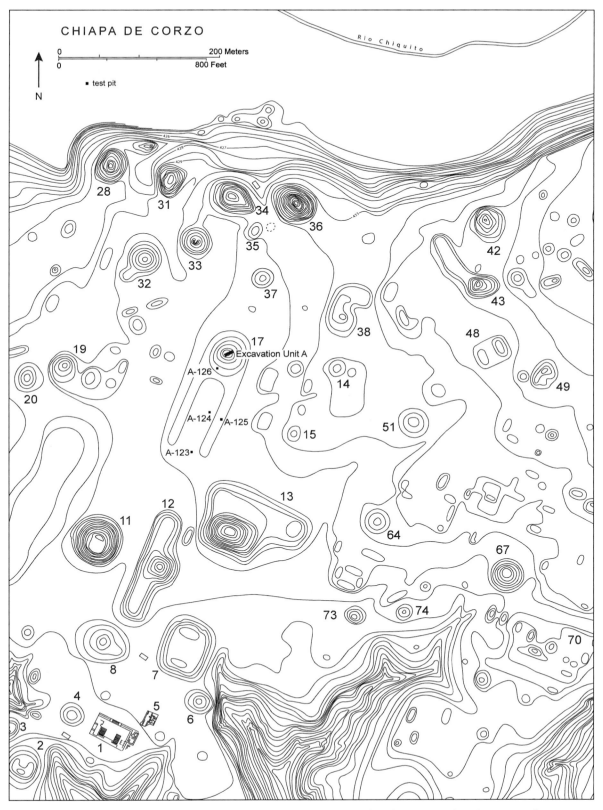

Figure 3. Map of Chiapa de Corzo showing the site before destruction for new road and construction of the Nestle factory. Test pit locations from Lowe 1962b:53, fig. 31.

## MOUND 17

The rather modest pyramid known as Mound 17 had two long, parallel, low wing platforms that extended from it to the southwest. As described in following chapters, Mound 17 contained a long and interesting sequence of human construction and material remains. It was used for at least eight centuries and was part of the original ceremonial complex at the site, along with Mounds 7, 11, 12, 13, and 36. Mound 17 lay almost midway between two mound-plaza complexes (see Figure 3).

Mound 17 was equidistant on an alignment with the center of Mound 36 to the north and the western edge of the Mound 12 basal platform to the south. Another axial alignment that may have been of significance is that comprising Mound 34 to the north, Mound 17 in the middle, and Mound 13 to the south. This alignment is almost true north-south. As apparent, Mound 17 was a central platform in the heart of ancient Chiapa de Corzo. It was probably part of the original spatial scheme upon which the ceremonial center was predicated.

As reported in the next chapter, three separate units of excavation were undertaken in the winter of 1969 into Mound 17. Four phases of human occupation and construction were recognized in the mound itself. Mound construction probably began in the Dzemba or Chiapa II-B phase (850-750 BC); there was a meter of Chiapa II fill below the earliest Escalera phase building. By the Escalera or Chiapa III phase (750-500 BC) Mound 17 was almost four meters high and had a floor plastered with fine clay on top. This early pyramid represents over half of the total height Mound 17 attained in its history.

The early map of the Chiapa de Corzo site (Figure 3; also, Lowe and Agrinier 1960: fig. 67) represents Mound 17 as 7 m tall and 54 by 60 m at the base, with two long extensions to the south just over 100 m long. The parallel wings were about 13 m wide and 1.25 m high; they were 30 m apart. Each wing required about 390 cubic meters of fill to construct. The 4 m high Escalera phase pyramid contained about 7,700 cubic meters of fill, some of which dated to Chiapa II-B times. These data provide a rough estimate of 8,480 cubic meters of fill for the greater Escalera phase building. The first Escalera phase construction under Mound 17 clearly represented a significant labor investment, all of which casts doubt on our previous proposal (Clark and Lee 1984) that construction of monumental architecture at Chiapa de Corzo began in Escalera times. Excavations undertaken at Chiapa de Corzo long after the salvage operations at Mound 17 confirm that some buildings' cores were constructed in Chiapa II-B times (Bachand and Lowe 2011).

Mound 17 in the Escalera phase was part of the monumental civic-ceremonial center, along with Mounds 7 (Lowe and Agrinier 1960:9), 11 (Bachand and Lowe 2011), 12 (Mason 1960a), and 13 (Hicks and Rozaire 1960; Mason 1960b). Within each of these mounds something on the order of half their height was achieved by Escalera times. It seems remarkable that in less than 200 hundred years so much building activity took place at Chiapa de Corzo. It was only doubled, in terms of mound volumes, in the following 600 years of construction, remodeling, and maintenance of these platforms.

A question which remains for Chiapa de Corzo is, where is the ballcourt? It is difficult to imagine a major site without at least one ballcourt. There is no obvious ballcourt at Chiapa de Corzo. One explanation for the pair of long, low platforms that projected south from Mound 17 is that they may have been the sides of an open-ended ballcourt (Figure 3). If so, the court would have been unusually long and wide. If Mound 17 were the northern backstop to a ballcourt, this court could have accommodated scores of players. The wings connected to Mound 17 look similar to a pair of long mounds at La Venta, Tabasco (see Chapter 6). The La Venta parallel mounds are taller than those at Chiapa de Corzo. If these constructions were not ballcourts, they certainly were esplanades. Spectators standing on these long mounds could have watched processionals to the associated platforms and their summit buildings.

# CHAPTER 2

# EXCAVATIONS AND ARCHITECTURE

This chapter is devoted to the excavations undertaken at Mound 17 and evidence of structures within the mound. Following NWAF conventions for describing architecture, superimposed structures in mounds are designated by capital letters corresponding to their phase (e.g., F for Francesa) and by sequential numbers for multiple structures of a single phase.

Substages, discernible modification or enlargement phases of particular stages are identified with appended arabic numbers, and superimposed supplementary and building platforms are identified by the addition of lower-case letters. Modified segments of the latter platforms are again indicated by the addition of arabic numerals. The arabic numeral indentifiers of substages are applied in inverse order to that of their construction, i.e., in order of their discovery. As an example, an architectural discovery labeled 1-H9 indicates Mound 1, Stage H [Horcones] primary platform in its ninth-from-final modified form. (Lowe and Agrinier l960:4, 6)

Mound 17 and its area were tested by four test pits in the early NWAF explorations. Salvage excavations involved three separate trenches designated as A, B, and C (Figures 3-5). These excavations are described in this order. To salvage Mound 17, excavations were begun in two different areas. Much of the lower edges of the mound's eastern, southern, and western edges had been removed by a bulldozer before salvage began (Frontispiece). One sub-structure (Structure 17-H1) was already exposed, and men were placed to clean part of the remaining stairway and the front of this structure (Figure 5). A second group of workmen began to excavate in a grid-controlled area, four meters wide by ten meters long on top of the mound (Excavation Unit A). Later, a two meter extension was made on the northeast end of this excavation to aid in access for the workmen and to facilitate removal of backdirt.

After the facade of Structure 17-H1 had been cleaned and part of its stairway was visible, a second trench, 3 m wide and 18 m long (Excavation Unit B), was laid out from the southwest corner of Excavation Unit A down the slope to the sterile surface at the foot of the mound left by the earth removal phase of the factory site preparation. This excavation unit was later expanded beyond its original rectangular limits as needed to uncover evidence of architectural features. Excavation Unit C was made to clear the stepped facade of sub-structure 17-F1 that had been exposed in profile on the east corner of the mound by the bulldozer.

## PREVIOUS EXCAVATIONS IN MOUND 17

Only one 2 by 2 m test excavation (A-126) had been made in Mound 17 proper prior to the salvage operations reported here (Figure 3; also, Lowe 1962b: fig. 31). In 1959, Donald Brockington excavated this small test pit in the southwestern edge of Mound 17 and located a Horcones phase construction and two caches of ceramic vessels dating to the same phase (Lowe 1962b:54-56). The upper fill from the test pit contained both Istmo and Jiquipilas phase sherds dating to the Protoclassic and Early Classic periods, respectively.

Pit 126 was intended to gather sherds from immediately in front of Mound 17, thus to gather information about the mound without touching it. However, the pit hit what must be the front wall of a small platform projecting southward from the mound. It seems obvious that there was a small platform in front of the mound and that one offering was put immediately in front of the platform under its southwest corner. Another offering was put in front of the platform. The two offerings are not

Figure 4. Section of the Chiapa de Corzo site affected by Nestlé, S.A. and the location of Mound 17.

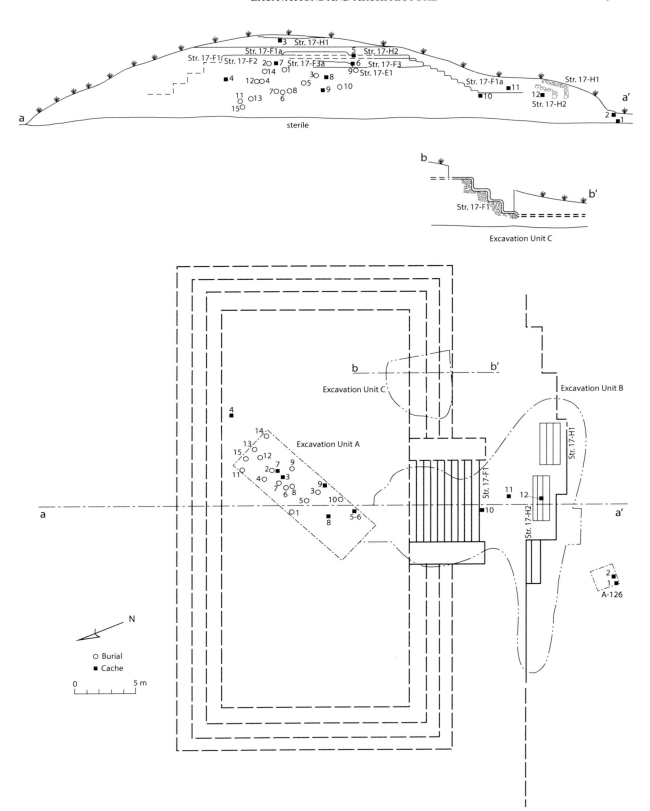

Figure 5. Reconstructed plan and sections of Mound 17, Chiapa de Corzo, showing the locations of excavation units, caches, burials, and architectural features.

Figure 6. Work in progress in Excavation Unit A; men working, with bulldozer in the background.

connected in any way, other than the fact that both are of the same period, Chiapa VI ... the depth of Offering 2 was much shallower than that of Offering 1. Gareth Lowe told me that this is the first time that an offering of Period VI has been found away from the vicinity of Mounds 1 and 5. The poorness of the two offerings is apparent. Lowe believes that the large offering in Mound 5 is of late Period VI [see Lowe 1962b]. These offerings from Pit 126 may be from a slightly earlier time of the same Period VI. (Brockington n.d.)

Three other 2 by 2 m test excavations were dug in or near Mound 17 (Figure 3). Test Pit 125 was on the easternmost of the two, long low parallel platforms which projected south from the main mound (Lowe 1962b:53, fig. 53). The other two test excavations (123 and 124) were placed between these parallel platforms or "wings" (Figure 3). Test Pit 125 on the east wing encountered an Escalera phase burial. Dili phase artifacts were found under the burial and just above the sterile caliche layer. The Escalera phase deposit overlying the burial reached within 15 cm of the modern surface. The upper 15 cm of the deposit of the east wing contained both Francesa and Guanacaste phase ceramics.

The evidence provided by excavation A-125 suggests that a buried Escalera-phase platform accounts for the eastern wing of Mound 17. Sherd content was very low and a dense rock fill characterized the structural core overlying the Dili-phase occupational deposit. This rock fill certainly does not represent a natural accumulation of household refuse. (Lowe 1962b:56)

The eastern platform appears, then, to have been an Escalera phase construction. The western platform was never tested, but it most likely dated to the Escalera phase also. These two long mounds had already been destroyed before the 1969 salvage excavations began.

The two test pits dug in the court between the wings encountered sherds of the same era.

Test Pit 123 was excavated in seven levels to a depth of 1.05 m. Levels 5-7 had sherds from the Chiapa II and III phases. Some Chiapa IV and Colonial sherds were found in Level 4 and higher (Brockington n.d.). "It is apparent that considerable filling in has taken place in the vicinity of the Mound 17 East Wing. Its locale must originally have been a hollow, since pit A-124, dug only 20 m. to the west, encountered the sterile caliche bedrock at a depth of only 60 cm. below the surface. The A-124 excavation produced exclusively Dili and Escalera-phase sherds" (Lowe 1962b:56). Test Pit 124 reached a depth of 75 cm and five levels. Few sherds were found. Those in the three lowest levels date to Chiapa II times, and most of those in Level 2 were also of this phase (Brockington n.d.). These data indicate that the surface between the wings of Mound 17 dated to Chiapa II times. A Chiapas II level was also found underneath the eastern wing and beneath Mound 17.

## SALVAGE EXCAVATIONS

### Excavation Unit A

This 4 by 10 m trench was laid out on top of Mound 17, with the long axis oriented roughly east-west (Figure 6). The trench was subdivided into ten 2 by 2 m sections, numbered 1 through 10 from west to east (Figure 7). Excavation in each square proceeded by 20 cm levels.

After the trench had reached a depth of three meters, the northeast end was extended outward another two meters. This additional excavation removed the one meter thick balk unit of mound fill that had separated the trench excavation from the bulldozer cut, thereby allowing us to place the trench backdirt in the path of a bulldozer and trucks for easy removal from the mound (Figure 6). This area of mound fill was lowered progressively as the floor of the trench excavation was lowered to allow easy access for workmen and the removal of backdirt. In the very bottom of this extension of Excavation Unit A, we discovered an extremely important burial crypt (Burial 17-11). This excavation also exposed architectural features, caches, and other burials, as described below (Figures 8-9).

### Excavation Unit B

Excavation Unit B was staked out once the front stairway (Structure 17-F1) of Mound 17 had been located, cleared, and mapped. The excavation began as a trench 3 m wide and 18 meters long (Figures 5, 10 and 11). After this trench reached a meter in depth it was expanded outward along both sides of the trench in order to expose the northwest balustrade and later architectural units near the southern end of the trench (Structures 17-H1 and 17-H2) and to explore the possibility of interred caches in front of and under the stairway. Three caches (17-10, 17-11, 17-12) were located almost centered on top of the stairway's axis. These offerings were probably dedicatory to the three different architectural additions discovered in this area of the excavation. When finished, Excavation B measured 25 m across at its widest part, near the front of the mound, and was 18 m long and 4.5 m deep.

### Excavation Unit C

Some fifteen meters east of Excavation Unit B a bulldozer cut exposed a cross-section of Structure 17-F1 (Figures 5, 12, and 13). This sub-structure, formed of a thick whitish-gray layer of plaster over crude boulder masonry, contrasted greatly with the darker mound fill above and below it. To investigate this plastered sub-structure, an area approximately six meters square was cleaned off in order to photograph and map it. No caches, burials, features, or special artifacts were located in these architectural excavations.

## MOUND 17 ARCHITECTURE

Three major phases of construction were identified in Mound 17. The earliest clear building stage found dates to the Middle Preclassic Escalera phase (Figure 2). Later major additions, the most significant series of construction stages in the mound's history, date to the Francesa phase. Either there was no construction during the following Guanacaste phase or it was of minor importance at this mound since no architectural additions were found that could be equated with this time

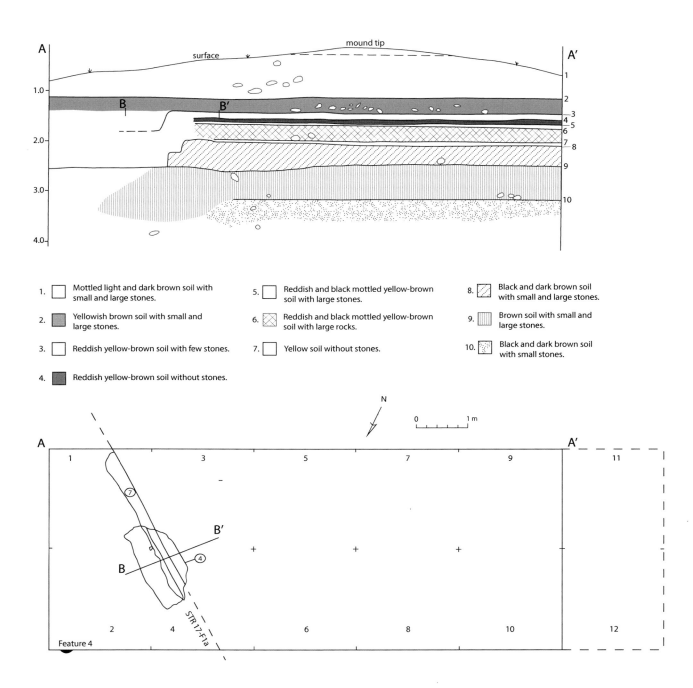

1. Mottled light and dark brown soil with small and large stones.

2. Yellowish brown soil with small and large stones.

3. Reddish yellow-brown soil with few stones.

4. Reddish yellow-brown soil without stones.

5. Reddish and black mottled yellow-brown soil with large stones.

6. Reddish and black mottled yellow-brown soil with large rocks.

7. Yellow soil without stones.

8. Black and dark brown soil with small and large stones.

9. Brown soil with small and large stones.

10. Black and dark brown soil with small stones.

Figure 7. Plan and profile of Excavation Unit A, Sections 1-10.

Figure 8. Burial 17-6.

period. The third and final building units or structures found in the mound are of the Horcones phase and consist of relatively thin veneers of construction that covered the entire mound.

### Dili and Dzemba Phases

No architectural features of Mound 17 can be assigned with certainty to these phases.[3] Nevertheless, the slightly more than one meter of cultural deposits above sterile caliche, in which the earliest burial (Burial 17-15) was deposited, is suggestive of a construction unit earlier than the Escalera phase, Structure 17-E1 (Figure 5). Whether this hypothetical structure dated to the early Escalera phase or to the preceding Dzemba phase was not determined. The dense rock fill found in Pit 125 in the eastern wing sounds similar to the stone rubble fill in the Chiapa II-B (Dzemba) phase mound found under Mound 11 (Bachand 2013).

[3] At the time of the excavation the Chiapa II phase had not been sub-divided into II-A (Dili) and II-B (Dzemba), hence all observations of artifacts of this era were described as Dili phase. It is likely that any construction for the Chiapa II phase actually dates to II-B times, and we have made this adjustment in the following discussion.

Figure 9. Cache 1 (17-3).

Sherd evidence below Mound 17 indicated that it rested on a fairly dense occupation area from the Cotorra and Dili phases. Below this layer was found a layer of sterile black clay, as if this section of the site had earlier been a low lying swamp or pond.

### Escalera Phase

A series of three floors (Str. 17-E1, E1a, and E1b) and the back corner of another structure (Str. 17-E2, not shown in Figure 5) are the only evidence of architecture for this phase in Mound 17. The superimposed floors that served as the upper surface of Structure 17-El (Figure 5) were 3.7 meters above sterile and represented more than half of the total height of the mound in its final form. The floor was made of a fine tan clay plaster 2-3 cm thick. It entirely covered a black and brown earthen platform core that had a few small water-worn pebbles scattered throughout its fill.

Brockington's excavation (A-125) in the east wing of Mound 17 demonstrated that the

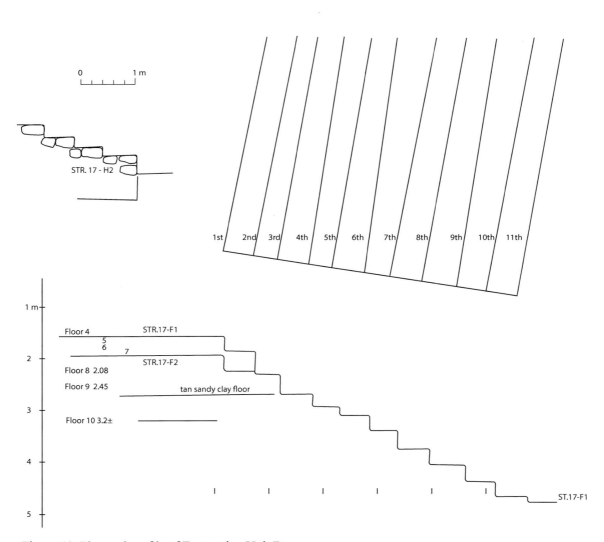

Figure 10. Plan and profile of Excavation Unit B.

basic form, orientation, and related volume relationship between the main platform and its projecting "wings" was established by the Escalera phase (Lowe 1962b:56) and maintained for over 800 years throughout many periodic building additions.

The three burials in Mound 17 identified with the Escalera phase, (17-5, 17-11, and 17-15) lie well below the upper level of the Escalera platform. Burial 17-5, the highest of the three, was only a meter below the level of the floor. None of these burials, however, was covered by preserved floor representing Structure 17-E1 and, therefore, they were not stratigraphically "sealed" by Escalera architecture. Nonetheless,

accompanying burial goods established their date to this phase.

**Francesa Phase**

Less than 50 cm above the floor of Structure 17-E1 was found the surface of the earliest of three Francesa phase buildings. This building, Structure 17-F3, was made of brown earth and had both large and small stones as aggregate in its fill. The thin floor capping this building unit was made of a tan clay and was well finished on its upper surface. One burial (17-9) was covered over by the floor of Structure 17-F3 but above the floor of Structure 17-E1.

Figure 11. Men uncovering Structure 17-F1 stairway. Note bulldozer proximity to Excavation Unit B.

Figure 12. Excavation Unit C, Mound 17. Note three-stepped terrace body of Structure 17-F1.

Figure 13. Structure 17-F1 in cross-section.

An addition, made perhaps immediately after Structure 17-F3, was a broad, low platform or temple base labeled Structure 17-F3a. This structural element was 40 cm thick, including a 10 cm layer of tan clay capped, in turn, by another 2 cm thick layer of tan clay plaster that covered the entire structure. The platform had two 20 cm high steps on the south edge of the mound, suggesting that Structures 17-F3 and 17-F3a had the same orientation and perhaps the same shape as the later and more complete Structure 17-F1 (Figure 5). All Francesa burials, including one intrusive Guanacaste burial, were found below the finished surface of Structure 17-F3a. All but three of the caches found in the center of the mound were also found below this level. Only one of these three caches dates to the Francesa phase (Cache 17-6), and it was in close vertical association with the building unit just mentioned. The other two caches (17-3 and 17-5) were higher up in subsequent building units and date to the Horcones phase.

Structure 17-F2 was an enlargement of Structure 17-F3a that completely enveloped the earlier structure and added about 30 cm to its height. The matrix of this building unit consisted of bright reddish and black-colored earth, with large stones sparsely intermixed. The floor that encased this unit consisted of a 2 cm thick layer of fine tan clay, which overlay a 10 cm thick layer of dark brown clay. Directly above these two layers was a 12 cm thick, well-prepared floor made of reddish clay and black earth, with occasional large stones within it. Immediately above this was a second floor of reddish ocher-colored earth, about the same thickness as the previous layer, but without stones. These two thin floors represent minor refloorings or refurbishings of the Structure 17-F2 building. The shape, volume, and placement of the southern stairway, which was undoubtedly the main facade of Mound 17 during the Structure 17-F2 stage of development, was the same as for Structure 17-F1.

Structure 17-F2 was one of the best preserved sub-structures of Mound 17 and also the best known Francesa building from Chiapa de Corzo. In plan it was shaped like a large rectangle, 22 m wide at the base by 41 m long, with three stepped-terrace walls or bodies. The terraces were each one meter high and were covered with a 20 cm thick, roughly finished, white lime plaster. This plaster covered masonry walls made of roughly dressed limestone rocks laid up in a lime mortar, similar to the plaster used on the terrace walls. All together the terrace walls formed, in profile, a clear, thick whitish layer that contrasted greatly with the surrounding mound fill, so this construction layer was easy to follow and expose. The same kind of building construction was found at Mound 7 at Chiapa de Corzo (Lowe and Agrinier 1960:10) and, not far away to the west, at the coeval site of San Agustín (Navarrete 1959).

Access to the top of Structure 17-F2 was provided by a broad southern stairway, at least 6.5 m wide, flanked on both sides by low, broad balustrades (1.9 m wide). These balustrades were only 30 cm higher than the steps. Individual steps of the stairway averaged 20 cm high with 40 cm long treads. The entire stairway was covered with a thin layer of the same grayish white plaster that covered the terrace walls. The stairway surface, however, was much smoother than those of the terrace walls. All the edges and corners of the steps and the balustrades were rounded off, leaving a smooth looking finish with little angularity, other than the stairway's basic shape.

The two uppermost steps of the southern stairway access to the top of Structure 17-F2 were overlain by the two highest steps of a later addition, Structure 17-F1. From this point on the two structures merged downslope using the same lower nine steps to complete their stairways. This addition slightly elevated the height of Structure 17-F1 and also lengthened it a bit, but left unchanged its original width.

The southern stairway of Structure 17-F1 is the only access known for this structure (Figure 11). Mound 17 may have had other stairways, but the leveling operation by bulldozer prior to our salvage operation had removed all other edges of the mound except in the area of the southern stairway. The additions made to the Structure 17-F2 platform to produce Structure 17-F1 consisted in raising the level of the original platform some 30 cms, adding two more steps to the stairway (which covered the top two steps of the same stairway of Structure F2), and building a small, low secondary platform for a superstructure in the middle of the platform. The superstructure's secondary platform, labeled Structure 17-F1a in Figure 5, was 5.5 m wide, 30 cm high and probably rectangular in plan. The length of this superstructure is unknown. It was made of a reddish ocher-colored earth fill with a few rock inclusions. The floor which sealed this building addition was 10 cm thick and capped with a 3-4 cm layer of very smooth white stucco.

### Guanacaste Phase

None of the identified architectural remains found in Mound 17 date to this phase.

### Horcones Phase

The earliest Horcones construction, Structure 17-H2, raised the height of the Francesa structure by 30 cm and extended the mound by 6.5 m in front of the stairway. The lime plaster floor of this building was 5 cm thick. Although badly preserved and uneven, we traced the floor 16.5 m across the top of Mound 17 in one direction. The floor probably extended out in all directions for about the same distance. The nature of the floor suggests that the top of Structure 17-H2 was unencumbered with permanent superstructures such as temples or altars. There was no evidence on the floor of masonry footings or postholes of superstructures. If a superstructure was present, it was not placed on the center of the platform – an uncommon arrangement at Chiapa de Corzo, except when there were two or more superstructures. Symmetry was the architectural norm at Chiapa de Corzo in all periods. When more than one superstructure was present on top of a mound at Chiapa de Corzo they were spaced around the edge of the platform, leaving the center free and unencumbered. This is precisely the area of Structure H2 we originally found in our salvage excavations. Therefore, the negative evidence for superstructures is suggestive but not conclusive.

The number and nature of the exterior retaining walls for Structure 17-H2 are unknown. A fragment of the south stairway, the only one known in this building phase, consisted of four steps of about 25 cm in height and in tread length, each made of a single stone slab riser. The lowest step had two courses of stones as the step riser. One stone may have extended below the plaza surface with the other extending above it, thus creating a step the same height as the other stairway steps. This thick riser also suggests that it was the stairway foundation and, consequently, the beginning of the stairway and the mound.

The final building increment in Mound 17 for which there was architectural evidence, Structure 17-H1, was an exterior basal terrace wall 1.1 m high that extended about 2 m in front of Structure 17-H2. Structure 17-H1 also added 40 to 60 cm to the mound height over the stairway of Structure 17-H2 and 80 cm to the total height on top of the mound in the center. The basal terrace platform wall was 35 cm thick and composed of dressed limestone laid up in a limey clay mortar. It was thinly plastered over with smooth lime stucco.

The Structure 17-H1 central facade projected out from the basic rectangular outline of the structure on the south side in three stages, with a reduction in the length of the facade with each advancing projection. The first projection was 1.2 m long and had a 4.7 m long frontal surface. This first facade projection had a two-terrace profile. Where the first step of this projection abutted against the basal terrace platform wall it was 50 cm below the top of the wall. The first step of this first projection was 50 cm long or deep and then it dropped down to the second terrace which was 75 cm long, which in turn reached the ground level in 50 cm (Figure 5). The second facade projection moved out from the first 2.4 m and had a 4 m long frontal surface. The third addition which finished the facade projected out 1 m and was 6.4 m wide. The second and third facade projections

maintained the same level as the basal terrace wall of the platform.

The remains of what may have been a low, three step stairway were joined to the third facade projection wall by a thin coat of lime plaster. The terrace wall was slightly over 1 m high at this point, and as no other access was found to reach the steps in the vicinity, it is possible that the three-stepped element identified as a possible stairway was, instead, an architectural embellishment. The proximity of this unit, perpendicular to the upper edge of the southernmost projecting platform body, would seem to disqualify it as an architectural adornment since there would not have been enough space to turn the corner to run parallel to the east face of the projecting stages, if it continued around the platform on other sides as could be expected. Since Structure 17-H1 was not the final construction stage in Mound 17, it is possible that later building activity destroyed the lower steps of this postulated stairway.

The building feature reported by Gareth Lowe (1962b:54-56, fig. 33) as Structure 17-H would seem to be related to Structure 17-H1. It appears to have been a low, stepped basal flange at the bottom of the main platform; it was only about two meters above the sterile caliche layer, while the lowest extension of Structure 17-H1 is over three meters above the same level.

## Istmo Phase

Overlying Structure 17-H1 was another 30 cm of fill, undoubtedly the remains of later construction units made on Mound 17 for which there is no other evidence. No architectural elements, burials, or offerings were found that related to this mixed fill. Lacking architecture, burials, or cache offerings we cannot conclusively date this final building stage. We think it may date to the following Istmo phase, the period of greatest construction activity at Chiapa de Corzo. No potsherds in this fill date later than those of the Istmo complex. The lack of architectural activity at Mound 17 after the Istmo phase perhaps indicates that the focus of community building activity had shifted to other parts of the site.

## CHIAPA DE CORZO ARCHITECTURE

A primary goal of all NWAF work at Chiapa de Corzo was to determine the age and uses of its numerous buildings and platforms. Correlation of individual building histories allows one to trace the growth and development of Chiapa de Corzo as a ceremonial center, a topic addressed in Chapter 6. Here, we focus on technical aspects of construction – the materials and techniques used through time in platform and building construction. The salvage excavations in Mound 17 and, most recently, excavations in Mound 11 (Bachand and Lowe 2011) add to the knowledge of building techniques and histories for the site, going back to Chiapa II times. Over the course of ten centuries at Chiapa de Corzo there were significant changes in materials and techniques used in constructing buildings and platforms, with an evolution from dirt and clay pyramids to buildings faced with cut stone covered with painted plaster (Lowe 1959:11-15). The best, most complete, and earliest construction history is available for Mound 11 located southeast of Mound 17. Mound 11 is the earliest attested pyramid known for the site (Bachand 2013).

### Dili and Dzemba Phases

Traces of the earliest buildings and platforms at Chiapa de Corzo have been found just above sterile soil in some deep excavations in the south plaza and through some pyramids. As described, a stratum of fill or midden dating to Dzemba (Chiapa II-B) times underlay Mound 17 and could have been a layer from a small platform rather than being just a thick midden. Chiapa II phase fill also was found under the eastern wing of Mound 17 and near the surface of the court or procession alley between the mound's two long southern extensions. We lack construction details. Counter to our previously published opinion (Clark and Lee 1984:265), we suspect that the earliest structure in Mound 17 may have been built in Chiapa II rather than Chiapa III times. Fill for such a platform would have been earth mixed with Chiapa II domestic midden, thus the platform would have dated toward the end of the phase. Of course, Chiapa II midden may have been scooped up in Escalera times to make the first platform. For Chiapa II constructions of which we are certain, midden material was not used as mound fill.[4] Rather, a black, sticky, oderiferous swamp clay was used as the preferred material. The excavators describe the clay as smelling like petroleum, and this after more about 3000 years in its transplanted construction context (Bachand 2013:20). The color of this clay, or its known watery origins, may have been an important aspect of the construction. Platforms built over swamp muck may have symbolized mounds or mountains arising from a watery underworld, as known for later Mesoamerica (e.g., *altepetl* or "water-mountain") (see Clark and Colman 2012).

Short vertical walls of stone slabs mortared with sticky black clay were built in Chiapa II times. These were assigned to the Dili phase which has since been subdivided into two phases, II-A and II-B. Some of these constructions likely date to Chiapa II-A or Dili times, and others to Chiapa II-B or Dzemba times. They have been found just north of Mound 1 (Excavations 83 and 121) and just southeast of Mound 36 (Excavation 128-129) (Lowe 1962b: figs. 21 and 31; Lowe and Agrinier 1960:15). The earliest mound at the site dates to this time. A Chiapa II-B phase pyramid 4 m tall was found as the core structure of Mound 11 (Bachand and Lowe 2011:19). It was constructed over a core of stone rubble and thick black clay. This excavation has not yet been described in detail, but the profile of the excavations shows a counter-intuitive situation. The lowest level of the mound and the earliest construction (Chiapa II-B) was of stone rubble fill; later constructions were of earth and clay with fine clay floors. Vertical stone steps covered with clay date to Dzemba and Escalera times and gave way to clay steps. The earliest use of stucco may date to Escalera times, but this is not clear. The Chiapa III and IV phase manifestations of Mound 11 appear to have been largely constructed of earth

---

[4] The clearest Dili constructions (Chiapa II-A) are those which incorporated black clay. It is not clear from excavations whether earth fill was used as common fill behind walls in constructing platforms, such as the one identified under Mound 36.

and clay, with fine clay veneers. The pyramid was terraced.

Mound 36, the northernmost tall mound at the site (Lowe 1962b:57-59), rests on a low, broad platform built in Chiapa II times. The pyramid on this platform reached its final 9 m height by 450 BC (Chiapa IV) and was built over an earlier pyramid dating to 700 BC (Chiapa III). This platform was oriented 28 degrees east of true north, an orientation followed by later buildings at the site (Sullivan 2009). Excavations through the summit of Mound 36 did not reach sterile layers, so it was not determined whether there is an even earlier platform covered in the interior of the mound (Lowe 1962b:58). The tallest mounds at Chiapa de Corzo achieved their final heights in Francesa times. The platform under Mound 36 dates to the Chiapa II phase, probably near the end of the phase now designated as Chiapa II-B, and shares the style of "Olmec" decorative stone work described for Chalcatzingo and Teopantecuanitlan in the Mexican Highlands (see Grove 1984, 1989:143; Martínez Donjuán 1994). At Chiapa de Corzo, horizontal sandstone slabs set in black clay mortar bracket a double row of river cobbles (Lowe 1962b:57-59, fig. 37, Plate 29h). On the south side of Mound 36, "immediately below the surface there are constructed walls made with large stone slabs up to a meter long, with other rows of horizontal slabs. Below the northern side of Mound 36 there are large terraces made of enormous stones, where we find Cotorra-phase sherds [Chiapa I-A] in the fill" (Lowe 1991:115, translation JEC). The practice of making designs in walls by alternating horizontal and vertical stone slabs with round cobble insets mimics the more elaborate stone facings known from early La Venta in which squared serpentine blocks and basalt slabs were placed in alternating horizontal and vertical rows which also alternated with layers of clay and adobes to produce a mosaic effect (see Drucker et al. 1959:Plates 7, 10-13).

Other stone walls dating to Chiapa II times have been found at Chiapa de Corzo in the lowest levels of Trench 121 in the plaza north of Mound 1 and in Excavation 83, just north of Mound 1 (Lowe and Agrinier 1960: 14 and 15, fig. 3). These appear to be normal walls for buildings made of river cobbles and show no evidence of designs. They do not appear to have been retention walls for cellular construction of platforms. The hard, black clay used in construction of the walls came from swampy soils at the site. Remnants of Chiapa II phase walls (probably Dili) have been found over the complete north-south extension of the final site, therefore Chiapa de Corzo was an extensive site by this time. The earliest platforms of its monumental center were also started at this time and constituted what Clark and Richard Hansen (2001) called the Middle Formative Chiapas (MFC) pattern (see Chapter 6).

The early mound complex at Chiapa de Corzo dates to Chiapa II-B times and likely comprised Mounds 11, 12, 13, 22, 36, and maybe 17. Mound 36, the northernmost pyramid, dates to Chiapa II through IV times. The southernmost mounds of the early complex, Mounds 11 and 12, constitute an E-Group. At the time Chiapa de Corzo was excavated in the 1960s, Mound 11 supported a municipal water tank and could not be excavated, but investigations in its flanking, complementary structure, Mound 12, uncovered a 3.5 m high platform that dates no later than to Chiapa III times (Mason 1960a:2-3). The length of this early structure has not been determined. Explorations in Mound 11 in 2010 went from the summit all the way through the mound down to bedrock and found 20 construction episodes. The earliest platform was 4 m high and was built during the Chiapa II-B phase (Bachand 2013). The large offering pits found on the eastern edge of Mound 11 are said to date to about 750 BC (Bachand 2013; Bachand and Lowe 2011:81). The latest construction layers of this mound date to Chiapa IV times, the main building phase for pyramids at Chiapa de Corzo.

### Escalera Phase

The dating of the core mounds at Chiapa de Corzo is more secure for the following Escalera or Chiapa III phase. Mound 17 was constructed by the beginning of this phase, and probably earlier (Lee 1969b). It was built in the middle of the plaza as a broad low platform with two 100 m long, parallel low platforms extending southward from it (Lowe 1962b:56). These

1.25 m high wings of Mound 17 may have been an early ballcourt. They were constructed with early midden (Chiapa II) and earth. These low, parallel mounds were just north and west of the broad platform at Mound 13. This latter structure has not been extensively explored so its beginning construction date has not been ascertained. One of the earlier buildings in Mound 13, dating to 700 BC, was a stepped earthen platform 6.2 m high (Lowe and Mason 1965:212). An even earlier platform was discovered inside it (Hicks and Rozaire 1960:5).

Nothing definitive is known of the size, shape, or profile of the exterior terrace walls of the Structure 17-E1 platform. But earthen platforms dating to Escalera times were contained within Mounds 7 (Lowe and Agrinier 1960:9), 12 (Mason 1960b), and 13 (Mason 1960a; Hicks and Rozaire 1960). The Escalera phase platform in Mound 13 "was a stepped earth platform, surfaced with smoothed mud or adobe plaster, of a yellowish color" (Hicks and Rozaire 1960:5). These three mounds are the principal public platforms that formed the formal civic-ceremonial precinct core at Chiapa de Corzo. Half or more of the cores of these three mounds is made up of construction dating to the Escalera phase. Therefore, by at least 700 BC the basic spatial layout of the principal monumental civic-ceremonial center at Chiapa de Corzo was established, and it was maintained thereafter for over a millennium (Clark 2016; Clark and Lee 1984:265, fig. 11.9). Mound 1A was also constructed in Escalera times. At the time it was a low platform with a wall made of a double row of adobes associated with a thin lime or ash floor (Agrinier 1975a:5).

Some information is available for another low mound for the Escalera phase which may have been an elite house mound. As part of an INAH salvage operation in 1982, Pedro Guzzy, Arnoldo González, and Marta Cuevas excavated a low platform (Mound 73) located in the southeast quadrant of the site (Figure 3) (González and Cuevas 1998). They discovered two construction episodes. They do not specify their ages, but an Escalera phase burial was found sealed under the northeast corner of the earlier stone-faced platform (González and Cuevas 1998:25-30). The burial looks like a dedication offering placed deliberately under the northeast corner, and just 40 cm below the intended outer floor flanking the platform (González and Cuevas 1998: fig. 7), consequently, it does not look like a case of a later building placed over an early burial by accident, but this is a possibility. The relationships between the burial and building appear deliberate and organic. The excavators do not specify the age of these constructions, but the implication is that the building and the burial are of the same age. They clearly knew the ceramic sequence and would have noticed any disjuncture between the ages of the two. González and Cuevas (1998:25, 30) describe the sequential buildings as follows:

> En la exploración del montículo 73 se identificaron dos épocas constructivas en las que se erigieron plataformas de forma rectangular. En la primera etapa constructiva el sistema que se siguió fue el de colocar el núcleo construyendo un muro o cajón de retención formado por piedra de río amarrada con lodo, después se rellenó el cajón con una capa de piedra similar con tierra suelta, encima de estos elementos se colocó un relleno de tierra apisonada mezclada con piedras pequeñas. La fachada del edifico se realizó mediante hiladas de piedra calliza careada, unidas con mortero de lodo y en la parte superior de la plataforma se colocó un piso de estuco blanco de 0.30 m de espesor; para el acceso a la parte superior se construyeron dos escalones. En la siguiente etapa constructiva se erigió una nueva estructura cubriendo totalmente la primera plataforma con un relleno de piedra caliza mezclada con tierra, sobre esta capa se colocó otro relleno a base de arcilla fina compactada. Debido a la avanzada destrucción de esta plataforma en la parte superior sólo se localizó una banqueta doble cubierta de estuco y adosada a un muro; de las fachadas sólo se encontró una parte del lado norte. La fachada está construida a base de piedras rectangulares bien labradas unidas con mortero de lodo.[5]

This is the earliest use of shaped limestone we know of in architecture at Chiapa de Corzo.

This has been seen as a trait dating to the Guanacaste phase. It would be nice to have more details of this salvage operation, but the profile drawings of the excavation are convincing evidence of the early use of stone in platform facades. The thickness of the stucco floor is probably a typographical error. The profile drawing shows three flooring episodes that together are about 10 cm thick.

### Francesa Phase

Francesa phase architectural remains are rare at Chiapa de Corzo and, when found, are only partially preserved. In the case of Mound 17, however, structures of this phase were quite well preserved and add to the knowledge of architectural development at Chiapa de Corzo.

Elsewhere, in the southwestern quadrant of Chiapa de Corzo, Francesa phase architecture is not present or is very poorly preserved. Mound 1, for example, which contains a complex and detailed building sequence after the Guanacaste phase, has only two clay floors of a low platform overlying refuse dateable to the Francesa phase (Lowe and Agrinier 1960:15). In Mound 1A, Agrinier (1975a:5) found the "remnant of a rude retaining wall 75 cm high and made of large rounded and angular stones bound with mud." At nearby Mound 3, three floors rested on sterile caliche bedrock and were contained between low walls made of clay adobes (Tucker 1970:11, fig. 3). This low platform was disturbed and badly preserved. Across the plaza east of Mound 3, and just to the north of Mounds 1 and 1A, lies Mound 5. Only domestic refuse and a few burials were found there dating to Francesa times. No architectural remains dating to the Francesa phase were found in Mound 5

(Lowe 1962b:7). The same absence of Francesa construction was verified for nearby Mounds 2A, 5A, and 5B, although burials of this phase were found beneath these mounds (Lowe 1962b:38, 42). These were off-mound Francesa burials subsequently capped by later platforms.

Mound 8, in the same quadrant experienced three distinct building episodes during the Francesa phase. The earliest was a 50 cm high, multi-roomed domestic structure with base walls of boulders, on top of which was constructed a platform about 1 m high surfaced with the same yellow clay and stones that occur throughout its fill. The final Francesa construction was a building increment that raised the platform 80 to 110 cm in height and was surfaced with irregular-shaped small stones (Lowe 1962b:49-50). Mound 13 in the same quadrant was rebuilt in Francesa times to a height of 7 m. "The structure was made entirely of black earth or adobe, and no special surface finish was apparent" (Hicks and Rozaire 1960:5).

Mound 7 is the only structure in the southwestern quadrant with a truly significant architectural development in this phase, but it in no way matches the completeness of the building remains of Mound 17. The beginning of Mound 7 was not in the Francesa phase, but earlier. Six burials and two caches were found in the fill of an Escalera phase platform 1.3 m high. A minimum surface area of 15 by 15 m is postulated for this Escalera platform, which may have had a stepped-terrace exterior (Lowe 1962b:45, 47-49). On top of this structure was built the first Francesa phase building; it appears to have been a primary platform 2.2 to 2.5 m high with a stairway on the east. The stairway had a balustrade and all was covered with a

---

[5] "The exploration of Mound 73 identified two construction phases in which they erected rectangular-shaped platforms. In the first construction stage the system followed was to place the core construction material in retention cells with walls made of river cobbles cemented with mud mortar. Afterwards, these cells were filled with a layer of like stone and loose earth, and on top of these was placed tamped earth fill mixed with small pebbles. The facade of the building was made with rows of well-placed blocks of cut limestone set in mud mortar. On top of the platform was placed a white stucco floor 30 cm thick. For access to the top of the platform they made two steps. In the following construction stage they built another platform that completely covered the first with a fill of limestone rocks mixed with earth. On top of this layer they put a fill of fine, compact clay. Given the great destruction of the upper part of this platform we were only able to identify a double bench covered with stucco, and a wall attached to it. As for the facades, we only found part of that on the north side. This facade was constructed with well-shaped rectangular stones set in mud mortar." [JEC translation]

"poor quality lime plaster" (Lowe 1962b:46). This was the first of three Francesa phase building additions which eventually raised the platform to a height of 3.4 m (Lowe 1962b:46). Sloping rock walls on both the east and west sides of the upper mound exterior and the yellow caliche layer have been suggested by Lowe (1962b:46) as the basic profile of the Structure 7-F2 building. The structural model of a beveled upper exterior on Francesa phase mounds at Chiapa de Corzo may be within the range of architectural possibilities if differences in building function are taken into account, but the broad and high upper stepped-terrace profile of Mound 17 supports an alternative hypothesis to Lowe's reconstruction.

With the architectural evidence of Mound 17 it is possible to reconstruct a different building exterior for Structure 7-F1 from the information presented in the plan and profile of Trench 1 by Lowe (1962b: fig. 27a). The three rock walls found in the west side of Trench 1 may have been about the same height as the terrace walls of Mound 17. The terrace tops or treads, if that is indeed what the space between the stair-stepped walls was, are almost twice as long as those in Mound 17. However, the top of the highest wall which has a slight inward slope, unlike that for Mound 17, corresponds almost exactly with the top of Structure 7-F. Our proposed reconstruction yields a profile similar to that recorded for Francesa phase Mound 17, albeit of slightly different proportions. This reconstruction of Francesa phase Mound 7 is also similar in profile and construction materials to the main platform at San Agustín (Navarrete 1959).

Mound 11 also witnessed significant rebuilding episodes during the Francesa phase and appears to have attained its final height of 12 m (Bachand 2013: fig. 6). It was also a terraced pyramid with stone steps covered with clay plaster.

In Mound 33 in the northwest quadrant at Chiapa de Corzo a 4 m high Francesa platform has been identified with a possible two-step profile (Lowe 1962b:56-57). The single wall present in the mound profile drawing, postulated to be the upper terrace wall of this platform, is about two meters high, somewhat higher than similar terrace walls in Mound 17. Unfortunately, no more will be known of this building as the owners of the gas station, which now occupies this ground, bulldozed this important Francesa phase mound flat. They also destroyed the smaller Mound 35 in the same leveling process (Figure 5).

Along with Mound 11, one of the tallest mounds at Chiapa de Corzo was Mound 36, located in the northwest quadrant. Nearly all of its 9 m was built up during the Francesa phase (Lowe 1962b:57-59). Little else is known of this structure since only one small test pit was placed at its summit.

**Guanacaste Phase**

Guanacaste phase building activity appears to have been limited at Chiapa de Corzo (Lowe and Agrinier 1960:10; Martínez and Lowe in press). Mound 1 was begun during this phase, and there was probably ritual use of Mounds 3, 7, 12, and 13 (Hicks and Rozaire 1960; Lowe and Agrinier 1960; Mason 1960a; Tucker 1970). Mound 32 was built in this phase and underwent three significant expansions during the phase (Martínez and Lowe in press). Evidence of mound construction and/or use demonstrates that the Chiapa de Corzo civic-religious precinct was in active use during this period. The placement of cut-stone steps on Mound 13 (Mason 1960b) and Mound 32 (Martínez and Lowe in press) suggests that construction techniques had advanced significantly over those of the Francesa phase in which adobe bricks, roughly worked stones, and clay floors were building elements in some structures (Hicks and Rozaire 1960:5).

In the southwest quadrant of Chiapa de Corzo remnants of a platform about 2 m high, found beneath Mound 3, date to the Guanacaste phase (Tucker 1970:11-13). This building, Structure 3-Gl, had a sloping, cut-stone wall over 1.3 m high with a slightly inset horizontal section at its top (Tucker 1970: fig. 3). The bottom of this inset strip coincided with a thin clay floor (labeled Structure 3-G2), thus it is difficult to say whether the inset section of the wall represented a later remodeling or a decorative element of the Structure 3-Gl structure. A looted tomb of the Guanacaste phase has been reported for Mound 3 (Lowe 1962b:38-39), as well as a possible rare Guanacaste phase building (Lowe and Agrinier 1960:10).

Mound 4, in the same area has a buried, red-stained floor which may date to the Guanacaste phase or the following Horcones phase (Lowe 1962b:40).

Another possible Guanacaste phase structure is hypothesized for Mound 8, also located in the southwest quadrant, to account for the upper 80-120 cm of mound fill which contained sherds of this phase (Lowe 1962b:50-51). In general, Guanacaste phase constructions are rare in the southwest quadrant. A telling example is Mound 5. This mound had elaborate architectural remains and ceramic offerings for the Horcones phase, but evidence of building activity in the Guanacaste phase was found in only one small pit on the east base of the structure. Here, excavations uncovered "a single-course, faced-stone, terrace on basal platform wall associated with undisturbed refuse of the Guanacaste phase" (Lowe 1962b:7).

In the northwest quadrant, Mounds 32 and 15 have the most complete sequence of buildings known for the Guanacaste phase at Chiapa de Corzo. For Mound 15, three low platforms arranged around a patio occur with three superimposed remodelings (all data from Glauner, Herman, and Clark in press). The earliest structures of this series, Structures 15-G1-3a, are three separate, individual platforms arranged around an open-corner patio measuring 9 by 9.5 m. The platforms average between 60 cm to 1 m in height and about 6 by 6 m to 7 by 7 m square. One has a long narrow porch on its southeast side that wraps around the sides of the main platform (Structure 15-G2a) and is about half as high as the platform. Another platform (Structure 15-G1a) has a one-step approach across the entire southeast side. This structure also has a narrow area, one short step above the main platform top, which extends across the entire platform rear. The third platform has no access or other modification to its basic square form.

The next remodeling in the sequence of two of the three buildings (Structure 15-G1-2b) was an addition to the southeast end of Structure 15-G2b which covered the earlier porch, amplified its upper surface toward Structure 15-G1a, and added a single, short, low one-step access to the southeast end. The Structure 15-G1b addition was an enlargement attached to the northeast side of the earlier building and almost joined the Structure 15-G3a and Structure 15-G2b buildings by filling in the patio. The same wide one-step access of the earlier building was used in this remodeling. The third platform, Structure 15-G3 had no visible addition during this stage of reconstruction.

In the last remodeling stage wide, but low aprons were placed around all three platforms tying them together in one or two new terraced areas at the foot of the earlier structures, all with accesses of narrow, low and short one-step stairways. Extensions were also constructed on the southwest sides of Structure 15-G2c and G3c which enlarged the principal platforms at their highest level.

Mound 32 was built in this phase and then refurbished and expanded three more times. Salvage excavations there consolidated the earliest platform, 32-G1, and it is now an island that divides the highway just south of the Pemex station whose construction destroyed Mound 33. In ground plan, Mound 32 is shaped like an inverted "T" and is thought to have been the platform for a small temple (all details from Martínez and Lowe in press). As evident today to all passersby, the early Guanacaste phase building has sloping walls just over 2 m high built of small cut limestone blocks of similar size. Originally, these were laid in mud mortar. This surface was covered with a thin lime plaster or lime-and-mud plaster. Floors were also of stucco. The mound had projecting wide balustrades flanking a wide, inset stairway, a design also known for the coeval temple platform at Mound 1A (Agrinier 1975a:23, fig. 21) and the later Horcones platform at Mound 1 (see Lowe and Agrinier 1960:20, fig. 11) built after the Mound 32 pattern. As with this later structure, Mound 32 has a "sunken patio" built with walls of river cobbles that served as a burial crypt; two tombs were found therein. Later building stages covered this sunken patio, and the platform was elevated another 2 m for Structure G4 and greatly expanded horizontally.

Other Guanacaste phase building remains were found in Mound 40 in the northeast quadrant of Chiapa de Corzo (Lowe 1962b:61-62) and Mound 26 (González and Cuevas 1998). In Mound 40 a small pit excavation revealed a series of four floors, two red-stained sand floors, a red-stained lime floor, and a stone slab floor which all overlie a 50 cm fill of boulders and Francesa phase trash. Lowe (1962b:62) suggests that these floors must have been on a low raised platform. Nothing is known of the exterior supporting walls of this structure. Little is reported for the Guanacaste phase of Mound 26 other than it had retention walls built of river cobbles (González and Cuevas 1998:33).

In the southeast quadrant of Chiapa de Corzo the only Guanacaste phase structure known is in Mound 67. It consists of a low earthen fill platform with two clay-lime floors and a red-painted adobe wall (Lowe 1962b:66). Although the mound may have been three meters high during the Guanacaste phase, no details are known of exterior walls or of overall building shape.

### Horcones Phase

Horcones phase architecture at Chiapa de Corzo is characterized generally by "primary platforms with vertical cut-stone walls of complex profile, lightly plastered" (Lowe and Agrinier 1960:table II). The complex profile of the walls was a new innovation from the earlier phase, known best for Mound 32, in which the walls were a simple slope or talud (Martínez and Lowe in press). Evidence of superstructures with cut-stone walls are also present, as are flat roofs, entrances with flanking columns, and some use of adobe bricks.

In the southwest quadrant of Chiapa de Corzo most of the principal platforms had Horcones phase buildings. The best known structure of this period, Mound 1, underwent at least 15 major stages of construction (Lowe and Agrinier 1960:10-27). The expansion of Mound 1 in Horcones times covered over Mound 1A. In Guanacaste times, Mounds 1 and 1A were twin temples that faced north (Agrinier and Clark 2014:88). The construction stages of Mound 1 consisted of secondary platforms, temple

superstructures on top of basal platforms, and different modifications of the perimeter and profile of the basal platform. At least nine major modifications were directed to the basal platform. The typical or most characteristic basal platform profile of the Horcones phase has been compared to that of a thatched hut: a slanting upper panel, recalling a thatched roof, joins a vertical, recessed wall which, in turn, rests on a low basal platform. These were of cut limestone and covered with plaster. Structures 17-H1 and 17-H2 did not have the profile of elaborate Mound 1 architecture. The simple rock wall and low-rising stairway of Mound 17 were a far cry from the complex domestic house profile characteristic of Mound 1.

Horcones phase building increments have been found on almost all mounds tested at Chiapa de Corzo, in keeping with the great ritual activity demonstrated during this phase in most other artifactual categories. Mound 5, which was built on a slight rise on the sterile bedrock on the east side of the main plaza at Chiapa de Corzo and in front of Mound 1, is the best known and most complex Horcones structure at the site. This special building functioned as a palace or receiving hall for the center of the civic-religious ceremonial precinct during this time (Clark and Hansen 2001). Mound 5 had a wide central stairway on its west side flanked by balustrades which provided access to the many room superstructure, its central hall covered with a flat roof (Lowe 1962b). Mound 5 was significantly different in form, and surely function, from Mound 17. Mound 17 was not as broad as Mound 5, and it was much taller, suggesting that the buildings on these two platforms were designed for different purposes.

In the southwest quadrant of the site Mounds 1A, 2A, 3, 4A, 7, 10, 12, and 13 all had Horcones phase construction elements (Hicks and Rozaire 1960:5, 6; Lowe 1962b; Mason 1960a:4; Tucker 1970:13-19).

In the northwest quadrant, Mounds 17, 26, and 33 also had Horcones buildings. Most of the architectural modifications needed for these buildings were not grand or obviously important, but together they indicate that during the Horcones phase Chiapa de Corzo was extensively occupied and was engaged in an active program of urban renewal.

INAH salvage operations in Mound 26 recovered evidence of a well-made Horcones phase building. It had shaped rectangular stones used in vertical walls. These were covered with plaster. The building had a porch flanked by two pillars. Unlike later buildings at Chiapa de Corzo and in the Soke area, these pillars made of squared limestone blocks were square rather than circular in transverse cross-section (González and Cuevas 1998:33, 41, foto 11).

This new building spree added a broad platform addition around the entire group of what was during the Guanacaste phase three separate low platforms (Structure 15-G1-3, Glauner et al. in press). This building added length, width, and height to two of the formerly isolated platforms (Structures 15-H1, H2). The third platform, Structure 15-G1, remained unchanged. The platform addition ranged in width from 1-6 m, depending on the section of the platform concerned, and in height from 25 cm to 1.5 m. This group now appeared to be a basal platform with three superstructures. It measured 10.8 by 30 m. The two platforms, which were enlarged, now measured, respectively, 8.7 by 13 m and 9.1 by 13.7 m; both were under 75 cm high.

The least known zone of Chiapa de Corzo site, the northeast quadrant, also had Horcones occupation, with evidence of architectural activity in Mound 40 (Lowe 1962b:62-63). In Mound 40 a 60 cm high, well-made stone wall was covered with a thin, well-made lime stucco. The floor was made of the same lime material and connected to the wall.

In the southeast quadrant, Mound 67 contains evidence of a 4 m high Horcones structure faced with cut-stone walls and plastered with a thin lime stucco. Not much more is known of this platform, although the excavation was extensive. This mound experienced considerable building activity during the subsequent Istmo phase, and much of the Horcones phase architecture was destroyed in the process (Lowe 1962b:67-68). An excavation in the plaza area between Mounds 68 and 74 revealed evidence of two low basal platforms (labeled 38-H1 and 38-H2) of the Horcones phase (Dixon 1959:19; Lowe 1962b:72-73). The 38-H1 platform wall was a simple cut-stone wall with a vertical profile. In contrast, Structure 38-H2 had a typical Horcones phase platform wall with a "domestic-house" profile. It was also made of cut stone and rose over a meter high (Lowe 1962b:72-73, fig. 45).

## General Comments

We have only covered the evolution of architecture at Chiapa de Corzo for the span of time represented by Mound 17. Public architecture evolved by turning pyramids inside out. The earliest, flat-top platforms were largely of stone rubble cemented with clay and shrouded with clay. By Horcones times, mounds were of earth and clay covered with cut stone – stones worked with flat surfaces on all six faces so they could be set in mud mortar like bricks. These expensive facades were plastered over with stucco and painted. The sizes and shapes of basal mounds changed through time (see Lowe and Agrinier 1960 for Mound 1) as did the size and shape of summit buildings. We lack information for early summit buildings, and information for domestic architecture for Chiapa de Corzo is rare for all phases. The famous inverted "T" shape of temple platforms was present by Guanacaste times, as best known for Mounds 1A and 32.

The largest mounds at Chiapa de Corzo gained most of their stature during the Francesa phase and grew very little after that. The same appears to be true of other Chiapas Middle Preclassic centers. The emphasis in later building projects at Chiapa de Corzo was on surfaces rather than on stature or size. Architectural labor and masonry was invested in shaping limestone and sandstone blocks to make regular stone facades to cover with plaster. There was an evolution in these techniques, of course, with earlier stone veneers of rough or "uncut" stone hidden under the plaster. The idea of stone buildings with plastered surfaces appears to have been a Maya idea adopted by the people at Chiapa de Corzo during the Late Preclassic period (Chiapa V) and carried on through the Protoclassic period (Chiapa VI and VII).

# CHAPTER 3

# CACHES

In this chapter we group and describe caches found in the salvage excavations with those recovered in earlier work and then summarize cache patterns in Mound 17 and at the site by phase. In the NWAF Chiapa de Corzo work the term and concept of "cache" has been used as originally defined by A. Ledyard Smith (1950:91) and, later, by William Coe (1959:78-79) to refer to one or more objects (usually ceramic vessels at Chiapa de Corzo) which appear to have been interred together as a votive offering unassociated with a burial. "Caches at Chiapa de Corzo fall principally into two classes or types, 1) dedicatory offerings, and 2) terminal offerings, the latter seemingly confined to the Horcones and Istmo occupations" (Lowe 1960b:55). This distinction between dedicatory and terminal offerings is followed here for the 10 caches found in the salvage excavations of Mound 17 and two found previously. We follow the cache numbering system for the site and include caches found at this mound prior to the 1969 excavations. In the field Lee identified Caches 1-5 and 10-14 (see Lee 1969b: fig.2). We also include two caches found in earlier work. We have renumbered these caches as a continuous sequence from 1 to 12.

Dedicatory caches are groups of ceramic vessels placed together, generally in upright positions, and related to building construction activities. Terminal caches, none of which were found in Mound 17, are ceremonial dumps of ceramic vessels and other artifacts usually broken in place, as if they were part of some ritual destruction just prior to their immediate burial. The actual behaviors involved with these caches were different, and the difference may have been important conceptually. Dedicatory caches required digging a hole into an existing surface, placing objects, and then covering it over. For terminal offerings, objects were level on an open surface and then covered over. It is as if the building to be rebuilt was considered already buried.

In Mound 17 several caches appear to have been unrelated to specific architecture building episodes (17-3, 17-4, 17-6, 17-8, 17-9). We suppose these offerings served some other dedicatory or votive function. These caches are classified here as "offerings" rather than specifying a type of cache. The Mound 17 caches are described in the order of their discovery, and then considered phase by phase, to highlight offeratory practices at Mound 17 during Preclassic and Protoclassic times. We then consider them in relation to other Chiapa de Corzo caches. The first two caches were discovered in 1959 by Brockington in exploratory test excavations at the mound in unit A-126 and reported by Lowe (1962b:54-56). No traces of test excavation A-126 were detected during the salvage excavations of Mound 17 that would have allowed us to correlate Brockington's test pit and its contents precisely to our excavations. These caches were 1.2 and 1.4 m above sterile caliche. The location shown in Figure 3 is our best guess.

In this chapter and the next, an MRE number follows the listing of some artifacts. These are museum registration (Museo Regional del Estado) numbers required by INAH during the 1980s and 1990s when the final paperwork was completed for turning the Mound 17 artifacts into the INAH Regional Museum at Tuxtla Gutiérrez. In all the paperwork and information for these objects they are listed by these MRE numbers, hence, we provide them here to facilitate future research.

Figure 14. Cache 17-1, republished from Lowe 1962b:pl. 28f.

## MOUND 17 CACHES

### Cache 17-1 (Figures 14 and 15)

**Type:** Dedicatory (?).

**Phase:** Horcones.

**Location and Context:** "60 cm. below southwest corner of Stage H structure in Mound 17 excavation A-126" (Lowe 1962b:55, fig. 33, pl. 28g). "Offering is in the southwest corner of the pit. It begins at a depth of 1.12 m and continues downwards to about 1.40 m. It is 18 cm from the south side of the pit and enters the western wall for some 10 cm. It goes 45 cm east of the west wall of the pit and continues some 85 cm north of the south wall. The offering consists of 17 vessels or so, partly clustered and partly one inside the other. Most seem broken ...

Photos were taken of the work in various stages. All coordinates are from the SW stake of the pit and from level of the NW stake, which is Point Zero for all the measurements of this pit" (Brockington n.d.).

**Contents:**

1. Polished brown bridge-spout jar, with vertical grooves and circular depressions on the shoulder (Fig. 15a).

2. Orange flaring-wall bowl with thickened lip, found inverted inside of Vessel 6 (30 cm diam.) (Fig. 15b).

3. Coarse buff inner-horn burner bowl (18.5 cm diam.) (Fig. 15c).

4. Black round-side bowl (28 cm diam.) (Fig. 15d).

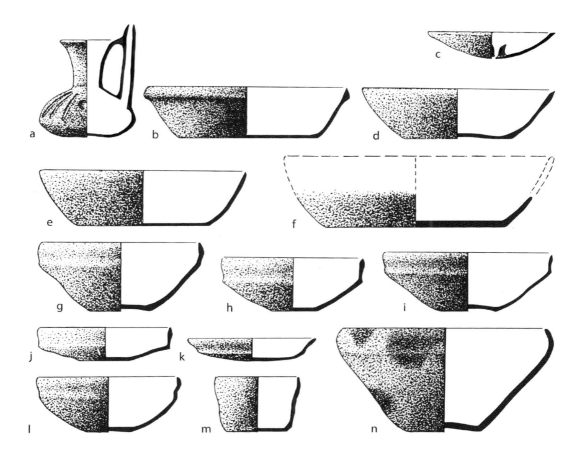

Figure 15. Cache 17-1, republished from Lowe 1962b:fig. 34.

5. Black round-side bowl (30 cm diam.) (Fig. 15e).

6. Brown slip round-side bowl (39 cm diam.) (Fig. 15f).

7. Coarse buff standing-wall bowl (22 cm diam.) (Fig. 15g).

8. Coarse buff standing-wall bowl (21 cm diam.) (Fig. 15h).

9. Coarse buff standing-wall bowl (25 cm diam.); this vessel was nested in a bowl of similar dimensions (Fig. 15i).

10. Coarse buff standing-wall bowl (20 cm diam.) (Fig. 15j).

11. Coarse buff dish found upright in Vessel 8 (19 cm diam.) (Fig. 15k).

12. Coarse buff bowl found inverted under Vessels 2 and 6 (21 cm diam.) (Fig. 15l).

13. Coarse buff cup (12 cm diam.) (Fig. 15m).

14. Coarse buff basin with orange-to-black firing clouds (30 cm diam.) (Fig. 15n).

15. White-rim-black round-side bowl (not illustrated).

16. Coarse buff standing-wall bowl the same size as Vessel 9, and nested in Vessel 9 (not illustrated).

17. Coarse buff standing-wall bowl similar to Vessel 7 (not illustrated).

**Remarks:** "The vessels were originally placed upright or inverted, closely clustered as if deposited within a pit ... The caches rested upon a deposit of fine white ash. Within and among the vessels were three obsidian flake blades" (Lowe 1962b:55, fig. 34, Pl. 28g).

Figure 16. Cache 17-2, republished from Lowe 1962b:pl. 28g.

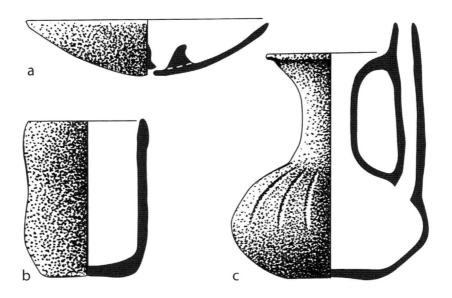

Figure 17. Cache 17-2, republished from Lowe 1962b fig. 35.

### Cache 17-2 (Figures 16 and 17)

**Type:** Terminal (?).

**Phase:** Horcones.

**Location and Context:** "Just south and 20 cm. below base of Stage H wall encountered in excavation A-126 at the base of south slope of Mound 17 ... Apparently placed in intrusive pit" (Lowe 1962b:55, fig. 33, Pl. 28f). "A second offering was revealed in the south side of this pit, and the pit was therefore extended to recover it ... The offering was found at a depth of approximately 95 cm from Point Zero and about 72 cm from the surface of the ground. This offering is a mass of random sherds, especially on top. It appears that the vessels are a bit more together (lower down), although still badly broken. This offering was cleaned all around it down to what seems to be the bottom. The scattered, broken sherds on top were simply removed. Large pieces will still be logged as they come out. One stuccoed and painted (red) sherd was found on the top of the offering" (Brockington n.d.).

**Contents:**

   1. Coarse buff inner-horn burner bowl (22 cm diam.) (Fig. 17a).

   2. Rude coarse buff vertical-wall vessel (12 cm diam.) (Fig. 17b).

   3. Polished brown bridge-spout jar with grooved shoulders (Fig. 17c).

   4. Fragments of vessel similar to Vessel 2 (not restored) (16 cm diam.).

   5. Fragments of another vessel (14 cm diam. and 10 cm high) similar to Vessel 2 (not restored), found face-down beneath Vessel 4.

**Remarks:** "Mass of [five] smashed pottery vessels ... Five obsidian flake blades, bits of carbon, miscellaneous sherds, and fragments of worked shell were included in the offering" (Lowe 1962b:55, fig. 35, Pl. 28f).

## Cache 17-3 (Figures 9 and 18)

**Type:** Offering.

**Phase:** Horcones.

**Location and Context:** Excavation Unit A, on the line between Sections 8 and 10, 65 cm from corner of Section 9 at a depth of 36 cm.

**Contents:**

1. Cintalapa Grooved-composite: Cintalapa Variety bowl; height 5.6 cm, diameter 14.6+ cm (Fig. 18a). MRE-4478.

2. Nambiyugua Smoothed: Nambiyugua Variety cylinder; height 17.6 cm, diameter 13.9 cm (Fig. 18b). MRE-4479.

**Remarks:** Vessel 1 was found mouth down over Vessel 2. Similar shaped vessels were part of Horcones phase Cache 1-24 in Mound 1 (Lowe 1960: 60-1). A vessel from Feature 223, Trench 121, in the plaza in front of Mound 1 is almost identical to item 2 of this cache. The form of Vessel 1 was more common in the Francesa phase (Warren 1978; see Agrinier 1964:31-32, B. 149). It could have been an hierloom vessel. Vessel 2, however, is definitely Horcones phase; it is the same ceramic type as the famous sherd from Chiapa de Corzo that has post-fired incised glyphs on it (MNA0000125) found in a Horcones phase trash dump (Lowe 1962a, and personal communication). Warren (1978) places the Nambiyugua type in the succeeding Istmo phase, but it would seem on the basis of the published evidence to have begun in the Horcones phase.

## Cache 17-4 (Figure 18)

**Type:** Offering.

**Phase:** Guanacaste.

**Location and Context:** Three meters beyond end of Excavation Unit A, Section 10.

**Contents:**

1. Libertad Black-brown: Red rim Variety jar neck; height 3.5 cm, diameter 10.0 cm (Fig. 18c).

2. Libertad Black-brown: Red rim Variety bowl; height 5.5 cm, diameter 10.6 cm (Fig. 18d). MRE-4480.

**Remarks:** These vessel fragments were collected from a cut left by the bulldozer. These vessels have red painted rims similar to the vessels from Burial 17-14 (items 4 and 5). This type differs from Libertad Black-brown: Libertad Variety only in the addition of a fugitive red, exterior painted rim. Two other vessels were also found.

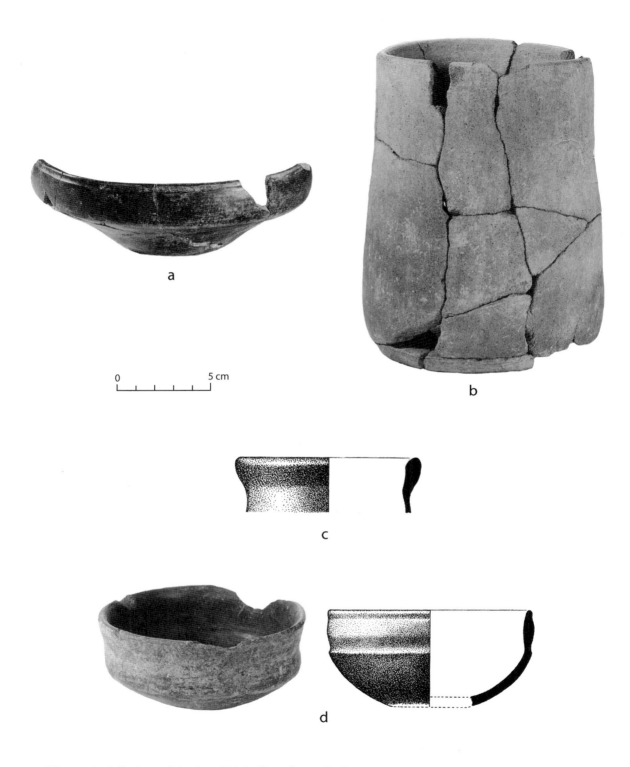

Figure 18. Offerings of Caches 17-3 (a, b) and 17-4 (c, d).

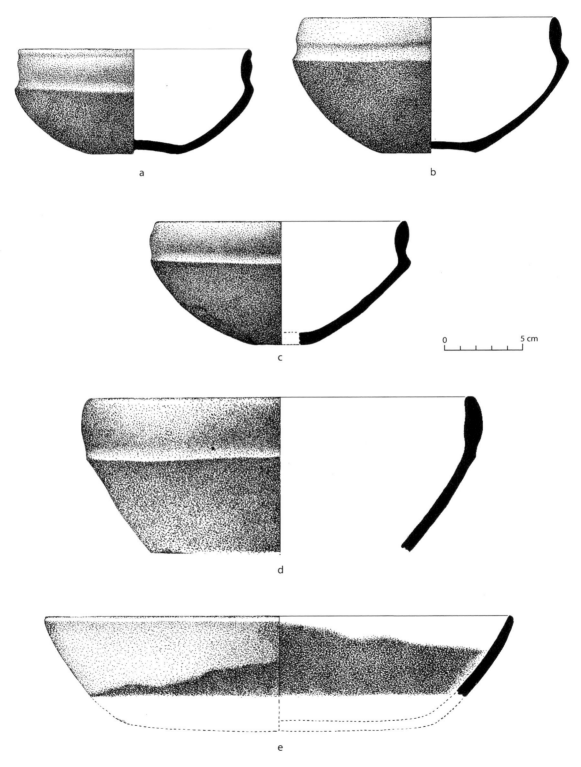

Figure 19. Cache 17-5.

### Cache 17-5 (Figure 19)

**Type:** Dedicatory Offering.

**Phase:** Horcones.

**Location and Context:** Excavation Unit A, Section 2, depth 1.2 m.

**Contents:**

1. Nambiyugua Smoothed: Nambiyugua Variety bowl; height 8.7 cm, diameter 16.6 cm (Fig. 19c). MRE-4481.

2. Nambiyugua Smoothed: Nambiyugua Variety bowl; height 11.5+ cm, diameter 26.1 cm (Fig. 19d). MRE-4482-1, 2.

3. Nambiyugua Smoothed: Nambiyugua Variety bowl; height 9.2 cm, diameter 17.5 cm (Fig. 19b). MRE-4483.

4. Nambiyugua Smoothed: Nambiyugua Variety bowl; height 6.5 cm, diameter 13.5 cm (Fig. 19a). MRE-4484.

5. Cueva Grande Smudged: Cueva Grande Variety bowl fragment; height 7.6+ cm, diameter 30.4 cm (Fig. 19e). A large sherd was found in association, but it is probably intrusive.

**Remarks:** The vessels were broken and found in rock fill 30+ cm above Cache 17-6. The cache was intrusive through Francesa phase sub-structure 17-F1 into Str.17-F1a. All vessel drawings are based on partial rim profiles. Vessels similar to Vessels 1-4 were found at Chiapa de Corzo in Horcones phase Tombs 1, 4, and 6 (Lowe and Agrinier 1960; Agrinier 1964:37).

Figure 20. Cache 17-6.

### Cache 17-6 (Figures 20 and 21)

**Type:** Offering.

**Phase:** Francesa.

**Location and Context:** Excavation Unit A, Section 2, depth 1.5 m.

**Contents:**

1. Mundet Red: Polished Variety jar; height 19.3 cm, diameter 22.3 cm (Fig. 21a). MRE-4486.

2. Mundet Red: Polished Variety jar; height 18+ cm, diameter 20+ cm (Fig. 21b). MRE-4487.

**Remarks:** This cache was apparently intrusive through Structure 17-F1b floor, although the rims of the vessels were almost level with the floor.

a

b

0                    5 cm

Figure 21. Cache 17-6.

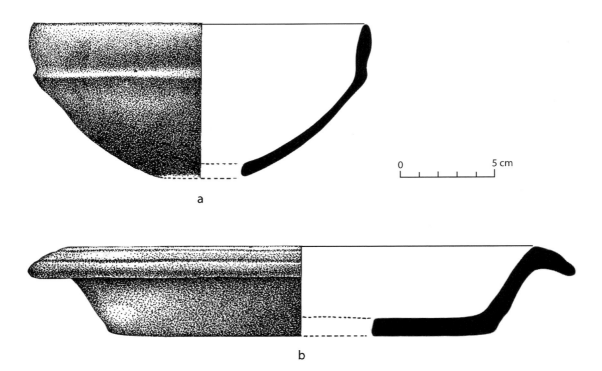

Figure 22. Cache 17-7.

### Cache 17-7 (Figure 22)

**Type:** Dedicatory Offering.

**Phase:** Francesa.

**Location and Context:** Excavation Unit A, Section 2, depth 2.3 m.

**Contents:**

1. Cintalapa Grooved-composite: Cintalapa Variety bowl fragment (reconstruction drawing); height 8.5 cm, diameter 18.5 cm (Fig. 22a).

2. Ocosingo Incised: Ocosingo Variety flaring rim plate fragment; height 5.0 cm, diameter 29.0 cm (Fig. 22b). MRE-4489.

**Remarks:** The bowl (Vessel 1) was found 10 cm northeast of the plate (Vessel 2).

Figure 23. Vessel 2 of Cache 17-8 and unidentified bowl.

### Cache 17-8 (Figures 23 and 24)

**Type:** Offering.

**Phase:** Francesa.

**Location and Context:** Excavation Unit A, Sections 3-4, depth 3.22 m.

**Contents:**

1. Cintalapa Grooved-composite: Cintalapa Variety bowl fragment; height 5.8 cm, diameter 25.3 cm (Fig. 24a). MRE-4490.

2. Tzutzuculi White-to-buff cylinder (badly broken); height 26.6 cm, diameter 16.2 cm (Fig. 24b). MRE-4491.

**Remarks:** Vessel 1 was placed mouth down over the mouth of Vessel 2 to make a lip-to-lip container. The photograph suggests that another small dish was part of this offering.

a

b

0 _____ 5 cm

Figure 24. Cache 17-8.

Figure 25. Cache 17-9.

## Cache 17-9 (Figures 25-27)

**Type:** Offering

**Phase:** Francesa.

**Location and Context:** Excavation Unit A, Section 6, depth 4.1 m.

**Contents:**

1. Tzutzuculi White-to-buff cylinder; height 23.1 cm, diameter 19.8 cm (Fig. 26d). MRE-4472.

2. Mundet Red: Polished Variety cylinder; height 19.7 cm, diameter 13.9 cm (Fig. 26e). MRE-4584.

3. Libertad Black-brown: Libertad Variety bowl; height 6.2 cm, diameter 21.5 cm (Fig. 26c). MRE-4492.

4. Matenica Modeled: Matenica Variety effigy jar; height 11.4 cm, diameter 7.7 cm (Fig. 26a). MRE-4493.

5. Matenica Modeled: Matenica Variety effigy jar; height 15.l ± cm, diameter 9.7 ± cm (Fig. 26b).

**Remarks:** This was the deepest offering in Excavation A and likely the oldest.

Figure 26. Cache 17-9.

Figure 27. Field drawing of Cache 17-9 showing positions of the vessels in situ.

a                                                b

0 _____ 5 cm

Figure 28. Cache 17-10.

## Cache 17-10 (Figure 28)

**Type:** Dedicatory offering.

**Phase:** Francesa.

**Location and Context:** Excavation Unit B, Section 6, depth 1.5 m from surface.

**Contents:**

1. Tzutzuculi White-to-buff cylinder, fragmentary, height 24.2+ cm, diameter 23+ cm (Fig. 28b). MRE-4494.

2. Mundet Red: Matte Variety partial cylinder, badly broken; height 21.6 cm, diameter 19.6 cm (Fig. 28a). MRE-4495.

**Remarks:** The vessels were buried at the foot of the front stairway to Structure 17-F1. The bases of the vessels were 90 cm below the top of the first step. They rested on a floor of fine tan sand.

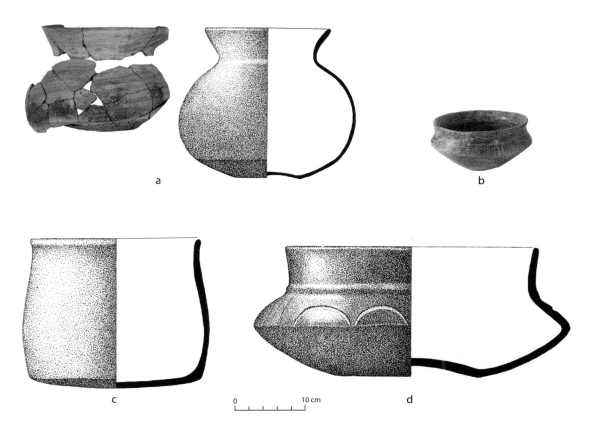

Figure 29. Cache 17-11.

### Cache 17-11 (Figure 29)

**Type:** Dedicatory offering.

**Phase:** Horcones.

**Location and Context:** Excavation Unit B, Section 7, depth 1.1 m from surface.

**Contents:**

1. Nandalumi White-brown: Nandalumi Variety jar, fragment; height 24+ cm, diameter 26.8+ cm (Fig. 29a, drawing restored). MRE-4496. (Horcones phase).

2. Nandalumi White-brown: Nandalumi Variety cylinder, fragmentary (drawing restored); height 22.4 cm, diameter 26.6 cm (Fig. 29c). MRE-4503. (Horcones phase).

3. Cintalapa Grooved-composite: Cintalapa Variety bowl; height 6.1 cm, diameter 13.1 cm (Fig. 29b). MRE-4497. (Francesa phase).

4. Cintalapa Grooved-composite: Cintalapa Variety bowl fragments; height 9.1 cm, diameter 22.6 cm (Fig. 29d, reconstruction drawing). MRE-4498. (Francesa phase).

**Remarks:** The vessels were buried in the fill of Structure 17-H2 and found on a tan sand floor. All items of the cache were below the level of the top step of the stairway of Structure 17-H2. The cylinders (items 1 and 2) rested directly on the sand floor, the two bowls (items 3 and 4) were 20 cm higher up in the fill and some 15 cm to the east. While the Cintalapa type is most characteristic of the Francesa phase, Warren (1978) says this type continued until the end of the Horcones phase. The Nandalumi type only dates to the Horcones phase. It is possible that the placement of his Horcones phase cache encountered a Francesa phase cache and that the older vessels were included in the new offering.

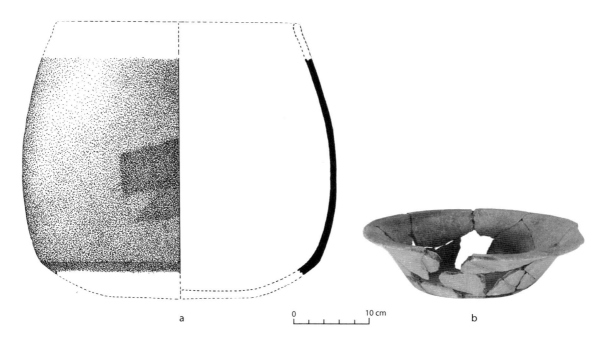

Figure 30. Cache 17-12.

### Cache 17-12 (Figure 30)

**Type:** Dedicatory offering.

**Phase:** Horcones.

**Location and Context:** Excavation Unit B, Section 8, depth 1.5 m from surface.

**Contents:**

1. Teopisca White: Teopisca Variety large open mouth jar, fragmentary; height 28+ cm, diameter 41.8+ cm (Fig. 30a, reconstruction drawing). MRE-4656.

2. Teopisca White: Teopisca Variety plate; height 9.4 cm, diameter 29.5 cm (Fig. 30b). MRE-4499.

**Remarks:** This offering was found in the center of Excavation B at the top of the stairway and on the mound axis.

### MOUND 17 CACHE PATTERNS

Ten caches were found in the salvage excavations of Mound 17, dating to three of the four phases recognized in the building constructions. No caches dating to the Escalera phase were found, but five dating to the Francesa

phase were recovered. One Guanacaste phase cache (17-4) was recovered, and four dating to the Horcones phase were present in the excavations (17-3, 17-5, 17-11, and 17-12). At the time of the salvage excavations in Mound 17 these 10 caches represented a 7.5 percent increase in the total caches known from these three phases for Chiapa de Corzo. Since then many more caches have been reported. By phase, the Mound 17 caches represented a 50 percent increase for the Francesa phase, a 100 percent increase for the Guanacaste phase, and a 6.5 percent increase for the Horcones phase. Considered with caches from other mounds, the Mound 17 caches add to our understanding of Chiapa de Corzo ritual practices and their changes through time.

### Escalera Phase

No caches of this phase were found in Mound 17.

### Francesa Phase

Five caches (17-6, 17-7, 17-8, 17-9, 17-10) with a combined total of 14 ceramic vessels dated to the Francesa phase (Table 1). Each

Table 1. Summary of the Mound 17 caches.

| Cache | Bowls | Jars / Cups | Cylinders | Plates | Other | Total vessels |
|---|---|---|---|---|---|---|
| *Francesa* | | | | | | |
| 17-6 | - | 2 | - | - | | 2 |
| 17-7 | 1 | - | - | 1 | | 2 |
| 17-8 | 2 | - | 1 | - | | 3 |
| 17-9 | 1 | 2* | 2 | - | *effigy jars | 5 |
| 17-10 | - | - | 2 | - | | 2 |
| *Guanacaste* | | | | | | |
| 17-4 | 4 | - | - | - | | 4 |
| *Horcones* | | | | | | |
| 17-1 | 12 | 2 | 1 | 1 | 3-horn incense burner, 3 shell fragments, 5 obsidian blade fragments | 17 |
| 17-2 | - | 1 | 3 | - | 3-horn incense burner | 5 |
| 17-3 | 1 | - | 1 | - | | 2 |
| 17-5 | 5 | - | - | - | | 5 |
| 17-11 | 2 | 1 | 1 | - | | 4 |
| 17-12 | - | 1 | - | 1 | | 2 |
| Total | 28 | 9 | 11 | 3 | 2 | 53 |

cache had at least two ceramic vessels. Cache 17-9 consisted of five vessels. No other types of artifacts were associated with Francesa phase caches, only pots. Vessel forms included bowls, jars, cylinders or vases, and plates. The most frequent forms were bowls and cylinders, occurring in three caches each, but found together in only two caches. Jars were also present in one of these bowl-cylinder caches. In contrast, bowls co-occurred with all other vessel forms. Jars and cylinders were found alone in one cache each. The single occurrence of a plate was in association with a bowl.

Cache 17-9 is the Francesa cache with the most vessels. Two are small modeled jars portraying anthropomorphic heads; one has a tubular mouth or mouth piece, such as seen on whistling pots. The tubular mouth indicates

that these effigy vessels portray a blowing or whistling mode.

Six different ceramic types/varieties are represented in the 13 Francesa phase cache vessels (Table 1). The most frequent type is Mundet Red: Matte Variety (3 cylinders). Next in abundance comes Cintalapa Grooved-composite: Cintalapa Variety (2 bowls). The other four types/varieties are represented by a single vessel form: a Libertad Black-brown: Libertad Variety bowl, two Mundet Red: Polished Variety jars, two Matenica Modeled: Matenica Variety jars, and one Ocosingo Incised: Ocosingo Variety plate. The typological makeup of these Francesa phase caches does not seem particularly significant. Cylinder vessels are always Mundet Red: Mundet Variety, and bowls tend to be Cintalapa Grooved-composite.

Since the cylindrical form occurs in other ceramic wares and types at Chiapa de Corzo it appears that Mundet Red cylinders in Francesa caches were deliberately selected, if not ritually prescribed, for certain kinds of caches.

Caches 17-8 and 17-9 were intruded into Structure 17-E almost on the east-west mound axis. Cache 17-10 was located just under the plaza floor of Structure 17-F1 near the central north-south axis of the mound. Cache 17-10 was in close alignment with Cache 17-8 on this same axis. These caches may have been related to the cardinal directions and unidentified celestial phenomena, perhaps commemorating some religious belief related to them.

### Guanacaste Phase

Only one cache was found dating to this phase. It consisted of two Libertad Black-brown bowls and two unidentified bowls. Cache 17-4 appears to have been transitional from the previous phase where Cache 17-9 also contained bowls of this type in its inventory. Cache 17-9 differs in other ways from the Francesa phase caches. As mentioned, it had more vessels than any other Francesa cache and contained two unique anthropomorphic effigy jars. The presence of Libertad Black-brown bowls in Caches 17-4 and 17-9 suggests they were close to one another chronologically, albeit different in function. The position of Cache 17-4 in Mound 17 provides few clues as to its purpose.

### Horcones Phase

With the two caches excavated by Brockington (Lowe 1962b:54-56) in 1959, there are six Horcones phase caches known for Mound 17. The four Horcones phase caches (17-3, 17-5, 17-11, 17-12) discovered in 1969 together had 13 ceramic vessels: eight bowls, two jars, two cylinders, and one plate. Two caches had two vessels, one had four, and the other had five. At least two vessels were placed in each cache. Both two-vessel caches featured different vessel forms. Cache 17-3 consisted of a bowl and a cylinder vase, and Cache 17-12 had a jar and a plate. Cache 17-5 consisted of only bowls, five in number. The remaining Cache 17-11 consisted of four vessels, with three forms represented:

two bowls, one jar, and one cylinder. Bowls were by far the most frequent form (9) in Horcones caches, followed by jars (2) and cylinders (2).

Horcones caches recovered in 1969 included five different ceramic types. These are (1) Cintalapa Grooved-composite, of which there were two bowls, (2) Nambiyugua Smoothed, represented by four bowls and two cylinders, (3) Cueva Grande Smudged, with one bowl, (4) Teopisca White, represented by one jar and one plate, and (5) Nandalumi White-brown, present in the form of one jar and one cylinder.

An interesting change occurred in the distribution of ceramic types during the Horcones phase. Three pottery types are represented by two vessel forms. In previous phases each ceramic type was limited to one vessel form. In Horcones caches, however, Nambiyugua bowls and cylinders are found. Nandalumi White-brown is represented by jars and cylinders. Teopisca White jars and plates are also present. The Cintalapa Grooved-composite and Cueva Grande types are represented only by bowls.

Comparison of the 1959 caches to the 1969 caches reveals a significant difference. More vessels were found in the two 1959 caches. The larger cache contained 17 vessels; the smaller cache five vessels. This smaller cache was also accompanied by other kinds of artifacts, "... five obsidian flake blades, bits of carbon, miscellaneous sherds, and fragments of worked shell" (Lowe 1962b:55). Both 1959 caches also had bridge-spout jars and three-horned incense burner bowls. Neither vessel form was present in earlier phases.

During the 600 years that elapsed from early Francesa to late Horcones times, cache offerings in Mound 17 became more heterogeneous in content and more conservative in number of ceramic types represented. Why this was so we do not know, but changes in the religious observations appear implicated.

Placement of caches on axial alignments remained a feature of paired caches. Caches 17-3 and 17-11, the former on top in the center of the structure and the latter much lower down near the front, were virtually on the north-south axis of Mound 17 (Figure 5). This shared spatial relationship becomes even more interesting when it is recognized that these two caches share two ceramic types and vessel shapes. This pairing may point to repeated or cyclical religious observances related to the cardinal directions and/or movements of celestial bodies. Alternatively, caches could have been placed in different locations at the same time as part of the same ritual event.

## CHIAPA DE CORZO PRECLASSIC CACHES AND OFFERINGS

More than 250 caches and offerings have been discovered at Chiapa de Corzo in controlled excavations. Most were placed after the Middle Preclassic. Very few caches or offerings are known for the early Middle Preclassic, and none is known for the Early Preclassic. The earliest offerings were mostly of stone axes and other stones; ceramic vessels were very rare. But beginning in the Francesa phase, pots became the dominant offering item, as evident in the caching pattern described for Mound 17. Offered vessels were presumably containers for food and drink – the supposed principal items of the offerings. Later, other types of objects began to be included. In Protoclassic and Classic offerings, small stone cobbles became common items in caches.

As a shift from preceding discussion, for the site as a whole we consider caches and offerings rather than just "caches." NWAF work at Chiapa de Corzo was undertaken with the working concepts of "burials" and "caches," and diligent efforts were taken to distinguish between the two, and within each category to also specify types of caches and burials. The notion of "offering" crosscuts these traditional categorizations and exposes some of their limitations. As defined above, all caches qualify as offerings, but not all offerings qualify as caches. Anything "offered" would constitute an offering. The term "cache" denotes multiple items and deliberate placement and, when used in tandem with the notion of "burial," items unaccompanied with human remains. Objects commingled with human bones are described as burial "offerings" rather than "caches," even when there are no significant differences between the kinds of things placed in the heartings of buildings or with human remains.

These analytical categories get in the way of understanding ancient offering practices. For example, in Pierre Agrinier's (1964) summary of "burials" from Chiapa de Corzo he makes it clear that many of the "burials" were actually dedicatory offerings in the strict sense. Judging from accompanying burial goods, the Istmo phase or late Protoclassic period saw a dramatic increase in the placement of human bodies in buildings sans burial goods (Lowe 1964:65, Table V), a likely indicator that these bodies or bones were not "burials" but human "offerings" to the building in which they were placed.

The people at Chiapa de Corzo do not appear to have made the same sorts of distinctions between people and things that archaeologists who worked at the site made. Some of the difficulty is linguistic. Both "cache" and "burial" have analytical as well as everyday meanings. As deployed in NWAF reports, the terms have been used mostly analytically and descriptively to classify different kinds of remains. We wish to understand the events behind the deposition of the materials involved in cultural terms that would have been meaningful for the ancient persons involved. As described in the following chapter, some of the "burials" recovered from Mound 17 were, in truth, "offerings" and ought to be understood as such in the historic context and architectural setting in which they occurred. That said, it is not clear whether categorical distinctions were blurred in the opposite direction (e.g., whether some objects are "burials" rather than offerings or caches).

### Dili and Dzemba Phases

No offerings have yet been definitely assigned to these phases for Chiapa de Corzo. We suspect that some of the axe offerings at the foot of Mound 11, currently assigned to the following phase, may date to the Dzemba phase. Bruce Bachand (2013) presents an argument to the contrary. We follow his assessments of phasing here.

### Escalera Phase

The earliest offerings at Chiapa de Corzo have been assigned to the beginning of the

Escalera phase about 800-750 BC in Bachand's assessment of the chronology. They consist of jade, serpentine, andesite, limestone, and sandstone axes found in offering pits just to the east of Mound 11 on the transverse axis that bisects Mounds 11 and 12 (see Bachand and Lowe 2011). Most of these axes were "pseudo-axes," meaning stones carved in the shape and size of axes but not meant to be serviceable chopping tools. The meaning of these symbolic axes, and caches of them, remain to be worked out. The Chiapa de Corzo axe offerings bear strong resemblances to axe and pseudo-axe offerings at the coeval sites of San Isidro, Chiapas, and La Venta, Tabasco (Drucker et al. 1959; Lowe 1981, 1999). No pottery vessels were included in the earliest offerings at Chiapa de Corzo. Ceramic pots are also rare in offerings at the other two coeval sites just mentioned. Axes arranged in a horizontal cruciform pattern were found at the eastern base of Mound 11. This offering dates to around 800 BC (Bachand 2013). Included were two deep pits for placing layers of axes, similar to offerings at La Venta, San Isidro, and Ceibal (Bachand and Lowe 2011).

Ceramic vessels similar to those found in the cist tomb at La Venta were found in the capping levels of the massive axe offering pit at Chiapa de Corzo at the eastern foot of Mound 11 (Bachand and Lowe 2011:77). In the uppermost level of the pit containing Massive Offering 1 just east of Mound 11 was found a "burial" with some ceramic vessels which date to the very beginning of the Escalera phase. This burial is more likely a human component of an offering, likely a sacrificial victim. If so, this offering would be the earliest evidence at Chiapa de Corzo of human sacrifice and of dedicatory offerings containing both humans and ceramic vessels. Both items continued to be offered in buildings throughout the history of Chiapa de Corzo. The placement of axes in offerings or burials continued until the end of Escalera times, but not after.

Escalera phase offerings of any sort are rare at Chiapa de Corzo and at all coeval Chiapas centers (Clark 2016). A possible cache was located in Mound 7 (Lowe 1962b:49) and is thought to have been a terminal offering. It consists of a single neckless jar lying in a layer of ashes. Lowe posited the possibility that the pot was merely refuse rather than a deliberate offering. It may well have been, but we think it unlikely. It is worth pointing out that all the Escalera phase offerings associated with Mound 11 were found at the foot of the mound and not in the mound itself. One reason Escalera phase offerings may be so rare is that archaeologists have looked for them in the wrong places. They were non-architectural. An Escalera-Francesa offering is reported for Mound 15 (Glauner et al. in press), but it was outside the mound. The practice of placing caches of pots inside building layers to dedicate construction events appears to have begun in Chiapa IV times. Very few Chiapa IV caches have been found off-mound, although this was the preferred location of human burials for that period (Lowe 1964).

### Francesa Phase

Before the Mound 17 salvage excavations, 10 caches were known for the Francesa phase at Chiapa de Corzo. They were found in Mounds 5b, 7, 12, and 36. Of these caches, four were dedicatory, one was terminal, and five were not assigned to either type. They consisted primarily of ceramic vessels, but four caches contained other items. One cache had a marine bivalve, another a small white stone, a third was capped with a small flat rock, and a fourth was a complex offering. This last, more elaborate cache in Mound 7 consisted of two jade ear flares, a shell pendant, a jade bead, and a rectangular, sherd-backed pyrite mirror. These appear to be a set of elite jewelry. Eighteen of the 20 ceramic vessels found in these caches are bowls and cylinders. Two jars were also found, each in different caches. Hence, the cache mode for vessel forms was about two bowls and one cylinder per cache.

The Francesa phase caches found in salvage excavations of Mound 17 only have ceramic vessels and therefore conform with the general tendency at Chiapa de Corzo. Nonetheless, Francesa vessel form frequencies and their patterning from Mound 17 differ from those known for the rest of Chiapa de Corzo. Cylinders rather than bowls were the most frequent form in the Mound 17 caches. In

Table 2. Comparison of the frequency of caches at Mound 17 to those at the rest of the site.

| Phase | # for Md. 17 | % | # for all others | % |
|---|---|---|---|---|
| E | 0 | 0 | 14 | 10.3 |
| F | 5 | 41.2 | 40 | 29.4 |
| G | 1 | 8.3 | 10 | 7.4 |
| H | 6 | 50.0 | 72 | 52.9 |
| Total | 12 | | 136 | |

these same caches, jars were more frequent than bowls. Only one plate was found in the Mound 17 caches; plates are not otherwise represented in Chiapa de Corzo Francesa phase caches.

### Guanacaste Phase

No caches of this phase were reported for Chiapa de Corzo before the salvage excavations of Mound 17. Cache 2 from Mound 17 has been described above. Only more excavations at Chiapa de Corzo structures of this phase will provide information concerning the site-wide offering pattern. Glauner et al. (in press) report five Guanacaste phase caches for Mound 15, located about 150 m southeast of Mound 17.

### Horcones Phase

Even without the addition of the Mound 17 caches, the total number of caches at Chiapa de Corzo is highest for the Horcones phase (Table 2). Seventy-two separate caches from various mounds demonstrate a general Chiapa de Corzo trend towards larger and more complex caches through time. These caches are fairly evenly split between dedicatory and terminal offerings. Sixteen of these caches were placed in prepared repositories. These were constructed of two or more levels of prepared stone courses laid down in mud mortar to form walls. Slab cists with large tabular stones set on edge also served as cache containers, but rarely. Only two cases of this type of prepared repository are known for Chiapa de Corzo. The rectangular repository is the most frequent type at the site (10 examples), followed by the circular form (4 instances).

All but four prepared repositories contained dedicatory offerings. The four exceptions held terminal caches. Prepared repositories were a new feature for caches at Chiapa de Corzo during Horcones times and accord with the trend toward greater complexity and the increased frequency of caches, in general. Special repositories for offerings were not found in Mound 17. Two of the four exceptions just mentioned of terminal cache offerings in prepared repositories were found in Mound 5. The masonry "boxes" or hiding places in Mound 5 were much larger and deeper than normal rectangular repositories at Chiapa de Corzo. The fact that they contained two of the four known terminal caches accents their importance and perhaps also indicates a different function. The Mound 5 civic-ceremonial building or "palace" and its caches (13 in number, but perhaps only one large building-wide offering) is unique at Chiapa de Corzo (Lowe 1962b:23-24). Perhaps the exceptional Mound 5 caches should be excluded in gauging general trends at Chiapa de Corzo for Horcones phase caches.

The average number of ceramic vessels per cache rose during Horcones times from just over two per offering to over six. In Horcones phase caches, bowls were nearly ten times as frequent as incense burner bowls with interior horns, the next most frequent form. In descending order of frequency are cylinders, special forms (effigy vessels, flaring rim bowls, multiple compartment vessel, etc.), and plates. Bowls occur in about half the caches, but when present they average over 15 vessels per cache. The average occurrence of other vessel forms is about two vessels per cache for jars, cylinders, and incense burners, and one and one-half vessels per cache for special pots. There is a single instance of a plate form being included as an offering.

One of the most dramatic, new features in the Horcones phase caches at Chiapa de Corzo

was the inclusion of other kinds of objects
with pots. At least 16 caches (about 26% of
the total) included non-vessel objects. These
objects include obsidian blades (19 specimens
in four caches, expressed hereafter as 19/4),
anthropomorphic figurines (3/2), ceramic
"anvils" (5/3), marble or alabaster earspools
(13/3), ladle incense burners (2/2), a large
amber bead (1/1), a carved canine (1/1), flat
and cylindrical ceramic stamps (18/1), small
unworked pebbles or cobbles (4/5), and a deer
antler tine (1/1). Many of these artifacts were
included in Horcones caches from the palace
at Mound 5 and thus are not typical of Chiapa
de Corzo caches for this period. Two Mound 17
Horcones phase caches included obsidian blades.

Many new vessel forms were present in
the Horcones caches, including bowls with
mamiform tetrapod supports (3/3), armadillo
effigy vessels (3/2), anthropomorphic effigy
vessels, and a fish effigy on a flaring rim bowl.
Pots imported from outside the region occur
in two caches. One is an Usulutan effigy fish
bowl and the other is a gray, stirrup-spout
anthropomorphic effigy jar from Oaxaca (Lowe
1960b:60, fig. 62). The occurrence of imported
ceramic vessels at Chiapa de Corzo in Horcones
phase caches is indicative of the nature and
extent of commercial relations during this
phase. At the time, Chiapa de Corzo was well
connected via trading networks both to the
north and the far southeast. That the ancient
Chiapacorzeños had the purchasing power to
acquire what must have been costly goods is a
demonstration of their position in their region
and in Mesoamerica. Confirmatory evidence of
these foreign ties is also seen in goods placed
with the burials of honored dead, as described in
the next chapter.

## General Comments

Much of the significance of the Chiapa
de Corzo offering patterns is best appreciated
in relation to burial practices, a discussion we
defer until we have described these burials. Not
enough of the site has been excavated to place
much significance in the spatial patterning of
offerings per phase. Most of our information
comes from the southwest sector of the site.
Each mound there has a different history, as

described in Chapter 2. The pooled results from
many mounds there show significant changes
through time in the frequency of caches and the
kinds of objects placed in them. From Chiapa
III to IV times we posit a shift from durable
to perishable items. The earliest offerings
were stone axes and fragments of stone in
various numbers and assortments. Beginning
with the Francesa phase, ceramic vessels of
various shapes and colors became the main
objects of enduring quality. We presume these
contained food and drink. By Horcones times
they started to serve as containers for assorted
items, such as small roundish cobbles as sets
– thus getting back to the earliest caches and
stones as groups of items of probable ritual
significance. We have not yet attempted an
analysis of the changing symbolism of the
caches. We are still trying to organize the data
from all excavations undertaken over the years.
Our preliminary impressions are that ceramic
vessels appear to have been placed in offerings
as specialized containers for perishable items
and then to have evolved to the notion of generic
containers for all sorts of items by Horcones
times. It was at this same time that offering
boxes were constructed as integral elements
of public buildings to contain offerings. One
possible implication is that these could have
been multiple use facilities – like ossuaries for
offerings – with offerings being occasionally
replaced and refreshed, much like candles on an
altar.

The increasing frequency of offerings
through time at Chiapa de Corzo was
interrupted in Guanacaste times. Burials show
a similar reduction in frequency (see Chapter
4). All the information from Chiapa de Corzo
from this period indicates a period of significant
change from previous times, as discussed in
the next chapter. During the Guanacaste phase
Chiapa de Corzo appears to have come under
Maya influence of some sort. The nature and
impact of that "influence" are some of the major
questions that need to be resolved for the early
history of this ancient center. One key to the
answer may lie in changes in burial practices
and symbolism, a dataset that we add to in the
following chapter.

# CHAPTER 4

# BURIALS

Burials at Chiapa de Corzo were distinguished from caches by the presence of human remains. Our treatment of burials follows the format of the previous chapter for caches, starting with descriptions of burials in numerical sequence and followed by phase-by-phase summaries. Fifteen human interments, mostly in stratigraphic position, were located in Mound 17, all in Excavation Unit A. Only one burial (17-11) was in a formally prepared crypt. The other 14 burials were apparently placed in simple pits excavated into extant mound fill. Perhaps due to the hurried nature of the excavations, no evidence of mortuary pits of the simpler grave type was found. The locations of these burials are shown in Figure 5. We also include here the burial CC-26 found by Brockington in Test Pit 125 in the east wing of Mound 17.

Burials are considered in the order they were encountered rather than by phase. With the exception of the burial CC-26 found in Test Pit 125, burial numbers assigned in the field were specific for Mound 17 and not part of the pre-existing burial number sequence reported by Pierre Agrinier (1964) for Chiapa de Corzo. To prevent confusion with other numbered burials from Chiapa de Corzo, we prefixed a "17" to each burial (the practice for caches) to distinguish them from burials in the master list for the site (Agrinier 1964). We have since assigned Chiapa de Corzo (CC) numbers to the Mound 17 burials to include them on the master list for the site [CC numbers shown in brackets]. In the following descriptions, identifications of the age and sex of the human remains come from an analysis made by Phillip Walker (his report is Appendix 1). As with the artifacts reported for caches, most artifacts included as burial offerings have MRE numbers.

Many burials had rather elaborate mortuary offerings. The most elaborate of these, Burial 17-6, ranks among the most complex known from Chiapa de Corzo (cf. Agrinier 1964). Surprisingly, no trace of a formal tomb or crypt was found around this burial. Following descriptions of individual burials, the final sections of this chapter summarize Mound 17 burial patterns by phase and then place them in the context of the full burial population from the site.

## MOUND 17 BURIALS
### Burial CC-26 (Figure 31)

**Type:** Simple interment in fill.

**Sex:** Not determined.

**Age:** Adult.

**Orientation:** Head to the south, face up.

**Position:** Not determined.

**Location:** Approximate center of Mound 17 east wing, 16 cm below the surface (see Lowe 1962b:56).

**Phase:** Escalera

**Contents:** "Single incomplete (roughly one-half) polished orange 'cuspidor' bowl [Lowe 1962b: fig. 32], fragments of which were mixed with the burial" (Lowe 1962b:56).

**Remarks:** "The bones of the burial were all badly broken, and only a few were present. The burial looks all mixed up. The sherds are also broken and scattered. It looks like a disturbed and scattered burial and offering. This burial with its offerings was located 83 cm from the south wall of the [Test Pit 125], 64 cm from the west wall, and 16 cm below the surface. The

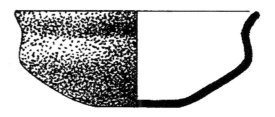

Figure 31. Burial 26 offering.

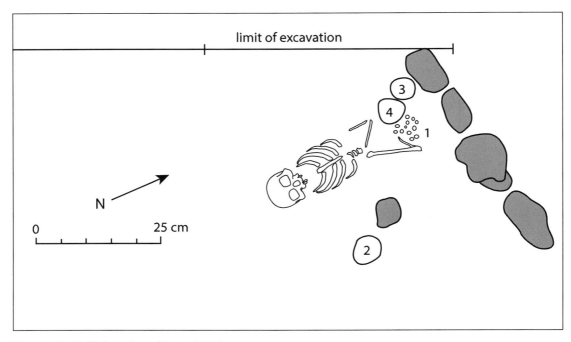

Figure 32. Field drawing of Burial 17-1.

bones and the sherds were placed in separate bags. The bones represent part of the skull and some other bones that must be fragments of long bones. A single offering of a badly broken bowl was slightly covering the west side of the burial. All must have been disturbed. The bones and sherds extended down 12 cm to 28 cm below the surface" (Brockington n.d.). "Burial 26 was thought by the excavator to have been disturbed and reburied in relatively recent times, but it is equally plausible that it was a secondary burial interred anciently in the platform surface" (Lowe 1962b:56).

### Burial 17-1 [CC 183] (Figures 32-33)

**Type:** Simple pit, individual.

**Sex:** Undetermined.

**Age:** Infant, six months.

**Orientation:** Head to the south, face up.

**Position:** Extended, on back.

**Location:** Near north edge of Excavation Unit A, Section 5, depth 2.55 m.

**Phase:** Francesa.

**Contents:**

1. 52 Jade sub-rectangular beads, width 0.4 cm, diameter 0.6 cm (Fig. 33b). MRE-4533.

2. Cintalapa Grooved-composite: Cintalapa Variety bowl; height 6.5+ cm, diameter 18.2 cm (Fig. 33a, rim reconstructed in drawing). MRE-4428.

3. Cintalapa Grooved-composite: Cintalapa Variety bowl; height 8.6+ cm, diameter 11.2 cm (Fig. 33d). MRE-4429.

4. Cintalapa Grooved-composite: Cintalapa Variety bowl; height 10.6 cm, diameter 24.8 cm (Fig. 33c, reconstruction drawing). Sherds placed in the NWAF type collection.

5. Human bones. MRE-4658.

**Remarks:** The jade beads were scattered over what would have been the feet, and Vessels 3 and 4 were just to the west of this area.

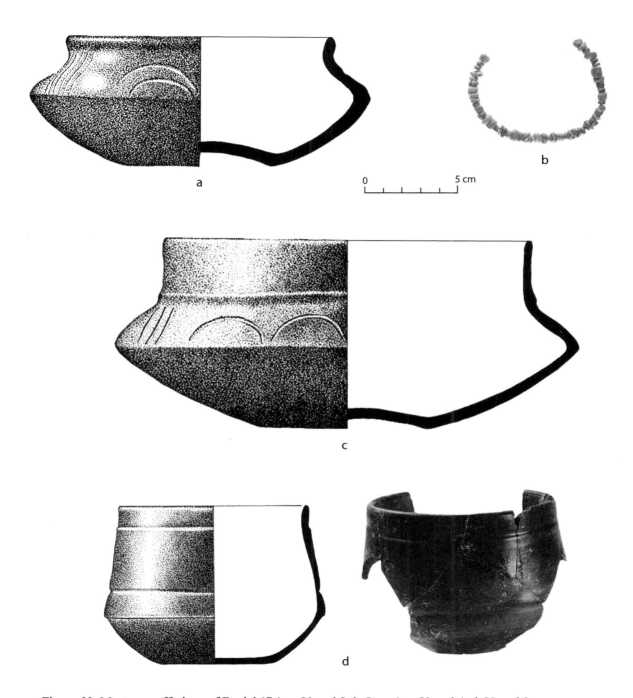

Figure 33. Mortuary offerings of Burial 17-1; a. Vessel 2, b. Item 1, c. Vessel 4, d. Vessel 3.

## Burial 17-2a and 17-2b [CC 184]
## (Figures 34-37)

**Type:** Simple pit, multiple.

**Sex:** Undetermined.

**Age:** a) Child 6-7 yrs, b) Youth 5-10 yrs.

**Orientation:** a, head to east, face turned to the north; b, head to west, face up.

**Position:** Extended, on back. 17-2a, head turned to right side.

**Location:** Excavation Unit A, Sections 9-10, depth 2.5 m.

**Phase:** Early Guanacaste.

**Contents:**

1. Shell pendant with inlaid jade placed over mouth of Burial 17-2a. One valve (*Spondylus* cf. *calcifer*); length 7 cm, width 6.1 cm (Fig. 34b). MRE-4534.

2. Two jade bracelets; right, 44 disk beads, thickness 0.4 cm, diameter 0.7 cm (Fig. 34d) left, 30 beads, 14 tubular, length 1 cm, diameter 0.6 cm; 16 disk, thickness 0.4 cm, diameter 0.7 cm (Fig. 34f). MRE-4535, MRE-4536.

3. Jade mosaic fragments (6), 3 simple, 2 perforated, 1 tubular bead; bead placed near mouth, length 2.3 cm, width 1.1 cm, thickness 0.31 cm (Fig. 34g). MRE-4537.

4. Shell pendant with inlaid jade, incised decoration, and red pigment; carved designs depict human arms and legs. One valve (*Spondylus* cf. *americanus* or *princeps*); length 7.9 cm, width 5.3 cm (Fig. 34c). MRE-4538.

5. Gastropod shell pendant (*Fasciolaria princeps*), spire cut off and three suspension holes drilled about opening, traces of red pigment; length 12 cm, width 4.9 cm (Fig. 34a). MRE-4539.

6. Mundet Red: Polished Variety bowl; height 10.0 cm, diameter 14.7 cm (Fig. 34o). MRE-4431.

7. Cintalapa Grooved-composite: Cintalapa Variety bowl; height 7.2 cm, diameter 16.6 cm (Fig. 34n). MRE-4432.

8. Cintalapa Grooved-composite: Cintalapa Variety bowl; height 4.2 cm, diameter 11.9 cm (Fig. 34j). MRE-4433.

9. Cintalapa Grooved-composite: Cintalapa Variety bowl; height 4.5 cm, diameter 10.2 cm, (Fig. 34i). MRE-4434. Placed mouth down on Vessel 10 in a lip-to-lip arrangement.

10. Nicapa Orange-Resist: Unspecified Variety bowl; height 3.4 cm, diameter 13.6 cm, (Fig. 34k). MRE-4435.

11. Rafael Incised: Rafael Variety flaring-rim plate; height 3.5 cm, diameter 19.0 cm (Fig. 34m). MRE-4436. Placed on chest, mouth up.

12. Cintalapa Grooved-composite: Cintalapa Variety bowl, height 5.7 cm, diameter 14.2 cm, (Fig. 34l). MRE-4437.

13. Small white pebble.

14. Jade bead, tubular; length 1.4 cm, diameter 1 cm, central hole diameter 0.5 cm (Fig. 34h). MRE-4540.

15. Two small white stone ear flares, probably of alabaster. One found on top of the head of Burial 2a, the other underneath the head.

16. Twelve shell beads (*Olivella* sp.); length 1.4 cm, diameter 7 cm (Fig. 34e). Found near the midsection of 17-2b. MRE-4505. The beads appeared to be in two rows.

17. Skeleton of snake (species unknown) inside items 9 and 10.

18. Bones MRE-4659; teeth MRE-4660; 17-2b teeth MRE-4662.

**Remarks:** This double burial consisted of a child burial (2a) over a few poorly preserved bones of another youth (2b). Burial 17-2b was directly under Burial 17-2a. The mortuary offerings definitely associated with Burial 17-2b were items 1, 2, 3, 4, 5, 14, and 16. The burial was placed in a simple pit dug into a light tan clay matrix. All of the whole vessels appear to have been with Burial 17-2a.

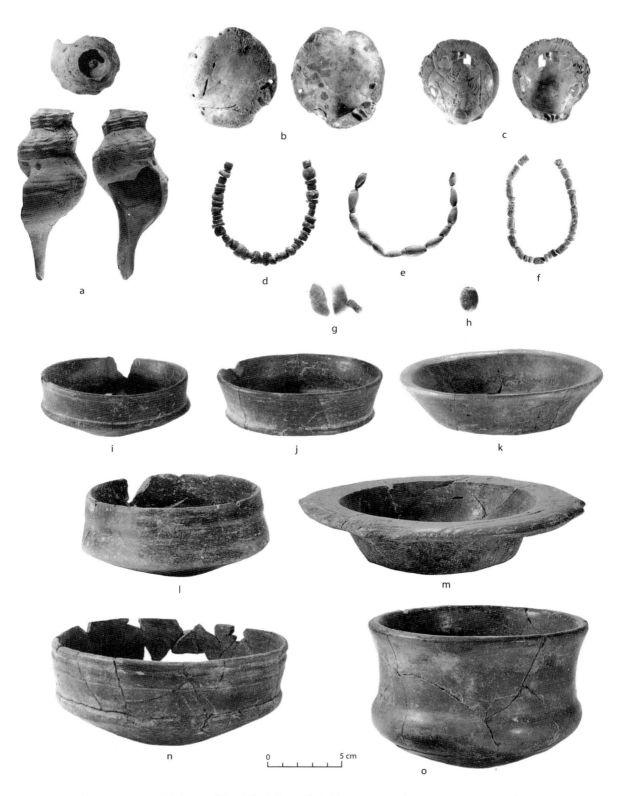

Figure 34. Mortuary offerings of Burial 17-2a and 17-2b; a. Item 5, b. Item 1, c. Item 4, d. Item 2, e. Item 16, f. Item 2, g. Item 3, h. Item 14, i. Vessel 9, j. Vessel 8, k. Vessel 10, l. Vessel 12, m. Vessel 11, n. Vessel 7, o. Vessel 6.

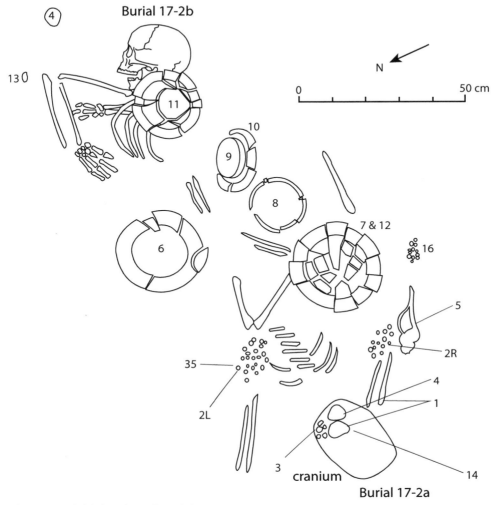

Figure 35. Field drawing of Burial 17-2.

Figure 36. Mortuary offerings of Burial 17-2. One vessel is from Burial 17-1 (see fig. 33c).

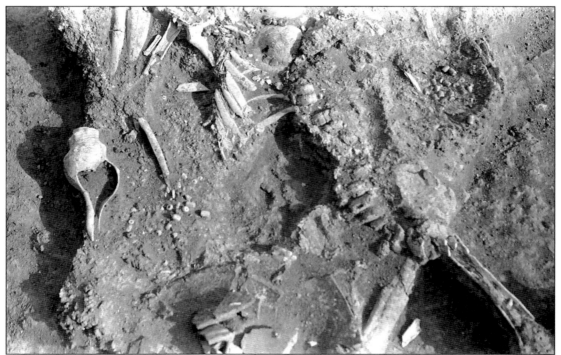

Figure 37. Photographs of Burial 17-2.

### Burial 17-3 [CC 185] (Figures 38-41)

**Type:** Stone lined pit, individual.

**Sex:** Undetermined.

**Age:** Adult, 25+ yrs.

**Orientation:** Head to the north, face up.

**Position:** Extended, on back.

**Location:** Excavation Unit A, Section 6, depth 3.22 m.

**Phase:** Francesa.

**Contents:**

1. Tzutzuculi White-to-buff jar; height 25.3 cm, diameter 28.0 cm (Fig. 41a). MRE-4438.

2. Copoya Coarse jar, fragmentary; height 18.0 cm, diameter 25.4 cm (Fig. 41e). MRE-4449.

3. Mundet Red: Polished Variety jar; height 20.8 cm, diameter 21.4 cm (Fig. 41b). MRE-4439.

4. Quechula smudged: Quechula Variety vase; height 15.0 cm, diameter 14.9 cm (Fig. 40a). MRE-4440.

5. Mundet Red: Polished Variety plate; height 4.9 cm, diameter 23.3 cm (Fig. 40e). MRE-4441.

6. Acambac Modeled: Painted Variety jar; height 24.3 cm, diameter 25.5 cm (Fig. 41c). MRE-4442. For type description see Lee (1974a:41, fig. 43a).

7. Mundet Red: Matte Variety cylinder; height 15.9 cm, diameter 9.7 cm (Fig. 40f). MRE-4443.

8. Broken, badly destroyed Mundet Red: Polished Variety jar; height 16+ cm, diameter 21+ cm (Fig. 40b, reconstruction drawing). MRE-4444.

9. Mundet Red: Polished Variety jar; height 13.7 cm, diameter 16.2 cm (Fig. 40c). MRE-4445.

10. Libertad Black-brown: Libertad Variety bowl; height 6.5 cm, diameter 19.0 cm (Fig. 40d). MRE-4446.

11. Mundet Red: Matte Variety jar; height 15.2 cm, diameter 24.6 cm (Fig. 41d). MRE-4447.

12. Bivalve shell fragments; maximum length 15 cm and width 8 cm. MRE-4506.

13. & 14. Teeth. MRE-4661.

**Remarks:** This is one of the most complex burials from Mound 17 and one of the few with a marked burial pit lined with stones. The large number of vessels is surprising given the absence of jade finery.

Figure 38. Field drawing of Burial 17-3, sketch not to scale.

Figure 39. Photograph of Burial 17-3.

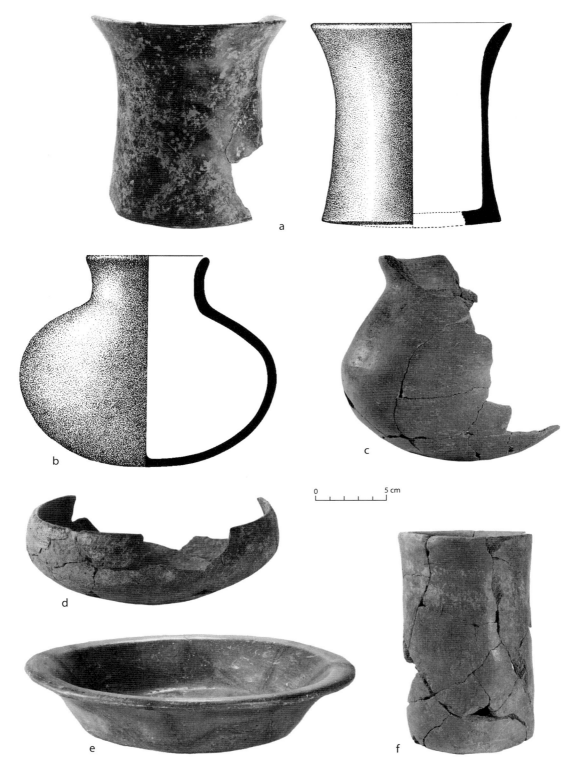

Figure 40. Mortuary offerings of Burial 17-3; a. Vessel 4, b. Vessel 8, c. Vessel 9, d. Vessel 10, e. Vessel 5, f. Vessel 7.

Figure 41. Mortuary offerings of Burial 17-3; a. Vessel 1, b. Vessel 3, c. Vessel 6, d. Vessel 11, e. Vessel 2.

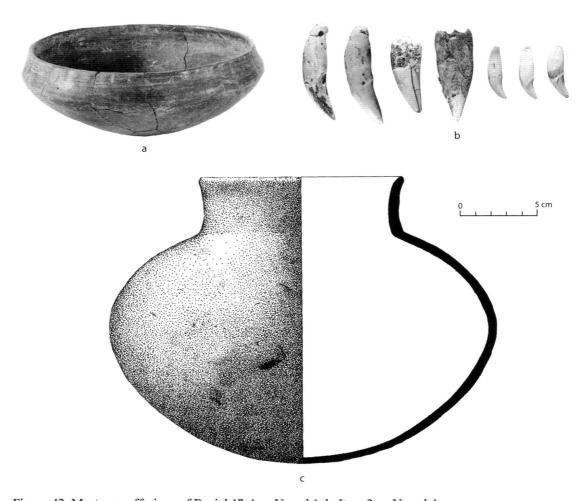

Figure 42. Mortuary offerings of Burial 17-4; a. Vessel 1, b. Item 2, c. Vessel 4.

### Burial 17-4 [CC 186] (Figures 42-44)

**Type:** Simple pit, individual.

**Sex:** Undetermined.

**Age:** Adult.

**Orientation:** Head to the west, face turned to the north.

**Position:** Extended, on back. Legs doubled up. Arms flexed, one on the other to the right. Head on right side.

**Location:** Excavation Unit A, Section 9, depth 3.7 m.

**Phase:** Francesa.

**Contents:**

1. Cintalapa Grooved-composite: Cintalapa Variety plate, with a few small remaining pieces of stucco in white and pastel red and green colors stuck to it; height 6.0 cm, diameter 15.9 cm (Fig. 42a). MRE-4448.

2. Canine-tooth necklace, seven teeth. Length 6.5 cm, width 1.5+ cm (Fig. 42b). MRE-4507.

3. Small shell bead.

4. Mundet Red: Matte Variety jar; height 19.1+ cm, diameter 25.1+ cm (Fig. 42c, reconstruction drawing). Sherds placed in type collection.

**Remarks:** The tooth necklace was in front of the left hand on a rock slab.

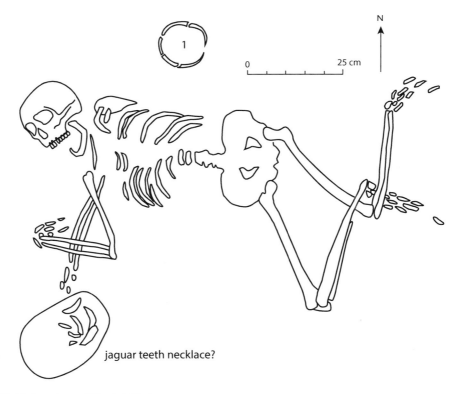

jaguar teeth necklace?

Figure 43. Field drawing of Burial 17-4.

Figure 44. Photograph of Burial 17-4.

Figure 45. Photograph of Burial 17-5.

### Burial 17-5 [CC 187] (Figures 45-47)

**Type:** Simple pit, individual.

**Sex:** Undetermined.

**Age:** Adult.

**Orientation:** Waist of body pointing east, body lacks thorax, right arm and skull.

**Position:** Extended, on back. Heels together, legs slightly drawn up separating knees widely. Arms at side.

**Location:** Excavation Unit A, Section 5, depth 3.8 m.

**Phase:** Escalera.

**Contents:**

   1. Nicapa Orange-Resist: Nicapa Variety plate; height 4.4 cm, diameter 20.5 cm (Fig. 46). MRE-4450.

   2. Human bones, MRE-4665.

**Remarks:** The vessel was found mouth up between the heels of the feet.

0       5 cm

Figure 46. Mortuary offering of Burial 17-5.

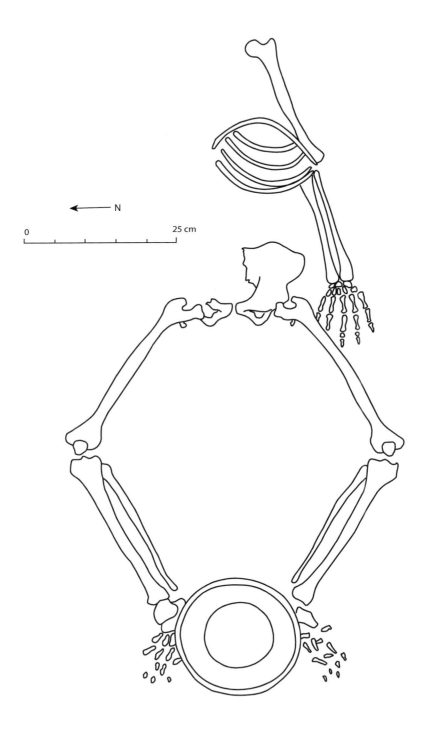

Figure 47. Field drawing of Burial 17-5.

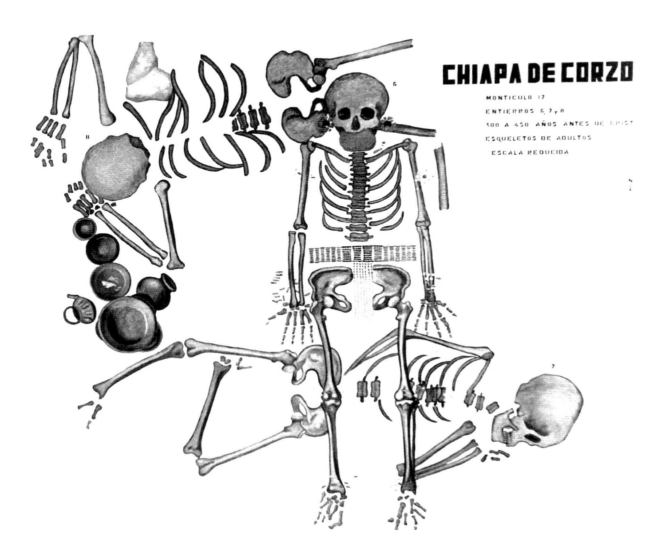

Figure 48. Reconstruction painting of Burials 17-6, 17-7, and 17-8 that was part of the museum exhibit of the materials salvaged from Mound 17.

**Burial 17-6 [CC 188] (Figures 48-61)**

**Type:** Simple pit, multiple, principal individual with two sacrificial victims as part of mortuary offering.

**Sex:** Male.

**Age:** Adult, 25± years.

**Orientation:** Head toward the southeast.

**Position:** Extended on the back, face up. Head of Burial 17-6 rested on the buttocks of Burial 17-8, while his legs were stretched out straight with the knees over the waist and chest of Burial 17-7.

**Location:** Excavation Unit A, Section 7, depth 4.7 m.

**Phase:** Francesa.

**Contents:**

1. Right anklet, 77 beads: 5 tubular jade beads, length 1.7 cm, diameter 0.7 cm; 36 disk jade beads, thickness 0.4 cm, diameter 0.7 cm; 36 disk shell beads, thickness 0.5 cm, diameter 0.7 cm (Fig. 56a). MRE-1852.

2. Left anklet, 67 beads: 5 tubular jade beads, length 1.7 cm, diameter 0.8 cm; 39 disk jade beads thickness 0.4 cm, diameter 0.7 cm; 23 disk shell beads, thickness 0.3 cm, diameter 0.6 cm (Fig. 56b). MNA000159, MRE-4509.

3. Right kneelet, 24 beads: 4 large tubular jade beads, length 2.6 cm, diameter 1.2 cm; 5 teardrop shell beads, length 1.5 cm, diameter 1 cm; 4 subspherical shell beads, thickness 0.5 cm, diameter 0.9 cm; 11 hemispherical shell beads, thickness 1 cm, diameter 1.5 cm (Fig. 56c). MNA000160, MRE-1845.

4. Left kneelet, 20 beads: 3 teardrop shell beads, length 1.8 cm, diameter 0.9 cm; 4 subspherical shell beads, thickness 0.7 cm, diameter 0.9 cm; 13 hemispherical shell beads, thickness 0.6 cm, diameter 1.5 cm (Fig. 56d). MRE-1843.

5. Right bracelet; 88 subspherical jade beads, thickness 0.4 cm, diameter 0.5 cm (Fig. 56e). MRE-1851.

6. Left bracelet, 74 beads and a pendent: 1 *Olivella* sp. shell pendant, length 1.1 cm;

diameter 0.6 cm; 3 tubular jade beads, length 1.3 cm, diameter 0.6 cm; 37 disk jade beads, thickness 0.7 cm, diameter 0.4 cm; 34 disk shell beads, thickness 0.8 cm, diameter 0.5 cm (Fig. 56f). MRE-4513.

6a. Second left bracelet (single strand, doubled over) of 97 jade and 117 shell disk beads; thickness 0.5 cm, diameter 0.8 cm (Fig. 56g). MRE-1848.

7. Jade bead belt (Figs. 53 and 55). This two piece belt was found in the burial in such a state that its original shape and construction are accurately known. The belt consisted of a waist band with hanging tassels in the front center. The waist band was constructed of 30 columns of tubular jade beads. Each column was nine beads high. Each column had the longest beads at each end of the column with progressively shorter beads towards the center of the column. The four central columns of beads are much larger than the other columns. The beads in these four columns were decorated with two types of surface grooves. One decoration consists of long spiral grooves which run from one end of the bead to the other, narrow ridges separate paired grooves. Two of these spiral beads are further differentiated by a small groove at each end of the bead which defines the non-spiraled tip of the bead. The second groove decoration consists of three or four broad grooves which encircle beads and leave a raised ridge between each pair of grooves. The central ridges of these beads are often larger than the ridges near the ends. All other column beads are plain, undecorated tubular beads. Each end of this bead waist band was finished off by two plain tubular beads arranged as though they were the ends of the next column, which had no other beads. The band was composed of 283 jade beads. The sash which hung from the lower row of the two central columns of beads comprised both jade and shell beads arranged in seven long tassel-like columns. Each of these long columns was made up in order (from the top to bottom, as suspended) of one truncated conical jade bead, three or four plain tubular jade beads, one or two subspherical jade beads, ten shell disk beads alternating with ten jade disk beads, and finally

20-24 small subspherical and disk jade beads. There are 341 beads in the sash, making 624 bead elements in the entire belt. MNA000161.

8. Left armlet, 38 beads: 4 teardrop shell beads, length 1.4 cm, diameter 0.9 cm; 3 subspherical shell beads, thickness 0.7 cm, diameter 0.8 cm; 2 hemispherical shell beads, thickness 0.6 cm, diameter 1.2 cm; 16 small tubular jade beads, length 0.9 cm, diameter 0.6 cm; 13 disk jade beads, thickness 0.4 cm, diameter 0.6 cm (Fig. 56h). MRE-1846.

9-10. Now parts of No. 7, jade belt.

11. Right armlet, 11 beads: 3 teardrop shell beads, length 1.7 cm, diameter 0.9 cm; 2 subspherical shell beads, thickness 0.7 cm, diameter 0.9 cm; 3 hemispherical shell beads, thickness 0.7 cm, diameter 1.2 cm; 3 constricted tubular jade beads, length 1.3 cm, diameter 0.6 cm; 3 tubular jade beads, length 0.9 cm, diameter 0.5 cm (Fig. 56i). MRE-4516.

12. Necklace; 88 small irregular and subspherical pearls, maximum diameter 0.4 cm, minimum diameter 0.15 cm; 1 large subspherical jade bead, thickness 0.6 cm, diameter 1.5 cm (Fig. 56j). MRE-1849.

13. Necklace; 57 small irregular and subspherical pearls, maximum diameter 0.5 cm, minimum diameter 0.2 cm; 7 subspherical jade beads, thickness 0.6 cm, diameter 0.8 cm; 6 disk jade beads, thickness 0.3 cm, diameter 0.5 cm (Fig. 56k). MRE-1847.

14. Left mosaic jade earspool pieces; 1 disk and 8 irregular rectangular thin jade pieces. Disk, diameter 1 cm; largest rectangular piece, length 2.1 cm, width 1.1 cm, thickness 1 cm (Fig. 61a). MRE-1857.

15. Right mosaic jade earspool pieces; 5 rectangular and irregular formed pieces, length 1.4 cm, width 1.1 cm, thickness 0.3 cm (Fig. 61b). MRE-1857.

16. Shell mouth cover; 1 valve of a marine clam shell, ground and polished on the interior and exterior surfaces; two biconical holes 0.3 cm in diameter drilled through the edge for hanging as a pendant, four small cavities are drilled in the exterior surface to embed mosaic pieces; a crude rectilinear design is scratched into

exterior surface (Fig. 60a). MRE-1853.

17. Libertad Black-brown: Libertad Variety bowl; height 4.5 cm, diameter 13.5 cm (Fig. 57a). MRE-1839.

18. Nicapa Orange-Resist: Nicapa Variety plate; height 6.0 cm, diameter 23.4 cm (Fig. 58b). MRE-4451.

19. Libertad Black-brown: Libertad Variety hemispherical bowl; height 6.9 cm, diameter 12.8 cm (Fig. 57g). MRE-1837.

20. Nicapa Orange-Resist: Nicapa Variety bowl (fragmentary); height 7.7 cm, diameter 18.7± cm (Fig. 57e). MRE-4583.

21. Cintalapa Grooved-composite: Cintalapa Variety bowl; height 4.5 cm, diameter 11.7 cm (Fig. 57b). MRE-1838.

22. Mundet Red: Matte Variety jar; height 15.4 cm, diameter 17.5 cm (Fig. 57h). MRE-1836.

23. Libertad Black-brown: Libertad Variety bowl; height 5.5 cm, diameter 10.8 cm (Fig. 57d). MRE-1842.

24. Nicapa Orange Resist: Crystal Ash Variety jar with bridge-spout and basket handle; height 12 cm, diameter 15.8 cm (Fig. 59). MNA000162.

25. Unworked freshwater clam shell; length 8.6+ cm, width 5.9 cm (Fig. 60b). MRE-1856, MRE-4522 (fragments), MRE-1850.

26. Unworked freshwater clam shell; length 8.5 cm, width 4.9 cm (Fig. 60d). MRE-1854.

27. Nicapa Orange-Resist: Nicapa Variety plate; height 4.0 cm, diameter 23.3 cm (Fig. 58a). MRE-1835.

28. Nicapa Orange-Resist: Nicapa Variety plate; height 3.8 cm, diameter 20.3 cm (Fig. 57i). MRE-1834.

29. Cintalapa Grooved-composite: Cintalapa Variety bowl; height 5.5 cm, diameter 14.5 cm (Fig. 57f). MRE-1841.

30. Libertad Black-brown: Libertad Variety bowl; height 3.8 cm, diameter 11.3 cm, (Fig. 57c). MRE-1840.

31. Unworked freshwater clam shell; length 9.7 cm, width 6.1 cm (Fig. 60c). MRE-1855.

32. Teeth MRE-4664, Bones MRE-4669,

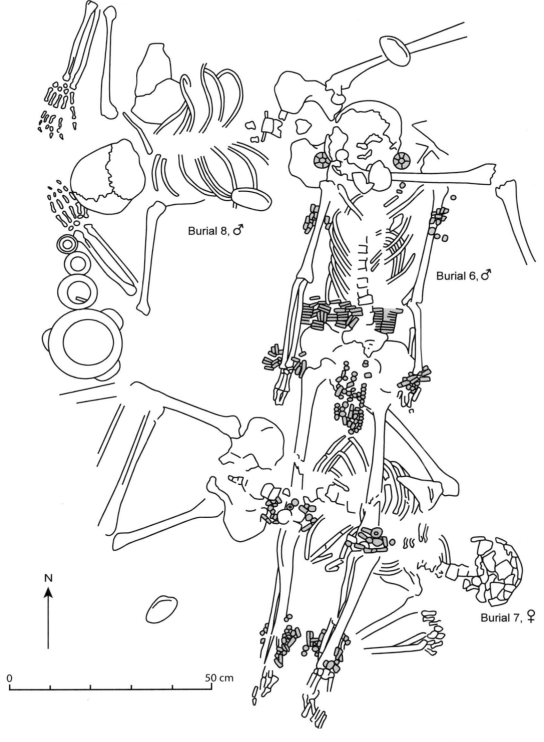

Figure 49. Field drawing of Burials 17-6, 17-7, and 17-8. Note that the spouted pot shown in the painting (Figure 43) is not shown in this drawing.

Figure 50. Photograph of the multiple burial of 17-6, 17-7, and 17-8.

Figure 51. Photograph of the multiple burial of 17-6, 17-7, and 17-8.

Figure 52. Photograph of the multiple burial of 17-6, 17-7, and 17-8.

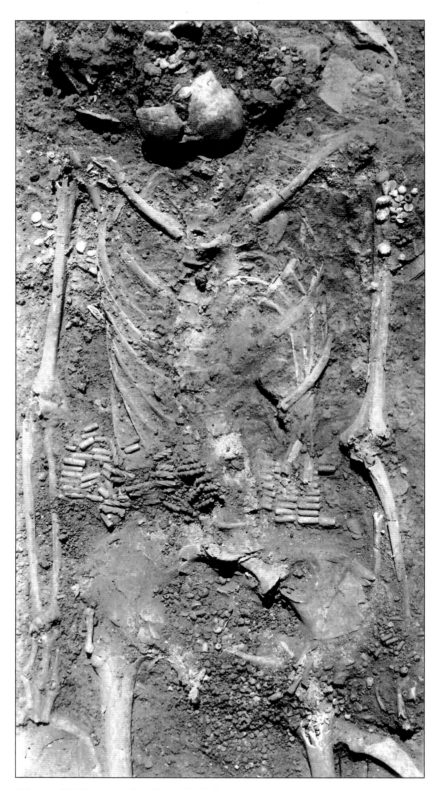

Figure 53. Photograph of Burial 17-6.

Figure 54. Photograph of the multiple burial of 17-6, 17-7, and 17-8.

Figure 55. Jade jewelry with Burial 17-6.

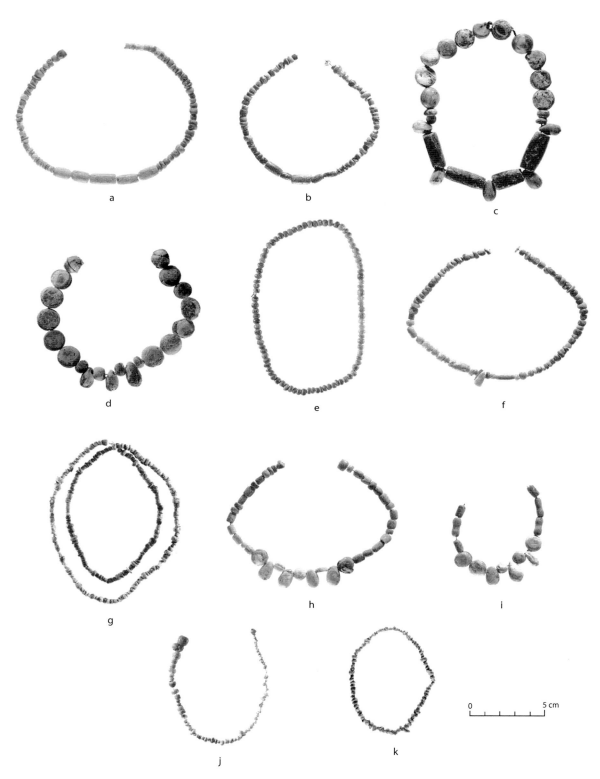

Figure 56. Mortuary offerings of Burial 17-6; a. Item 1, b. Item 2, c. Item 3, d. Item 4, e. Item 5, f. Item 6, g. Item 6a, h. Item 8, i. Item 11, j. Item 12, k. Item 13.

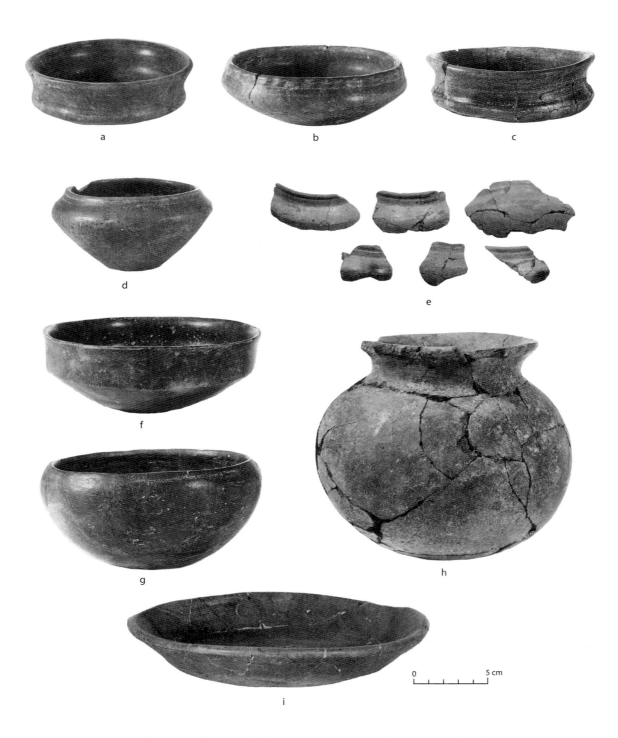

Figure 57. Mortuary offerings of Burial 17-6; a. Vessel 17, b. Vessel 21, c. Vessel 30, d. Vessel 23, e. Vessel 20, f. Vessel 29, g. Vessel 19, h. Vessel 22, i. Vessel 28.

a

b

Figure 58. Mortuary offerings of Burial 17-6; a. Vessel 27, b. Vessel 18.

Figure 59. Mortuary offerings of Burial 17-6; Vessel 24; jar with bridge-spout and basket handle.

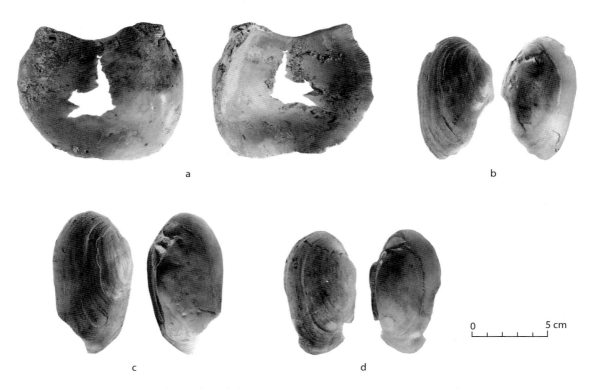

Figure 60. Mortuary offerings of Burial 17-6; a. Item 16, b. Item 31, c. Item 26, d. Item 25.

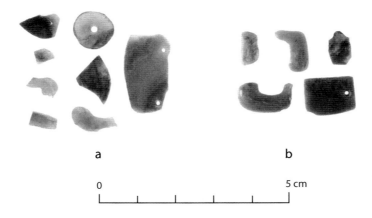

a                                        b

0                                        5 cm

Figure 61. Mortuary offerings of Burial 17-6; a. Item 14, b. Item 15.

Teeth w/paint MRE-4666.

**Remarks:** Burials 17-7 and 17-8, because of their position sustaining Burial 17-6, appear to have been sacrificial victims and are part of the mortuary offering of the individual of Burial 17-6. Fragments of two other individuals were found with this burial (17-6b), but they were not primary parts of this multiple burial. Rather, they were probably parts of earlier burials in the same area that were destroyed when the grave for Burial 17-6 was constructed. The mortuary offerings of this burial are in the State Regional Museum of Tuxtla Gutiérrez, Chiapas. Parts of it are on permanent display. The ceramic vessels are considered here as offerings for Burial 17-6 rather than for Burials 17-7 or 17-8, although they are closer to the skeletons of these burials.

### Burial 17-7 [CC 189] (Figures 48-54, 62)

**Type:** Simple pit, part of multiple Burial 17-6 offering.

**Sex:** Female (?).

**Age:** Adult, 40+ years.

**Orientation:** Head to the west.

**Position:** Extended on back. Head on left side facing north. Legs slightly doubled up. Right arm at side, hand on waist. Left arm doubled up, elbow out. The legs of Burial 17-6 rested on the

waist and chest of this burial.

**Location:** Excavation Unit A, Sections 7-9, depth 4.8 m.

**Phase:** Francesa.

**Remarks:** Remains of an apparently earlier burial in the same general area, unrelated to the Burial 17-6, 17-7, and 17-8 complex, were bagged with this burial (see Appendix 1). Child burial (4-6 years) teeth (Burial 17-7b). Teeth MRE-4667, teeth w/paint MRE-4668.

### Burial 17-8 [CC 190] (Figures 48-54, 63-64)

**Type:** Simple pit, part of multiple Burial 17-6 offering .

**Sex:** Male (?).

**Age:** Adult.

**Orientation:** East.

**Position:** Extended, on stomach. Face down. Legs apart. Arms doubled slightly, elbows out, hands beyond head.

**Location:** Excavation Unit A, Section 7, depth 4.8 m.

**Phase:** Francesa.

**Remarks:** The head of Burial 17-6 rested on the lower body of Burial 17-8. Labeling error in the field resulted in a child 6 years old (Burial 17-8b) being bagged with Burial 17-8 (see Appendix 1). Human teeth MRE-4670. It is not clear who

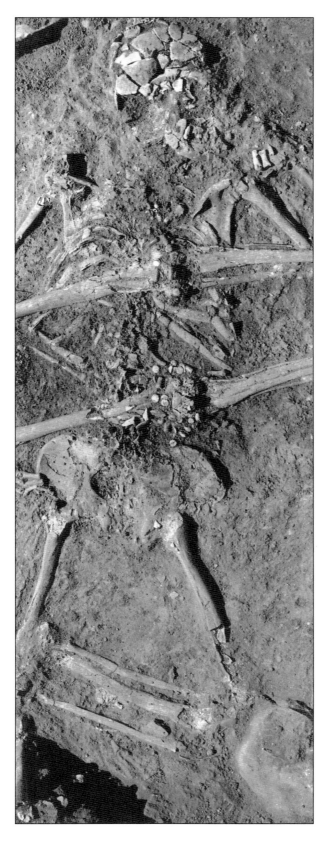

Figure 62. Burial 17-7.

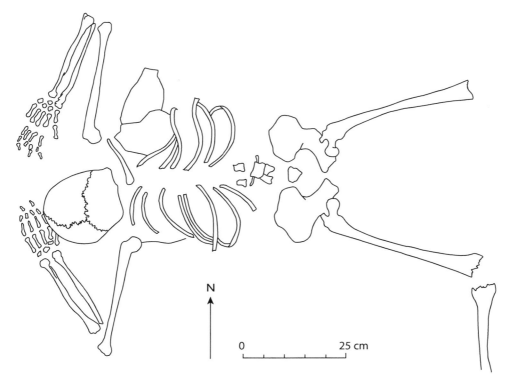

Figure 63. Field drawing of Burial 17-8.

Figure 64. Photograph of Burial 17-8.

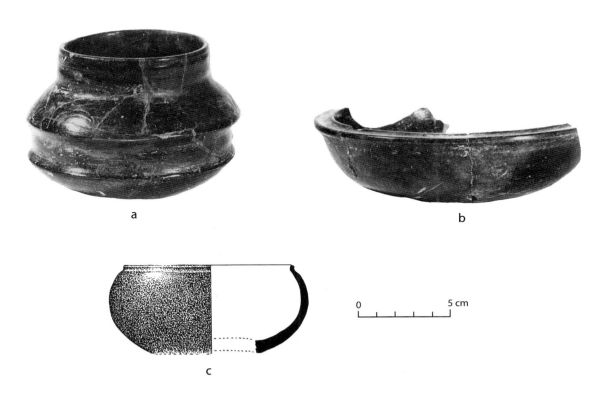

Figure 65. Mortuary offerings of Burial 17-9; a. Vessel 1, b. Vessel 2, c. Vessel 3.

determined the age and sex of Burials 17-7 and 17-8. They were not on the list of burials analyzed by Phillip Walker in Appendix 1. We added them to his tables based on descriptions here. In Walker's tables we have added letters to distinguish the main burials from the bone scraps found with them.

### Burial 17-9 [CC 191] (Figures 65-67)

**Type:** Simple pit, individual.

**Sex:** Male.

**Age:** Youth, 11 years.

**Orientation:** Head to the north, on side facing east.

**Position:** Extended, on left side.

**Location:** Excavation Unit A, Section 12, depth 3.0 m.

**Phase:** Francesa.

**Contents:**

1. Macanuda Incised: Macanuda Variety jar; height 8.4 cm, diameter 11.6 cm (Fig. 65a). MRE-4452.

2. Cintalapa Grooved-composite: Cintalapa Variety bowl; height 4.0 cm, diameter 14.0 cm (Fig. 65b). MRE-4453.

3. Cintalapa Grooved-composite: Cintalapa Variety bowl; height 4.5 cm, diameter 9.1 cm (Fig. 65c, drawing restored). MRE-4454.

4. Human bones MRE-4671, teeth MRE-4672.

**Remarks:** Vessel separated from body by a small open space and a large stone.

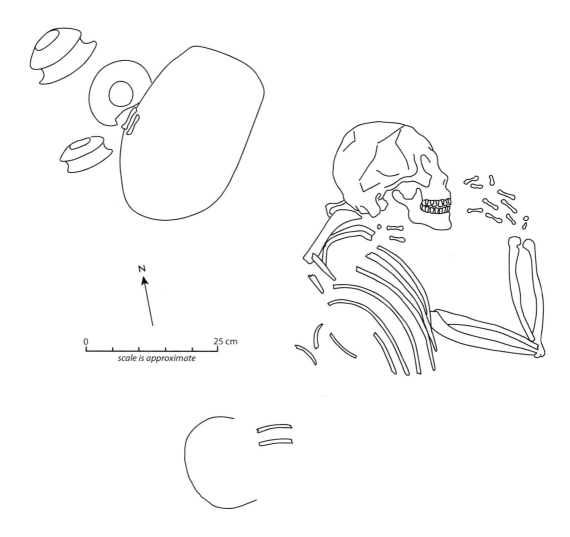

Figure 66. Field drawing of Burial 17-9.

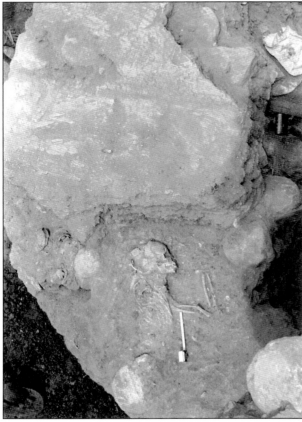

Figure 67. Photographs of Burial 17-9.

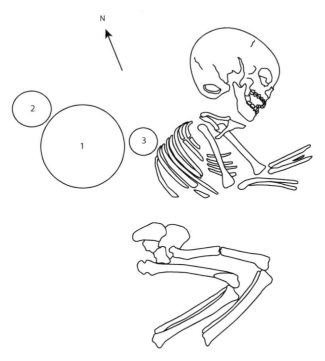

Figure 68. Field drawing of Burial 17-10, not to scale.

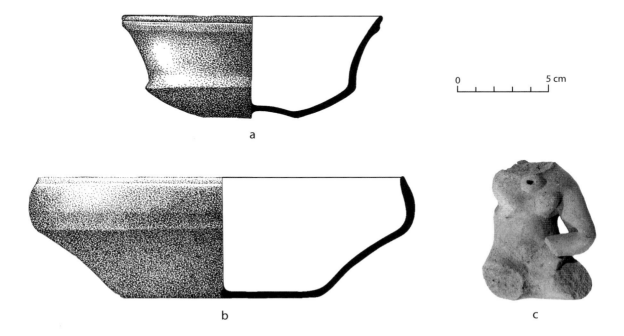

Figure 69. Mortuary offerings of Burial 17-10; a. Vessel 1, b. Vessel 2, c. Item 3.

### Burial 17-10 a-b [CC 192] (Figures 68-69)

**Type:** Simple pit, individual.

**Sex:** Male.

**Age:** Adult.

**Orientation:** Head is to the west.

**Position:** Extended, on left side. Head on side facing southeast. Arms slightly doubled up in front of chest. Legs folded up in front of pelvis.

**Location:** Excavation Unit A, Section 4, depth 4.18 m.

**Phase:** Francesa.

**Contents:**

1. Cintalapa Grooved-composite: Cintalapa Variety bowl; height 5.2 cm, diameter 14.4 cm (Fig. 69a, drawing restored). MRE-4455.

2. Cintalapa Grooved-composite: Cintalapa Variety bowl; height 6.9 cm, diameter 21.3 cm (Fig. 69b, drawing restored). MRE-4456.

3. One figurine body fragment; height 8.0 cm, width 6.21 cm (Fig. 69c). MRE-4523.

4. Human bones. MRE-4673.

**Remarks:** Figurine fragment may be intrusive. Parts of the dentition of a second adult individual were found with this burial.

### Burial 17-11 [CC 193] (Figures 70-80)

**Type:** Stone-lined crypt, individual.

**Sex:** Female.

**Age:** Adult, 40+ years.

**Orientation:** Head to the north.

**Position:** Extended, on back. Head up. Arms at side.

**Location:** Excavation Unit A, extension beyond Sections 9, 10, depth 5.47 m.

**Phase:** Escalera.

**Contents:**

1. Libertad Black-brown: Libertad Variety bowl; height 5.3 cm, diameter 10.2 cm (Fig. 78a). MRE-4457.

2. Cintalapa Grooved-incised: Cintalapa Variety bowl; height 9.2 cm, diameter 20.8 cm (Fig. 78d). MRE-4430.

3. Jade bead, subspherical; thickness 1.5 cm, diameter 2 cm, central hole maximum and minimum diameters 0.6-0.3 cm (Fig. 80b). MRE-4525.

4. Small polished black stone jar; height 3.8 cm, diameter 4.5 cm (Fig. 76a). MRE-4459.

5. Small stone monkey effigy tecomate, reconstruction drawing; height 4.5 cm, length 10 cm, width 6.5 cm (Figs. 73-75). Missing; stolen by female part-time worker from USA and apparently sold on the art market. It appears in an art catalog of a show in Geneva, Switzerland (Glaser 1998:39, fig. 26). The vessel is described as made of serpentine and of the "Olmec" culture.[6]

6. Alabaster tecomate jar; height 4.5 cm, diameter 7.0 cm (Fig. 76c). MRE-4460. Contents: 48 gms. of red pigment. MRE-4526.

7. Alabaster tecomate jar; height 4.2 cm, diameter 6.6 cm (Fig. 76d). MRE-4461. Contents: 26 grams of red pigment. MRE-4527.

8. Two subspherical jade beads and two subspherical shell beads; thickness 0.7 cm, diameter 1.2 cm (Fig. 80c). MRE-4524.

9. Jade beads (52); 4 tubular, length 1.4 cm, diameter 0.8 cm; 3 subspherical, thickness 1.7 cm, diameter 0.9 cm; 44 disk, thickness 0.6 cm, diameter 0.8 cm. (Fig. 80a). MRE-4528.

10. Mojón Fine: Mojón Variety miniature cylinder with lid; height 3.9 cm, diameter 5.5 cm (Fig. 76e). Currently on exhibit in the State Regional Museum of Tuxtla Gutiérrez, Chiapas. MNA000216.

11. Cintalapa Grooved-incised: Cintalapa Variety miniature bowl with dimple base; height 2.2 cm, diameter 4.5 cm (Fig. 76b). MRE-4462.

---

[6] One of the sponsors of the art show was the Nestlé company, a fact which may indicate motive and opportunity. The pilfered object could have easily been sold to one of the people working at Nestle, which sponsored the work at Mound 17, and made its way to Switzerland in a rather simple manner. I would not be surprised if the buyer had not witnessed the find itself or heard about it. (JEC)

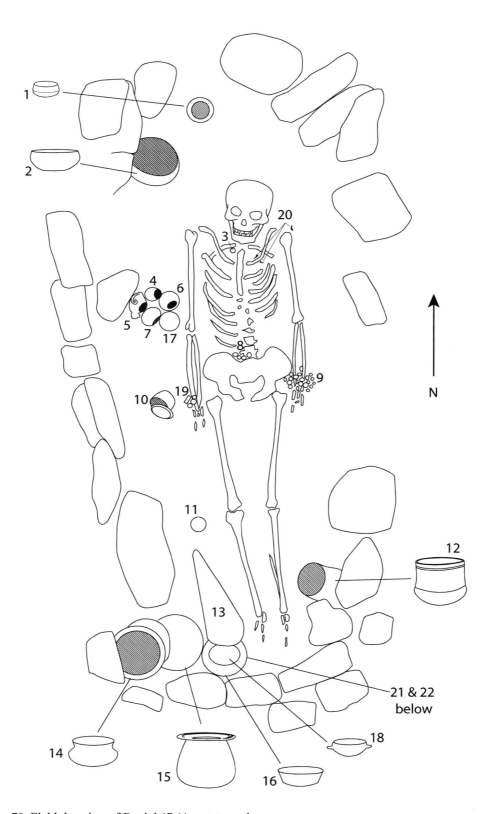

Figure 70. Field drawing of Burial 17-11, not to scale.

Figure 71. Photograph of Burial 17-11.

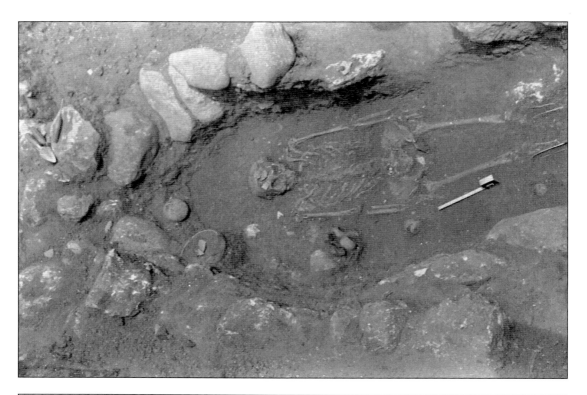

Figure 72. Photographs of Burial 17-11.

Figure 73. Small stone vessels with Burial 17-11.

Figure 74. Mortuary offerings of Burial 17-11.

Figure 75. Small stone monkey effigy tecomate with Burial 17-11.

Figure 76. Miniature ceramic and stone vessels from Burial 17-11; a. Item 4, b. Item 11, c. Item 6, d. Item 7, e. Item 10.

Figure 77. Ceramic vessels from Burial 17-11. The bowl on the upper left was published as from Burial 17-11 (Lee 1969b:20), but it is from Cache 17-9.

12. Cavada Incised: Cavada Variety bowl; height 11.2 cm, diameter 11.7 cm (Fig. 78c). MRE-4458.

13. Large wooden (?) spoon or ladle stuccoed in green on a white base-coat; length 30± cm, width 11 cm; badly preserved, recovery impossible.

14. Small jar with a rounded base. This vessel was on top of Vessel 15, mouth-up.

15. Cavada Incised: Cavada Variety jar; height 17.7 cm, diameter 21.3 cm (Fig. 79). MRE-4463.

16. Amatán Recessed: Amatán Variety bowl; height 7.1 cm, diameter 17.0 cm (Fig. 78e). MRE-4464.

17. Quechula Smudged: Quechula Variety cylinder; height 17.3 cm, diameter 18.1 cm (Fig. 78f). This has a polychrome, stucco design. MRE-4465.

18. Amatán Recessed: Amatán Variety, oval effigy bowl; height 4.7 cm, length 12.0 cm, width 8.7 cm (Fig. 78b). MRE-4466.

19. Seven jadeite, round disk beads and one large grooved subspherical limestone bead: seven disk beads, diameter 1.3 cm, thickness

6 cm, central hole diameter 0.3 cm, and one subspherical bead, diameter 2.1 cm, thickness 1.5 cm, central hole diameter 0.7 cm (Fig. 80d). MRE-4529.

20. Three-tooth (large rodent, probably *tepescuintle*) necklace with biconical hole in the root end of each tooth; length 1.7 cm, width 0.8 cm, thickness 0.6 cm (Fig. 80g). MRE-4530.

21. Freshwater clam shell fragments, one worked piece; length 7.3 cm, width 4 cm (Fig. 80h). MRE-4531.

22. Obsidian prismatic blade, proximal fragment; length 3.6 cm, width 1.5 cm (Fig. 80e). MRE-4532.

23. Limestone core fragment; length 3 cm, basal diameter 1.1 cm (Fig. 80f). It looks like a reamer. MRE-4582.

24. Human bones and teeth, MRE-4674.

**Remarks:** Crypt made of worked and unworked slabs of limestone. Walls were especially well preserved around the head and feet and along the west side. Ends of the crypt appear to have been rounded, but this may be due to its badly preserved nature and caused when it collapsed.

Figure 78. Mortuary offerings of Burial 17-11; a. Vessel 1, b. Vessel 18, c. Vessel 12, d. Vessel 2, e. Vessel 16, f. Vessel 17.

Item 15, the Cavada Incised: Cavada Variety jar with a wide everted rim is very similar to two jars on display in the new La Venta Museum in Tabasco.

Some of the items from Burials 17-11 and 17-6 appear to have become confused. In his draft manuscript, Lee had the spouted pot from Burial 17-6 with the Burial 17-11 items. As evident in Figure 77, he mixed a pot from Cache 17-9 with these materials as well. In contrast, Vessel 14 does not appear to have been reported, and there is no evidence in the photographs and drawings that Vessel 17 actually goes with this burial.

Figure 79. Vessel 15 of Burial 17-11, Cavada Incised jar.

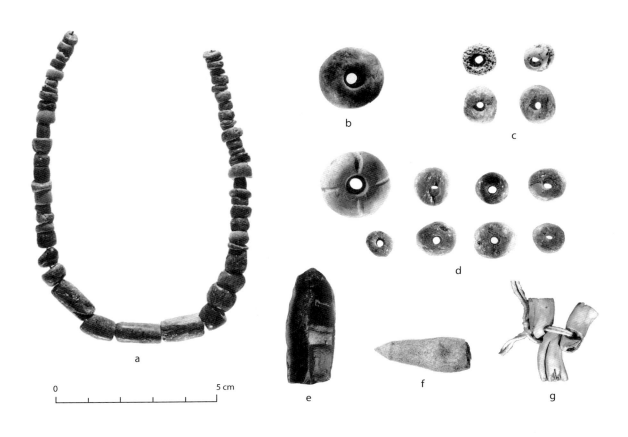

Figure 80. Mortuary offerings of Burial 17-11; a. Item 9, b. Item 3, c. Item 8, d. Item 19, e. Item 22, f. Item 23, g. Item 20, h. Item 21.

## Burial 17-12 [CC 194]
### (Figure 81, no burial drawing)

**Type:** Secondary.

**Sex:** Male?

**Age:** Adult.

**Orientation:** Undetermined.

**Position:** Undetermined.

**Location:** Excavation A, extension beyond Sections 9-10, depth 3.9 m.

**Phase:** Escalera.

**Contents:**

1. Enguti Incised: Crystal Ash Variety flaring rim bowl; height 2.2 cm, diameter 12.2 cm (Fig. 81a). MRE-4467.

2. Shell pendant mosaic base in the form of a human skull; length 4.4 cm, width 3.5 cm, thickness 0.4 cm (Fig. 81b). MRE-4508.

3. Thirteen jade and shell beads; 10 subspherical jade beads: thickness 0.7 cm, diameter 1.2 cm; 3 subspherical shell beads, thickness 1.1 cm, diameter 0.4 cm (Fig. 81d). MRE-4541.

4. Five jade and shell beads; 3 subspherical jade beads: thickness 0.4 cm, diameter 0.9 cm; 2 subspherical shell beads, thickness 0.9 cm, diameter 0.7 cm (Fig. 81c). MRE-4542.

5. Six shell mosaic fragments; length 2.6 cm, width 0.6 cm, thickness 0.3 cm (Fig. 81e). MRE-4543.

6. Three turtle carapace pendant fragments; length 3.4 cm, width 2.4 cm, thickness 0.1-0.3 cm (Fig. 81h). MRE-4544.

7. Shell mosaic fragments; length 4.9 cm, width 2 cm, thickness 0.5 cm (Fig. 81g). MRE-4545.

8. Obsidian blade fragment; length 1.8 cm, width 1.7 cm, thickness 0.4 cm (Fig. 81f). MRE-4510.

9. Human bones. MRE-4675.

**Remarks:** Badly preserved skeleton appears to have been secondarily scraped up into a localized area together with its offering. Burial 17-12 fill contained one figurine head, type I-Chiapa-A or A2, Dili phase. MRE-4557.

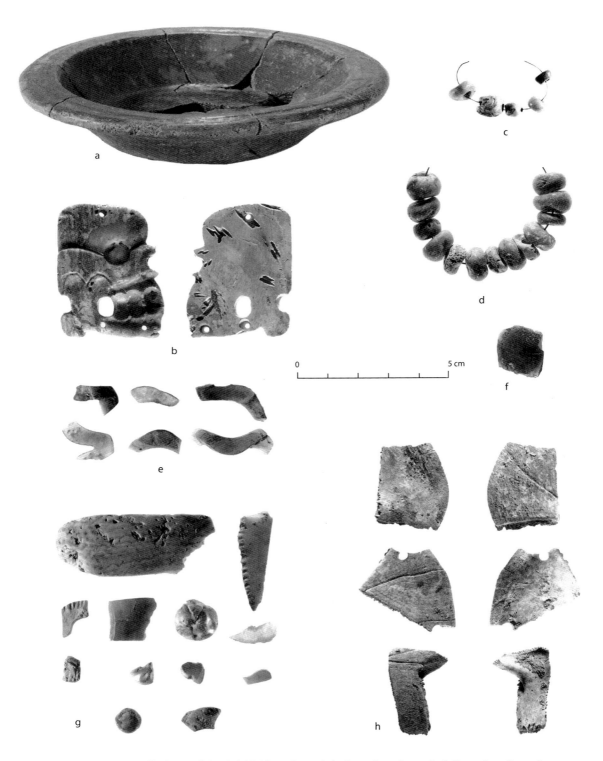

Figure 81. Mortuary offerings of Burial 17-12; a. Item 1, b. Item 2, c. Item 4, d. Item 3, e. Item 5, f. Item 8, g. Item 7, h. Item 6.

Figure 82. Photograph of Burial 17-13.

## Burial 17-13 [CC 195]
## (Figures 82-84, no burial drawing)

**Type:** Secondary.

**Sex:** Male.

**Age:** Adult.

**Orientation:** Undetermined.

**Position:** Undetermined.

**Location:** Excavation Unit A, extension beyond Sections 9-10, depth 5.20 m.

**Phase:** Francesa.

**Contents:**

1. Tapilula Smudged-white: Tapilula Variety bowl; height 9.2 cm, diameter 32.3 cm (Fig. 83c). MRE-4468.

2. Shell fragments incised with petate design; length 3.9 cm, width 2.7 cm, thickness 0.3 cm (Fig. 84b). MRE-4546.

3. Shell pendant (*Conus* sp.), notched hole in ends, spire cut off; length 6.6 cm, diameter 3.3 cm, thickness 0.4 cm (Fig. 84a). MRE-4547.

4. Shell fragments (species unidentifiable); length 7.5 cm, width 4 cm, thickness 0.1 cm (Fig. 84c). MRE-4548.

5. Cavada Incised: Cavada Variety jar; height 13.2 cm, diameter 18 cm (Fig. 83a). MRE-4469.

6. Tapilula Smudged-white: Tapilula Variety bowl; height 8.8 cm, diameter 23.8 cm (Fig. 83b). Resist decoration, new variety (?). MRE-4470.

7. Human bones, MRE-4676.

**Remarks:** Human remains were badly preserved as was the mortuary offering. All appeared to have been collected up from their primary location and placed in their new location. They are mixed up all together.

Figure 83. Mortuary offerings of Burial 17-13; a. Vessel 5, b. Vessel 6, c. Vessel 1.

Figure 84. Mortuary offerings of Burial 17-13; a. Item 3, b. Item 2, c. Item 4.

### Burial 17-14 [CC 196]
### (Figures 85-88, no burial drawing)

**Type:** Secondary.

**Sex:** Male.

**Age:** Adult.

**Orientation:** Undetermined.

**Position:** Undetermined.

**Location:** Excavation Unit A, extension beyond Sections 9-10, depth 2.8 m.

**Phase:** Francesa (Escalera?).

**Contents:**

1. Fragmentary white travertine flat bottom cylinder, badly broken; height 7.4 cm, diameter 9.9 cm (Fig. 88a). MRE-4471.

2. Nambiyugua Smoothed: Nambiyugua Variety jar; height 24.1 cm, diameter 27.0 cm (Fig. 88c). MRE-4504.

3. Mundet Red: Matte Variety jar; height 20.2+ cm, diameter 24 cm, very fragmentary, reconstruction drawing. (Fig. 88b). Sherds placed in NWAF type collection.

4. Quechula Smudged: Quechula Variety flaring wall plate; height 7.5 cm, diameter 35.0 cm (Fig. 87a). MRE-4474.

5. Quechula Smudged: Quechula Variety flaring wall plate; height 7.7 cm, diameter 33.6 cm (Fig. 87b). This plate has a painted stucco design. MRE-4475.

6. Shell owl's head made from one valve of a marine clam; length 8.1 cm, width 6.9 cm, thickness 2.4 cm (Fig. 85a). MNA000217.

7. Two large jade earflares; height 1.4 cm, diameter 6.3 cm (Fig. 85c). MRE-4549.

8. 18 shell beads (*Olivella* sp.); length 1.3 cm, diameter 0.6 cm (Fig. 86a). MRE-1844.

9. Canine tooth pendant fragment, decorated with an incised plaited design, 3 small suspension holes near the proximal end; length 3.8 cm, thickness 1 cm (Fig. 86c). MRE-4550.

10. Two small shell snakes (?); length 4.3 cm, width 0.8 cm, thickness 0.4 cm (Fig. 86b).

MRE-4551.

11. Three turtle carapace breast plate fragments, one with two suspension holes in one end; length 18 cm, width 5.2 cm, thickness 0.9 cm (Fig. 85b). MRE-4552.

12. Three large shell (*Morum tuberculosum*) beads (pendants) with spires removed and partially cut for single suspension holes; length 3.9 cm, diameter 2.4 cm (Fig. 86g). MRE-4553.

13. Two shell disk beads; diameter 0.8 cm, thickness 0.2 cm, central hole diameter 0.2 cm (Fig. 86d). MRE-4554.

14. Point of bone awl; length 2.8 cm, width 1.3 cm, thickness 0.4 cm (Fig. 86f). MRE-4555.

15. Worked shell fragment; length 2.8 cm, width 2 cm, thickness 0.05 cm (Fig. 86e). MRE-4556.

**Remarks:** Human bones, MRE-4677. Fragment of maxilla and teeth, MRE-4678. The ceramic bowls appear to be earlier than the jars. Future work may adjust the phase assignment of this burial.

Figure 85. Mortuary offerings of Burial 17-14; a. Item 6, b. Item 11, c. Item 7.

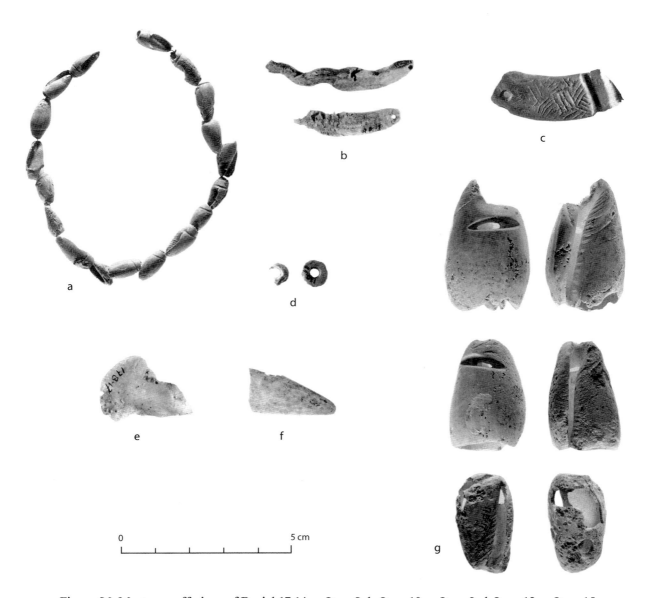

Figure 86. Mortuary offerings of Burial 17-14; a. Item 8, b. Item 10, c. Item 9, d. Item 13, e. Item 15, f. Item 14, g. Item 12.

a

b

0                    10 cm

Figure 87. Mortuary offerings of Burial 17-14; a. Vessel 4, b. Vessel 5.

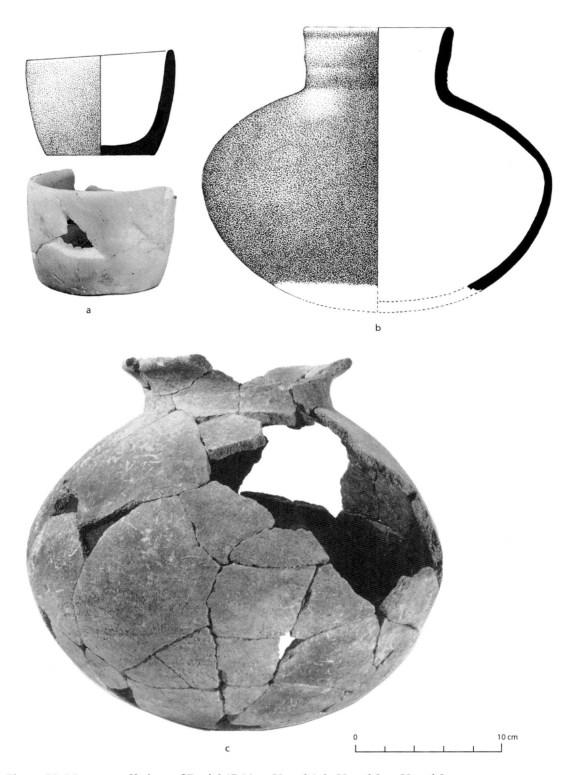

Figure 88. Mortuary offerings of Burial 17-14; a. Vessel 1, b. Vessel 3, c, Vessel 2.

Figure 89. Mortuary offerings of Burial 17-15; a. Vessel 2, b. Vessel 1.

### Burial 17-15 [CC 197]
### (Figure 89, no burial drawing)

**Type:** Simple pit.

**Sex:** Undetermined.

**Age:** Undetermined.

**Orientation:** Undetermined.

**Position:** Undetermined.

**Location:** Excavation Unit A, extension beyond Sections 9, 10, depth 5.8 m.

**Phase:** Escalera.

**Contents:**

1. Vergel White-to-buff: Vergel Variety jar; height 23.7 cm, diameter 29.0 cm (Fig. 89b). MRE-4476.

2. Vergel White-to-buff: Vergel Variety flaring wall bowl; height 5.8 cm, diameter 34.6 cm (Fig. 89a). MRE-4477.

**Remarks:** Human skeleton so badly destroyed that nothing could be saved nor could the normal attributes of sex, age, head orientation or body position be ascertained.

## MOUND 17 BURIAL PATTERNS

Fifteen burials, and some remains of bones and teeth, together representing at least 21 individuals were discovered in the 1969 salvage excavations of Mound 17, and all came from Excavation Unit A in the center of the structure (Table 3). Four of the burials (17-5, 17-11, 17-12, and 17-15) date to the Escalera phase. Another Escalera phase burial (CC-26), in very poor condition, was recovered by Brockington (Lowe 1962b:56) from the east wing structure of Mound 17. Ten primary burials (17-1, 17-3, 17-4, 17-6, 17-7, 17-8, 17-9, 17-10a, 17-13, and 17-14), as well as the minor remains of at least five other individuals (17-6b, 17-6c; 17-7b, 17-8b, 17-10b), date to the Francesa phase. Two individuals in a single Guanacaste phase grave were also exhumed from Mound 17 (Burials 17-2a and 17-2b).

Burials interred in civic-ceremonial structures in the center of almost any large site in Mesoamerica are generally those of elite individuals rather than commoners. We suspect, therefore, that most Mound 17 burials were from this social stratum. The following discussion summarizes trends concerning physical conditions of individuals buried in Mound 17: age, sex, and burial orientation. Patterns of Mound 17 mortuary offerings as they relate to coeval burials elsewhere at Chiapa de Corzo are discussed in the final section of this chapter.

### Escalera Phase

Of the five burials of this phase found in Mound 17 the sex of only two is known, one male and one female. At least three individuals were adults, and one was over 40 years old at the time of death. Body orientations are known for two individuals. A female was interred with her head to the north, and another adult was buried with its head to the east. Two individuals were extended full length, on their backs, one with the face up. In the other case the head was missing. The Escalera phase burials from Mound 17 were mostly adults, of both sexes, buried supine in extended positions.

### Francesa Phase

The 10 individual primary burials from the Francesa phase represent six males, one female, and three individuals of undetermined sex (Table 3). Seven of the burials were adults, one an infant, and one an adolescent. Two individuals, one adult and one youth, were buried with their heads to the north. Two adults were oriented to the west, another adult to the east, and another to the southeast. Seven of these burials were in extended positions; four were supine, two rested on their left sides, and one was prone. The heads of two burials faced up. In two instances the heads were turned on their left sides; in one case the face was down, and in another it was on the right side. The Francesa phase burials from Mound 17 were mostly adult males interred extended and supine.

### Guanacaste Phase

The probable age ranges of the two young individuals buried in the single Guanacaste phase burial overlap. Both were supine; the head of one was to the east and that of the other was to the west and face up. One individual was buried directly on top of the other.

## CHIAPA DE CORZO PRECLASSIC BURIALS

The 15 burials from the Mound 17 salvage excavations representing 21 individuals add to the extensive sample of Chiapa de Corzo burials from the heart of its civic-ceremonial center. Since most excavations at Chiapa de Corzo were placed in prominent mounds and adjacent plazas, few burials have been recovered from common residential sectors of the site. Hence, the site's burial sample is clearly biased towards the upper end of the social spectrum. It has been generally accepted that mostly elites were buried in the civic-ceremonial center, but even so, they were far from equal, as variations in the placement of graves and tombs, and of their accompanying mortuary goods show. Other "burials" clearly represented sacrificial victims, some of them possible prisoners or captives with hands tied behind their backs (see Lowe 1964:73). For the moment, the burial patterns of rural Chiapa de Corzo remain unknown for all

Table 3. Summary of the Mound 17 burials.

| Burial | Age | Sex | Type | Position | Pots | Jade | Shell | Other |
|--------|-----|-----|------|----------|------|------|-------|-------|
| *Escalera* | | | | | | | | |
| CC-26 | A | ? | Simple | ? | 1 | - | - | |
| 17-5 | A | ? | Simple | Extended | 1 | - | - | |
| 17-11 | A | F | Crypt | Extended | 14 | + | + | stone vessels, obsidian |
| 17-12 | A | M | Simple | Extended | 1 | + | + | turtle carapace, obsidian |
| 17-15 | ? | ? | Simple | ? | 2 | - | - | |
| *Francesa* | | | | | | | | |
| 17-1 | I | ? | Simple | Extended | 3 | + | - | |
| 17-3 | A | ? | Crypt | Extended | 11 | - | + | |
| 17-4 | A | ? | Simple | Extended | 2 | - | + | canine tooth necklace |
| 17-6 | A | M | Simple | Extended | 11 | + | + | 2 human adults as sacrifices |
| 17-7 | A | F | Simple | Extended | - | - | - | with 17-6 |
| 17-8 | A | M | Simple | Extended | - | - | - | with 17-6 |
| 17-9 | Y | M | Simple | Extended | 3 | - | - | |
| 17-10a | A | M | Simple | Extended | 2 | - | - | figurine fragment |
| 17-10b | A | ? | ? | ? | - | - | - | |
| 17-13 | A | M | Simple | Extended | 3 | - | + | carved shell |
| 17-14 | A | M | Simple | Extended | 5 | + | + | turtle carapace, stone vessel |
| *Guanacaste* | | | | | | | | |
| 17-2a | C | ? | Simple | Extended | 7 | + | + | |
| 17-2b | Y | ? | Simple | Extended | same | + | + | |

[Age: Infant, Child, Youth, Adult; Sex: Male, Female, Unknown]

pre-Hispanic time periods. The expectation of future excavations is that burials in the outskirts of Chiapa de Corzo will evince a much more limited range of burial goods and include more utilitarian goods. In most societies elites set the social agendas and styles, thus it would not be unexpected to find that commoners were buried in much the same manner as elites, but less ostentatiously – both in location and included offerings. These are issues for future research.

Based on a very conservative population estimate of 500 persons living at Chiapa de Corzo and with life expectancies of 20-25 years at birth, Clark (1983) estimated that over a 400 year period 8,000 to 10,000 people would have died at this site. "Clearly, not everyone was buried in the ceremonial precinct, or perhaps even buried" (Clark 1983:1). Chiapa de Corzo was occupied for 28 centuries rather than the four of this estimate, and it had several thousand inhabitants most of the time, thus, the total number of people who lived and died at Chiapa de Corzo would have been in the hundreds of thousands. Clearly, the 350 burials currently documented for Chiapa de Corzo do not represent even one-tenth of one percent of its former inhabitants. Consequently, any burial "patterns" detected for different phases at Chiapa de Corzo represent a small and unrepresentative sample of its former denizens (see Lowe 1964 for an early summary based on a burial sample of 162 individuals). The limitations of the small sample, of course, do not invalidate patterns in the burial practices which have been discerned, but the minuscule sample should serve as a check on over-generalization for Chiapa de Corzo society at large, for any time period. At best, the data from human burials provide insights into some burial practices of a privileged segment of its ancient society, the customs of the elite and likely leaders of the community. The burial record for Chiapa de Corzo provides important insights concerning changes in rulership through time, beginning with the Escalera phase in the Middle Preclassic. Burials recovered from Mound 17 have been of great importance for contemplating the first centuries of kingship and queenship at Chiapa de Corzo.

## Dili Phase

No burials of this period were found in Mound 17 in 1969 or at Chiapa de Corzo in any excavations after this date. The burial sample consists of four burials reported by Agrinier (1964) and interpreted by Lowe (1964). None of these was unambiguously associated with burial goods. A jade bead was found near the head of one burial, but the association is not certain. Nor were any burials "intentionally related to architecture; the proximity of Burials 117 and 130 to structures is fortuitous rather than intentional" (Lowe 1964:66). The 2010 excavations in Mound 11 discovered a Chiapa II-B phase building, but no burials or offerings were found clearly associated with it. Apparently, it was not until the following phase that burials and caches were interred in formal platforms and pyramids at Chiapa de Corzo.

## Escalera Phase

The early burial information from Chiapa de Corzo for this phase is listed by Lowe (1964, Table VI). These data indicate a ratio of adult burials to non-adults of 8:1. When the Mound 17 burials are added to Lowe's sample, the ratio becomes less skewed towards adults, a ratio of 22:6 or 3.7:1 (Table 4). Even so, the Escalera phase Chiapa de Corzo burial population represents an inversion of normal mortality rates for non-industrial societies. Infants and children have much higher mortality rates than adults and thus should be represented more frequently in burial populations than are adults, yet these sub-adults account for less than 25 percent of the Escalera phase human remains at Chiapa de Corzo. Burials of this phase from Mound 17 (Table 3) conform to the patterns described by Lowe (1964) in that most internments were of adults in formal platforms rather than off-mound. Twice as many adult burials were recovered in structures as in non-mound locations. Sub-adult burials occurred with equal frequency in buildings and plazas.

Lowe (1964:67) suggested that a "unity of thought for Escalearans is suggested by the fact that all of their known burials are extended and all those in architectural context are oriented north-south. Each of the ten [Escalera burials]

Table 4. Age of Preclassic and Protoclassic Chiapa de Corzo burials by phase.

| Age/Phase | D | E | F | G | H | I | Total | % |
|-----------|-----|-----|-----|-----|-----|-----|-------|------|
| Adult | 4 | 22 | 67 | 31 | 25 | 72 | 221 | 68.6 |
| Youth | - | 1 | 5 | 4 | - | 5 | 15 | 4.7 |
| Child | - | 4 | 17 | 14 | 9 | 15 | 59 | 18.3 |
| Infant | - | - | 6 | 2 | 1 | 5 | 14 | 4.4 |
| ? | - | 1 | 3 | 2 | 3 | 4 | 13 | 4.0 |
| Total | 4 | 28 | 98 | 53 | 38 | 101 | 322 | |
| % | 1.2 | 8.7 | 30.4 | 16.5 | 11.8 | 31.4 | | |

had a pottery offering with an average of three vessels per individual." In general, the Mound 17 burials follow a similar pattern; no burials were found that lacked some kind of offering, and none occurred with only ornaments or implements. The four Mound 17 Escalera burials found in the 1969 salvage excavations contained ceramic vessels and/or stone vessels and ornaments or implements as mortuary goods. A difference is evident, however, in the relative percentage of burials that only have ceramic vessels as their offering, 90 percent for Chiapa de Corzo in general (Lowe 1964); only half of the Mound 17 Escalera phase burials had these same objects as offerings. The other half had ceramic vessels and ornaments as grave goods. The actual burials are few, and therefore the pattern is weak, but the difference may be significant.

Bowls tend to be the most common ceramic vessels found with Escalera burials. Vessel colors are most commonly monochrome red, black, and brown, and there does not seem to have been a clear preference for any color. Other offered items include jade beads, small stone bowls, a rodent tooth necklace, a limestone tool, a wooden spoon, obsidian blades, and turtle

carapace pendants (Table 3). Fresh water shell fragments and a shell base for a shell mosaic were also included with burials of this phase.

Miniature vessels similar to those found with Burial 17-11 (three of which were of travertine) were included with Burial 6, an Escalera burial from Mound 7 (Lowe 1962b:42-49). The small vessels of Burial 6 "are tiny and suggest specialized usage such as for cosmetics or medicaments" (Lowe 1964:68). Finely ground red pigments were found in two of the travertine vessels interred with Burial 17-11. In Lowe's analysis, Burial 6 had almost twice as many ceramic vessels as the next burial with numerous offerings. Burial 6 was clearly the most important individual known for the Escalera phase prior to the Mound 17 excavations and the discovery of Burial 17-11. The presence of miniature "cosmetic" vessels among the grave goods of the female in Burial 17-11 suggests that the adult found in Burial 6 may also have been female.

Only one formal crypt was found in Mound 17, and it was for Burial 17-11, the earliest special burial known for Chiapa de Corzo.[7] The crypt was lined with unworked river cobbles laid two-courses high and oriented roughly

---

[7] The Escalera phase tomb found in 2010 in Mound 11 is coeval with Burial 17-11; both share some of the same kinds of pots. We think Burial 17-11 is earlier, but this opinion is biased by our oft-repeated hypothesis that the woman in this burial founded the royal linage at Chiapa de Corzo (see below), an idea we are loath to give up without clear evidence to the contrary. If so, then the male adult in Tomb 1 of Mound 11 could be her son, an hypothesis that can be checked through DNA analysis of extant remains stored in the Museo Nacional de Antropología in Mexico City. If Tomb 1 is earlier, then Clark's speculations about the founding of a royal line at Chiapa de Corzo are dead wrong.

north-south on the site's axis, just slightly east of the axial line through the center of Mound 17. The occupant of this tomb was an adult female. Burial goods included jade jewelry, carved small stone vessels, and ceramic vessels (Cheetham and Lee 2005: figs. 22-24; Lee 1969a: foto 9). The crypt and its stone lining and alignment remind one of burials and tombs reported for La Venta, Tabasco, especially Offering No. 5 (see Drucker et al. 1959: fig. 41). The goods found with Burial 11 reinforce this impression of connections to La Venta.

> Burial 11, was located approximately 2 m below the floor of an Escalera phase platform. This tomb [sic], formally prepared – the only one known for this phase at the site – contained the remains of a woman at least 40 years old. This member of the elite class was placed in an extended position, head to the north ... with a rich offering that included 62 jade beads and three alabaster vessels. More important for present discussion are the 10 accompanying ceramic vessels, three of which are identical to types imported from the Gulf Coast, particularly the fine gray wares. Also, another four fine-paste vessels were probably imported; these seven vessels have precise counterparts at La Venta. (Cheetham and Lee 2005:291, translation JEC)

A large jar with wide everted rim (Vessel 15) found in the crypt is also a precise copy of La Venta vessels, or an import (Lee 1969b: foto 9; compare to von Nagy 2003:840, fig. 6.9c). A similar pot was found in Tomb 1 of Mound 11 (Bachand 2013:32, fig. 8.6). David Cheetham and Lee's (2005) study of Escalera phase ceramics from Chiapa de Corzo identified 90 sherds in the NWAF type collections that represent imports. Of these, one was from the Maya lowlands and the rest were from the Gulf region. Most of these sherds came from the fill of Mound 17.

Clark proposed that the woman of Burial 17-11 came from La Venta as part of a marriage alliance between a leader at Chiapa de Corzo with a La Venta king. In this hypothesized history, the king sent a daughter or sister to found a cadet royal line at Chiapa de Corzo with royal blood from La Venta (Clark and Pérez 1994:271; Clark and Pye 2000:243-45). Cheetham and Lee (2005:291) found this proposal plausible and, based on their more thorough study of the artifacts, discovered many more connections to La Venta. They suggest that a group of retainers accompanied this La Venta noblewoman to Chiapa de Corzo and that she and they lived on or around Mound 17. If so, she was buried beneath the floor of her own dwelling. The creation of a cadet royal line would not have been an isolated event in La Venta foreign policy. The Middle Preclassic Olmec sculptures at Pijijiapan on the Chiapas coast and Monument 21 at Chalcatzingo (Cyphers 1984: fig. 5.2) depict elite women in elaborate dress and may portray bride exchange and marriage alliances with La Venta's kings (Clark and Pye 2000:245). These speculations can be tested through DNA analysis. There is no reason why royal sons could not have been similarly deployed or dispersed across Mesoamerica.

The recovery of two Escalera royal burials in Mound 11 in the 2010 excavations significantly changes the known burial patterns for this phase. An adult male accompanied by sacrificed individuals was found in Tomb 1. A royal woman, presumed to be his wife and queen, was found just outside of the tomb chamber. We think these royal burials in Mound 11 date to the period between Burials 17-11 and 17-6 described for Mound 17. The two royal burials were found juxtaposed in the heart of the Mound 11 Escalera phase pyramid. Tomb contents are still being analyzed. They include large, square pyrite mirrors with both burials, spondylus shells over the faces that appear to have been mosaic masks, and jade bead necklaces, bracelets, anklets, kneebands, and armbands. The male in Tomb 1 was supine, with his head to the north. He had a shell bead belt sash and was accompanied by 16 ceramic vessels and two human sacrifices – a two-month old baby and a young adult (Bachand and Lowe 2011:81-82). A beaded belt and paired human sacrifices are features described for Burial 17-6 dating to the following Francesa phase. The early king in Mound 11 had multiple dental

Table 5. Comparison of the frequency of primary burials at Mound 17 to those at the rest of the site. This does not include scraps of human bone and teeth found with primary burials.

| Phase | # for Md. 17 | % | # for all others | % |
|-------|-------------|------|------------------|------|
| D | 0 | 0 | 4 | 2.0 |
| E | 5 | 27.8 | 23 | 11.3 |
| F | 11 | 61.1 | 87 | 42.9 |
| G | 2 | 11.1 | 51 | 25.1 |
| H | 0 | 0 | 38 | 18.7 |
| Total | 18 | | 203 | |

inlays of jade and pyrite. His queen, buried just outside his tomb chamber, lacked the bead belt but had a stingray spine. No analogous item for self-piercing was found with the king.

The burial offerings from Mound 17 can be ranked rather crassly and materialistically in terms of the market value of included goods relative to one another, In descending order of value are Burials 17-11, 17-12, 17-15, and 17-5. Burial 17-11 was in a class by herself until the discovery of two burials in Mound 11. The individuals in these tombs had more goods, and more valuable goods, than included with Burial 17-11. They date roughly to the same time period but may be slightly later than Burial 17-11. These tomb burials appear clearly to have been of royal individuals. Burial 17-11 was interred with shell and jade jewelry, stone bowls, a wooden spoon, and a rodent tooth necklace as part of her mortuary offering. Burial 17-12 had obsidian blades as part of the mortuary offerings. All four Escalera phase burials from the 1969 salvage excavations were in an important public structure in the center of the civic ceremonial precinct. A working hypothesis might be that the individual of Burial 17-11 was an elite matron or priestess and that subsequent burials in the same mound were related kin or of lesser noble rank (Cheetham and Lee 2005; Clark 2016; Clark et al. 2000). The female of Burial 17-11 may have been of similar, if not more exalted rank, as the individual interred in Burial 6 in Mound 7. We draw attention to the possibility that Burial 6 may also have been female based on the similarities in miniature vessels full of

rouge found with both burials. Another Escalera elite female was found in Mound 11, just outside Tomb 1. All three burials appear to have been early members of the founding royal line at Chiapa de Corzo. Burials of elite women have not been identified at Chiapa de Corzo for any of the following phases. Clearly, something changed at Chiapa de Corzo with queenship by Chiapa IV times.

**Francesa Phase**

The 10 primary Mound 17 burials dating to the Francesa phase represented at the time of their discovery a 16 percent increase in the number known for Chiapa de Corzo. Other Francesa phase burials have been found in subsequent excavations. The Mound 17 Francesa phase burials are all from a major public structure and add significantly to our knowledge of community-wide burial patterns for this phase. Lowe (1964:68) reported six burials from major platforms out of a total of 61 Francesa burials. Most of the non-mound burials were found in the plaza just north of Mound 1. More were found there in the 2008 excavations (Bachand et al. 2008), consequently, the frequencies of burials for this and other phases have changed (see Table 5). The southern part of the main plaza at Chiapa de Corzo appears to have served as a cemetery in Francesa times. Factoring in the Mound 17 data, about 22 percent of the known Francesa phase burials were associated with architecture. The rest were buried off-mound but were still associated with the central (public) part of the site. Most of the burials in mounds were of adults; off-mound burials included individuals from a wider age-range. Adults comprised 50 percent of the Francesa phase individuals buried in mounds. The Mound 17 data change the adult burials in mounds to 62.6 percent. The percentages for all other age-grades fall off slightly, while retaining their relative relationship. This suggests that, regardless of the relative expense of the accompanying burial offering, a privileged social status was indicated by burial in the heartings of public buildings. What the nature of this status was we do not know. It may have been indicative of royal status or special religious or political rank. Lowe explores an alternative view.

> The evidence suggests strongly that Francesa phase individuals were interred in mound construction for some reason other than that of privileged status due persons of superior civil or religious rank. It is possible 1) that they were hierarchical workers of ordinary status whose death occurred at a moment convenient for inclusion in contemporary construction fill, or 2) that they do indeed represent civil or religious leaders but of relatively indigent circumstances. The latter situation of an even relatively impoverished priest or ruler class is one not often proposed in Mesoamerican culture history, but it nevertheless seems to me to be a probable in this instance. (Lowe 1964:68)

Another alternative is to rethink the categories of caches and burials. Some burials in public architecture may actually have been offerings of persons, rather than burials in the strictest sense, as the multiple burial in Mound 17 indicates.

Back to the notion of interring impoverished priests or fortuitous decedents in honored places, Lowe (1964:69) also pointed out, "It may be supposed that more elaborate Francesa tombs are located in the Chiapa de Corzo mounds of the period, some of which are known to be as large as any at the site (i.e., Mounds 8, 11, 36, core structures in 13, 33, 67) though all but Mound 11 have already been tested with negative indications." Recent excavations in Mound 11 did find elite burials there that date to the eve of the Francesa phase. Burial 4 was interred in Mound 11 in late Chiapa III times nearer to the top of the pyramid. The two individuals placed side-by-side have not been exhumed, but some burial goods have. This burial is of interest to show a later elite interment in the same mound and also because of a pendant that depicts an Olmec face carved in profile (Bachand and Lowe 2011:81), thereby indicating continued ties to the Gulf Coast Olmec in this phase.

The most elaborate Francesa burial in a pyramid is Burial 17-6. Other Francesa burials in pyramidal mounds have been found in the immediate vicinity at Mango Seco (Agrinier 1964) and in the same valley at San Agustín west of Tuxtla Gutiérrez (Navarrete 1959:4-7). The occurrence of special burials of high status individuals at smaller sites suggests an expansion of the Chiapa de Corzo polity and/or an increase in the number of individuals of high status. Burial 17-6 was certainly of a high status individual accompanied by two offerings of adult human lives and a trove of other items. The mortuary goods of this burial may fit a pattern in which we see only one or two high status individuals buried in pyramidal mounds during the Francesa phase at a given site. Perhaps the remainder of the mound interments were, as Lowe suggested, of "workers of ordinary status whose death occurred at a moment convenient for inclusion in a contemporary construction fill" (i.e., sacrificial victims without sacrifice) or true immolated bodies bloodied and dispatched to dedicate a new building addition, and thus buried with few personal possessions. Only Burials 17-7 and 17-8, those postulated as sacrificial offering to Burial 17-6, out of the 10 Mound 17 Francesa burials are thought to have lacked durable offerings. All the rest could claim at least a pair of pots. It is worth restating that their lack of goods is a presumption on our part. The ceramic vessels included with the three bodies in the burial were placed closer to Burials 17-7 and 17-8 than they were to Burial 17-6.

Burial 17-6 in Mound 17 is of particular interest. This multiple interment included a primary adult male, about 25 years of age, and the two mentioned sacrificed adults, Burials 17-7 and 17-8 (see Figure 17). The principal individual, Burial 17-6, was placed on his back in an extended position, with his head to the southeast. Several of his teeth had been filed, a mark of high status. His head rested on the buttocks of Burial 17-8 while his legs were stretched out with the knees over the waist and chest of Burial 17-7. Burial 17-8 is an adult male. He appears to have been thrown face down into the burial pit. Burial 17-7 is an adult female. These individuals were sacrificed and positioned in the burial in opposite orientations. One served as a headrest and the other as a footrest for Burial 17-6. A similar multiple burial is known for La Libertad, a coeval center up river (see Chapter 6), for the same period (see Miller 2014:134-151). Both burials date to the Francesa or Chiapa IV phase. In terms of mortuary offerings, Burial 17-6 was the "richest" recovered at Chiapa de Corzo until 2010 (see Clark 2000:50; Clark et al. 2000: fig. 19).

> [Burial 17-6] was adorned with bracelets on his wrists, biceps, knees, and ankles, all made of jade and shell disks. A small necklace of [57] pearls was around his neck while a [shell inlaid] clam shell covered his mouth. Mosaic jade earspools were on both sides of the head. A personal adornment of greater importance was a wide jade belt consisting of more than 250 tubular jade beads, with a central part of 36 long, spiral carved beads and rings. ... [and a sash made of 341 jade and shell beads] ... Nine ceramic vessels completed the mortuary offering. (Lee 1969b:19, 21, translation JEC; other details from Lee 1969a)

The principal individual also had two jade and pearl bracelets and three fresh water clam shells. One remarkable thing about this burial is that it was not placed in a special crypt – at least not one that was recognized in the hurried salvage operation. Evidence of a wooden tomb could easily have gone undetected in the excavations. This burial shares elements with the cist tomb burial at La Venta (Colman 2010:212-220; Wedel 1952:67, pl. 14). The jade bead belt-and-sash is especially significant. Later burials in Mound 17 were of individuals with jade jewelry with shells over their mouths (Lee 1969a). Burials 17-11 and 17-6 provide a picture of the early rulers at Chiapa de Corzo.

In terms of specific burial practices and practicalities, during the Francesa phase the norm at Chiapa de Corzo for final placement of the deceased was with the body extended supine and oriented east-west (Lowe 1964:70). The Mound 17 Francesa burials generally conform to this pattern, with some variations in orientation and body position. North and southeast, the latter a probable permissible variation on the east direction, occur as orientation. One body was prone, but this was of a sacrificial victim placed in an abnormal position to signal subservience to Burial 17-6.

Adding the Mound 17 data to those of the site little affect the mortality curves for Francesa phase Chiapa de Corzo because most of the burials recovered were of adults. In terms of overall percentages of age of death by cohorts, the Mound 17 burials fit nicely within the trends described by Lowe (1964) and shown in Table 4. The new totals do not change the relative number of infants, children, adolescents, and adults.

## Guanacaste Phase

Only two burials (17-2a and 17-2b) of Mound 17 date to Guanacaste times, thus they shed little light on burial practices for this phase. It is significant, however, that these were burials of children or adolescents, an unusual type of mound burial for any period at Chiapa de Corzo. The age distinctions for Burials 17-2a and 17-2b overlap, and there is uncertainty of precise age, but it is certain they were not adults.

Prior to the Guanacaste phase, the most frequent burial offering type at Chiapa de Corzo was of ceramic vessels only. The combination of ceramic vessels and personal ornaments was also found in 14 percent of the burials. As to burial locations, half of the burials were found associated with public buildings and half were off-mound burials. Many more adults than children were buried in mounds, so the Mound 17 situation is unusual for this phase. Architecture-related interments were favored for adults, while the opposite was true for children.

The mortuary offering of Burial 17-2a consisted of seven ceramic vessels plus many personal ornaments, an unusual combination for this era at Chiapa de Corzo (cf. Lowe 1964:72).

Jade, shell, and stone beads were present in only one other published burial of this phase. Burial 17-2a was a child, and the accompanying burial offering suggests he or she was of high social rank, an inference supported by the honor of being buried in Mound 17. The extended and supine position of the body of Burial 17-2a fits the general pattern for the Guanacaste phase, as also does the orientation of Burial 17-2b, whose head was to the west. Burial 17-2a was oriented to the east, a previously unknown orientation for burials of this phase at Chiapa de Corzo. Other reasons for believing that Burial 2a was of a unique status are the items of jewelry found, and especially the spondylus shell covering the mouth. This is a practice seen for royal burials at the site.

During the Late Preclassic and Protoclassic era, the kings at Chiapa de Corzo were interred in tombs below the floors of the main temple at Mound 1 (Agrinier 1964; Lowe 1960, 1962b; Lowe and Agrinier 1960). Most were "looted" in antiquity, so only limited information is available for their occupants and offerings. The earliest of these, Tomb 7, dates to the Guanacaste phase. It is the only one in Mound 1 not disturbed in prehistory. Eduardo Martínez and Gareth Lowe (in press) describe two tomb burials for this phase from Mound 32 that are earlier than the tomb in Mound 1. Other tombs of this phase were placed in Mound 3 (Tucker 1970).

Lowe (1964:72) pointed out that Tomb 7 of Mound 1, with its luxurious mortuary offering, was a formally constructed tomb placed below a stone-walled platform which was immediately constructed over it. This is the first substantial indication of special building activity linked directly to an elite burial at Chiapa de Corzo. The five high-status individuals of the Escalera phase described above may have been associated with building renovations, but the evidence is not as clear as for Tomb 7 of Mound 1. Tomb 7 appears to be one of those rare situations of preservation where the archaeological evidence, both burial and architectural, was fortunately protected over the centuries.

Tomb 7 was discovered in early investigations at Chiapa de Corzo and has only been described but not analyzed in any detail. The tomb was originally thought to date to the early Horcones phase (Agrinier and Lowe 1960:47), but this assessment was later pushed back to the end of the Guanacaste phase (Agrinier 1964:33), or about 150 BC. At this time a low platform existed in the Mound 1 location. Tomb 7 was cut through this platform and into the soft limestone bedrock beneath it (following information from Agrinier and Lowe 1960:47-50, figs. 47-53, Plates 24-28). The crypt for Tomb 7 was 3.25 by 1.45 m and aligned roughly north-south parallel to the site's axis but placed west of it. Above the bedrock, the east and west walls of the burial pit were shored up with four courses of large adobes, and the north and south ends were closed off with stone slabs. Large sandstone slabs covered the burial chamber. Some of these were carefully squared. Apparently, these sandstone slabs rested on wooden timbers for structural support. Wooden planks were also placed on the floor of the tomb perpendicular to its long axis, a practice also evident in the much earlier Tomb 1 of Mound 11 (Bachand and Lowe 2011:82).

The bones in Tomb 7 were poorly preserved, but the teeth indicate a young adult about 25 years old, about 1.70-1.80 m tall (Agrinier and Lowe 1960:50), and given this stature, undoubtedly male. He was placed in the burial chamber on his back, with his head to the south, and with his hands over his pelvis (Agrinier and Lowe 1960: fig. 48). The body was surrounded by vessels on all four sides. These included 34 ceramic vessels, one painted gourd or wooden bowl, and eight or more small vessels of perishable material on the south end by his head. Vessels were placed carefully in the tomb according to shape, color, and size. What the excavators found remarkable is that all 34 ceramic vessels had been imported, with most coming from the Gulf lowlands and the lowland Maya area, but there were also three bridge-spout gray ware jars from the Valley of Oaxaca and five painted Usulutan vessels from El Salvador (see below). Almost everything in this tomb had been imported.

Most of the burial goods were vessels or items of personal adornment. The few exceptions are particularly interesting. In the northwest corner of the crypt at the feet of the burial were found two chert, stemmed macroblade spear points from Colha, Belize, and an equally long obsidian macroblade from El Chayal, Guatemala. These were placed in a large pot. Just to the east of these was a large sheet of mica as well as two clam shells filled with mica fragments. In a small black jar in the northeast corner of the tomb were found two worked ulnas of a small mammal, and possibly an obsidian pressure blade [its location is not specified, but objects were placed in contrasting triads]. These may have been bloodletters. A small rod of limestone was also found nearby.

This tomb ignited after it was closed, hence many items, such as the planks, were carbonized. Traces of leather straps were seen on the forehead of the skull, probably straps of a headdress of perishable materials. A single strand of jade beads encircled the neck, and a pair of elaborate, composite earspools flanked the head. These consisted of jade earspools, amber cylinders (cautiously described as "resin" in the descriptions), and a large cross-shaped piece of shell. Four small tear-shaped pieces of mother-of-pearl were found by the face, as were 10 small, smooth pebbles. We think these pebbles may have been part of a rattle. To complete the assembly, a large sea shell was placed over the mouth of the buried individual, a practice seen for Burials 17-6 and 17-2a of Mound 17 and the king in Tomb 1 of Mound 11. All the adult burials were supine and oriented north-south. The burial in Tomb 7 had many fewer jade ornaments than those placed in Tomb 1 or with Burial 17-6, and there were no sacrificial victims included in his tomb, but an infant (Burial 24) may have been placed above the tomb (Agrinier 1964:72). "This may represent a dedicatory sacrifice connected with Tomb 7" (Agrinier and Lowe 1960:17).

On the basis of the foreign pottery, it might be conjectured that the offerings were sent to a famous personage, priest or ruler, from the widely separated source areas in Oaxaca, Veracruz, El Salvador and Guatemala (Lowe and Agrinier 1960:49).

But since there was no clustering of the objects in the tomb according to their source area, it seems much more likely that purely luxury goods already imported were placed with a highly honored personage as tribute or for his use in an afterlife. As with burial vessels, these probably contained food and drink, a postulate supported by the apparent presence of a zapote-like fruit in the offerings. The three chalcedony [chert] and obsidian spearheads were offered inside vessels and without shafts, suggesting their inclusion as wealth symbols rather than for their utility. The construction of Tomb 7, the placement of its occupant and offerings, and the apparently immediate construction of a stone-walled platform over it afford the first sure indication that we have of an elaborate architecturally related ceremonial funeral at Chiapa de Corzo.[8] (Lowe 1964:72)

Of special interest is the compelling evidence that the exact placement of Tomb 7 was remembered and commemorated through different remodelings of the structures in Mound 1 during the Horcones phase. Lowe and Agrinier (1960) described a possible offering placed above the tomb and the later subsequent removal of this offering and construction of a small stone and plaster platform or altar above this spot. All that remained of these activities in the two intrusive pits was the scapula of a giant tortoise (Lowe and Agrinier 1960:pl. 24c). Four royal tombs were placed in the top of Mound 1 during the Chiapa VI phase. None was on the axial line, and each was "looted" one or more times in prehistory. We think some of these tomb reopenings could have been by descendants of the deceased who removed valuable heirlooms and other memorabilia, including human bone (cf. Clark and Colman 2014). The elite burials discussed here reveal the continuity of royal interments at Chiapa de Corzo from 750 BC to AD 100. For the main plot of the Chiapa de Corzo story, it is of interest that the earliest

---

[8] This summary was published 5 years before the discovery of Burial 11 in Mound 17. The honor of the first architecturally related ceremonial funeral at Chiapa de Corzo likely goes to this queen.

elite burial known for the site was a female – the likely founder of the Chiapa de Corzo dynasty. Burial practices and mortuary offerings associate her with La Venta.

### Horcones Phase

Burial patterns during the Horcones phase changed dramatically, as evident in Agrinier's (1964) original inventory of Chiapa de Corzo burials. At the end of NWAF investigations at the site in 1961 only four Horcones burials had been recovered – and they were all of kings found in the four tombs placed in the center of Mound 1. This was a very skewed burial sample. There was clearly a shift at this time in the types of individuals interred in the main plaza at the site. The absence of Horcones burials in Mound 17 fits this pattern. Three of the four tombs in question were looted in antiquity, consequently, we have little idea of the full complement of objects once interred with these individuals. Sufficient skeletal remains were found, however, to show that each burial and his tomb was placed orthogonal to its predecessor. Thus, there was not a standard orientation of these royal bodies when placed in the underworld. Rather, they appear to have constituted a circuit around the central point of Mound 1. They were all interred in tombs with walls made of limestone blocks and adobes covered over with wooden beams (Lowe and Agrinier 1960:39-47).

Salvage operations in mounds off the main plaza recovered numerous Horcones phase burials that brought the total number to 38. Nine were found in Mound 3, 16 in Mound 15, and nine in Mound 26. These last two mounds are modest residential platforms north of the main plaza. None of these excavations has been published. González and Cuevas (1998) report that the nine burials of Mound 26 consisted of one infant, four "jóvenes," and four adults. Their middle category includes children and adolescents. Of the 16 Horcones burials found in Mound 15, Glauner et al. (in press) report that one was a child and the other 15 were adults. Most of these interments were simple extended burials with a few pots placed underneath the floors of houses, a practice that started by the Guanacaste phase. We lack information for Francesa phase dwellings at Chiapa de Corzo or

of any associated burials. Most known burials from this phase came from a cemetery placed in the main plaza just north of Mound 1. At the contemporaneous and closely related site of La Libertad upriver from Chiapa de Corzo, burials were interred beneath house floors in Chiapa III and IV times (see Miller 2014), thus we think this was an old practice of people "living with the ancestors," to evoke Patricia McAnany's (1995) description of this practice for Middle Preclassic Lowland Maya. At Chiapa de Corzo there does appear to have been a significant shift in burial practices by Horcones times in terms of the place of burials. We may be seeing a distinction between public space and private space and the sorts of individuals worthy of being buried in each. In fact, there also appears to have been a distinction between types of public space. Of all the mounds directly adjacent to the main plazas along the site's central axis, Horcones phase burials were only placed in Mound 1. Mound 17 received some ritual attention in terms of caches, but not as a site for human burials. Perhaps the larger message concerns the relationship between offerings and burials, a theme we consider in conclusion.

## OFFERINGS AND BURIALS AT PRECLASSIC CHIAPA DE CORZO

Site summaries of caches and burials presented in these last two chapters convey an inconsistent and even ragged history of ritual practices. The impression of the shifting importance of caches and burials for different phases could be due to the luck of the draw with what was found in different excavations in different mounds and plazas. Some mounds at Chiapa de Corzo were explored rather thoroughly (Mds. 1, 3, 5, 15) while most others were probed with only a test pit or two. Although Mound 17 was explored under extremely adverse conditions and unfavorable time pressures, the central part of this mound was excavated more extensively than those of most mounds. As a consequence we have evidence of caches and burials spanning much of the Preclassic and Protoclassic periods but few details of architectural history. The ritual practices of burying things and human bodies at Mound 17 do not appear to correspond to

Table 6. Summary of caches and burials per phase at Chiapa de Corzo.

| Phase | Chiapa | Caches | Burials |
|-------|--------|--------|---------|
| D | II-B | 0 | 4 |
| E | III | 14 | 28 |
| F | IV | 45 | 98 |
| G | V | 11 | 53 |
| H | VI | 78 | 38 |
| I | VII | 54 | 101 |
| J | VIII | 20 | 9 |
| L | IX | 2 | 3 |
| M | X | 34 | 6 |
| P | XI | 0 | 0 |
| R | XII | 0 | 0 |
| T | XIII | 0 | 10 |
| Total | | 258 | 350 |

each other very well, and this is a pattern of difference that applies to Preclassic Chiapa de Corzo in general, as evident in Table 6. For Mound 17 we found burials for the Chiapa III or Escalera phase but no offerings. In contrast, we found caches for the Horcones phase but no burials. For the Francesa phase there was evidence of both in abundance. This appears to have been the peak period of ritual activity at Mound 17 and for Chiapa de Corzo at large. The data from Mound 17 and the main sector of Chiapa de Corzo suggest that major changes in ritual activities occurred between IV and V times.

The data listed in Table 6 show two peaks in ritual activities dating to the late Middle Preclassic (IV) and the Protoclassic (VI and VII). We recommend that caches and burials be considered together conceptually as different kinds of ritual offerings. We think there was a significant relation between the two. In some phases they shared the complementarity just referred to, as most evident in the main plaza

in Horcones times. In this sector of the site for this time the only burials were kings and thus few in number. Otherwise, this part of the site witnessed a flurry of caching events. Thus, we get an absurd cache-to-burial ratio of 78:4. Compare this to the Francesa ratio weighted in the other direction of 45:98. Clearly two different kinds of things took place in this sector of the site in these different phases. In Horcones times the main plaza and its ringing mounds seem to have been off limits for offerings of human burials, but not for offerings of food and objects. More offerings are known for this phase than for any other. We think there was a complementary relationship between burials and offerings at this time which may have had its roots in earlier periods. Whether we are right or wrong in this opinion, the relationship between caching behavior and interment of burials is worth pursuing. It will be important also to include information for building additions and changes as well because they appear to have prompted many offerings of termination and rededication. Building itself may also have been a ritual activity. Most caches appear to have been associated with the growth of buildings; some burials may have been as well.

An interesting exercise is to sum the different kinds of ritual activities or offerings per phase. We see that things really get started at Chiapa de Corzo in Escalera times with its 42 known ritual events (Table 6). They took a major leap to 143 events in Francesa times, plunged to 64 during the Guanacaste phase, and then ramped up to 116 in Horcones times and to its high of 155 during the Istmo phase. After this, the number of ritual events known for Chiapa de Corzo dropped to below Escalera levels. These are gross statistics useful only for drawing attention to phenomena worthy of detailed investigation. Two questions raised by these numbers appear worth pursuing. What was the relationship between caches and burials to the construction or modification of public buildings? What was the relationship of all of these to social and political history at Chiapa de Corzo? Surely the investment in building the ceremonial center at Chiapa de Corzo, and continued efforts to add to or maintain its sacrality with additions of human blood, flesh, and bone had a significant impact on those who lived there.

Chiapa de Corzo's burial record most obviously tells a tale of kings who maintained sway at the site for nearly a millennium, but these were kings of different sorts. Early kings were Olmec and later kings may have been Maya. The last kings were Soke. Some of the means by which these kings of different dynasties maintained order are recorded in the annals of the site's building history and its caches. Clearly there are many more stories behind these events that deserve to be teased out than that of replaceable royals. To get at these and other histories all of the manifestations of ritual and technical activity at Chiapa de Corzo need to be compared to similar activities undertaken by people at neighboring centers. A comparison of site histories will eventually allow us to piece together the basic history of the people who built and lived at Chiapa de Corzo. Grounding our perspective in the findings at Mound 17, we start such a project for Middle Preclassic Chiapa de Corzo in our concluding chapter.

# CHAPTER 5

# MISCELLANEOUS ARTIFACTS

During the salvage of Mound 17 some artifacts, unrelated to caches or burials, but still deserving of study, were recovered from excavations and displaced fill from the mound's demolition. They were part of general fills which made up the different structures of the mound. We describe and illustrate them here by artifact class, beginning with ceramic artifacts and ending with chipped stone.

Most of the artifact types represented by the isolated finds in Mound 17 have been described in detail in Lee's (1969c) study of Chiapa de Corzo artifacts. In this publication the distribution and dating of each type at the site is provided, along with comparative information of their distribution in Mesoamerica. Consequently, we do not provide here a site-wide study of the miscellaneous artifacts from Mound 17. Most isolated artifacts rescued from mound fill were figurine fragments and partial pots.

## CERAMIC ARTIFACTS

### Ceramic Vessels

Type names for the vessel fragments come from Bruce Warren's unpublished study of Chiapa de Corzo ceramics on file with the NWAF in Chiapas, Mexico. These names are listed in his dissertation (Warren 1978). Brief descriptions of some of these types and related types can be found for coeval sites to the east (Bryant et al. 2005; Clark and Cheetham 2005) and to the west (Agrinier 2000).

1. Fragmentary Rodeo Patterned: Rodeo Variety flaring wall bowl; height 6.1 cm, diameter 28 cm (Figure 90a). Location: General back fill. Francesa phase. MRE-4501.

2. Fragmentary Enguti Incised: Enguti Variety everted rim bowl; height 5.4 cm, inside diameter 18 cm (Fig. 90c). Location: Alongside, but not clearly associated with Burial 17-2. Escalera phase. MRE-4500.

3. Fragmentary Mundet Red: Matte Variety jar rim; height 21.4+ cm, diameter 25+ cm (Fig. 90b). Location: General mound fill. Francesa to Horcones phase. MRE-4657.

4. Fragmentary Rafael Incised: Rafael Variety squash jar; height 4.5 cm, diameter 17.6 cm (Fig. 90e). Location: Ex. B, 2.5 m east of Step 6, Structure 17- F1, in mound fill. Horcones phase (probably). MRE-4502.

5. Fragmentary Soyaló Modeled: Soyaló Variety effigy vessel; height 4.5+ cm, width 7.3 cm, thickness 2.9 cm (Figure 92a). Escalera phase. MRE-4574.

6. Tzutzuculi White-to-buff: Tzutzuculi Variety cylinder, fragment; height 10.9+ cm, diameter 12.1 cm (Fig. 90f). Location: General mound fill. Escalera phase. MRE-4576.

7. Cavada Incised: Cavada Variety cylinder lid, fragment; height 2.5 cm, diameter 14 cm, (Fig. 90d, reconstruction drawing). Location: General mound fill. Francesa phase. MRE-4577.

### Anthropomorphic Figurine Heads and Fragments

The few figurines found at Mound 17 repeat types described for the site (Lee 1969c). The largest samples of Preclassic figurines for other Chiapas sites are from Mirador (Agrinier 2000; Peterson 1963) to the west, and upriver to the east at La Libertad (Miller 2014). Figurines are generally rare at Preclassic sites; they are abundant at the three sites mentioned. All of these are the largest centers in their respective regions. It is worth noting that the predominant style in each of these regions is significantly different.

1. Type: I-Chiapa-A; 1 (Fig. 92c). One badly eroded head which lacks its nose and ears. Length 4.2 cm, width 3.9 cm. Dili phase. MRE-4557. Provenience: with Burial 17-12, probably intrusive.

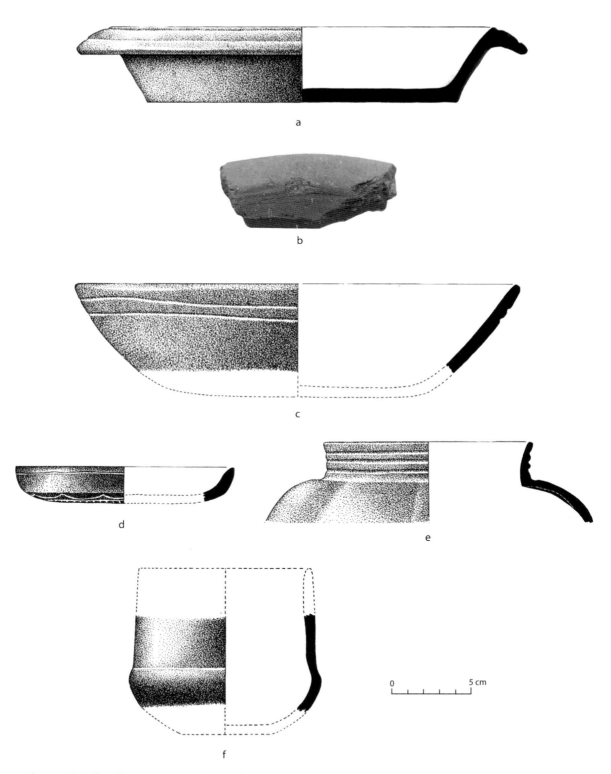

Figure 90. Miscellaneous ceramic vessels; a. Vessel 1, b. Vessel 3, c. Vessel 2, d. Vessel 7, e. Vessel 4, f. Vessel 6.

Figure 91. Miscellaneous figurine; large hollow figurine head.

2. Variety: I-Chiapa-A3; 1 (Fig. 92b). Torso, head, and upper arms of one figurine. Red paint in hair-do detail and on lower body clothing. Length 13.5 cm, width 8.1 cm. Dili phase. Provenience: Ex. A-3, depth 3.7 m. MRE-4558.

3. Variety: I-Chiapa-A10; 1 (Fig. 92d). New variety; similar to I-Chiapa-A except that it has a small round applique fillet in the center of the eye. Length 3.3 cm, width 4.8 cm. Escalera phase, or earlier. Provenience: with Burial 17-11, probably intrusive. MRE-4559.

4. Type: I-Chiapa-B; 2 (Fig. 92e, f). Two badly damaged heads. Both pierced laterally through the neck, probably for passing a cord for hanging around the neck of the wearer. Length 4.3 cm, width 3.7 cm. Escalera-Francesa phase. Provenience: Ex. A5, depth 4.25 m. MRE-4560-1,-2.

5. Type: I-Chiapa-B1; 2 (Figure 93 a, b). One figurine complete except for extremities. One hollow figurine head with red paint on its mouth. Most complete specimen, length 5.8 cm, width 3.1 cm. Francesa phase or earlier. Provenience: Most complete specimen, Ex. A5, depth 3.92 m. Hollow head, Ex. A5, depth 4.25 m. MRE-4561.

6. Type: I-Chiapa-F; 1 (Fig. 93c). One figurine head, broken from body. Also lacks rear of head. Length 5.3 cm, width 4.5 cm. Dili phase. Provenience: Ex. A8, depth 3 m. MRE-4566.

7. Type: I-Chiapa-H; 2 examples (Fig. 93 d, e). One of the heads has damage to nose and lips: length 5.9 cm, width 4 cm. Escalera phase, or later. Provenience: General back fill. MRE-4562, MRE-4567.

8. Type: II-Chiapa-B; 1 (Fig. 93f). One badly preserved, crude figurine head with hollow place in the top of the head. Length 5.7 cm, width 6 cm. Francesa to Horcones phase. Provenience: General mound fill. MRE-4563.

9. Type: II-Chiapa-B1; 1 (Fig. 93g). One head fragment which has the big nose style characteristic of this type. It also is considered a new variety because of two deep grooved wrinkles on sunken cheeks; related to the Mexica deity, Huehueteotl, the Old God of fire. Length 4.2 cm, width 3.4 cm. Francesa phase, or later. Provenience: Ex. B, Step 4 of stairway. MRE-4564.

10. Variety: III-Chiapa-E1; 1 (Figure 91). This large hollow figurine head was published as the frontispiece in Lee (1969c). The face and throat have a highly polished white slip, very similar to that found on Vergel White-to-buff pottery which dates from the Dili through Francesa phases. The back of the neck lacks white slip but is highly polished. The eyes, teeth, earplugs, and top and side hair ornaments are not slipped but are smoothed and retain the same pale whitish

Figure 92. Miscellaneous figurines; a. Vessel 5, b. Figurine 2, c. Figurine 1, d. Figurine 3, e, f. Figurine 4.

Figure 93. Miscellaneous figurines; a, b. Figurine 5, c. Figurine 6, d, e. Figurine 7, f. Figurine 8, g. Figurine 9.

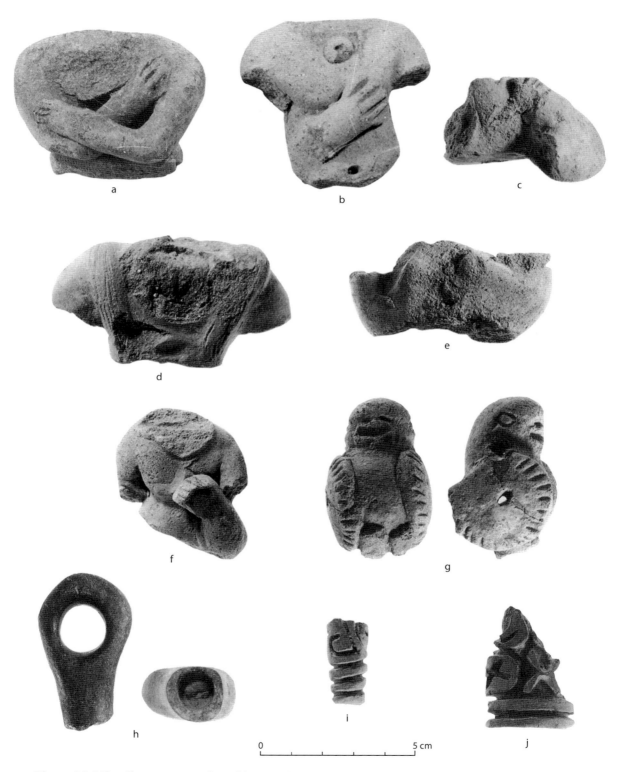

Figure 94. Miscellaneous ceramic artifacts; a-f. Figurine 12, g. Ocarina fragment, h. Single Ring, I. Cylindrical Stamp 2, j. Cylindrical Stamp 1.

Figure 95. Miscellaneous head and extremity fragments; 23.

buff color as the paste. The ear, lips, tongue, and the possibly tonsured area of the head are painted red and are not polished. The eyebrows and a dot on the upper lip are painted black. A cord and one-bead necklace about the neck are portrayed by applique fillets and are painted red. A small irregular hole pierces the top of the head. Two small dimples are clearly indicated, one near each corner of the mouth. Height 14 cm, width 10.8 cm, thickness 7 cm. Provenience: Mound 17 fill, about 5 m north of the east end of Excavation A, on a level below that of Burial 17-11. Turned up by bulldozer. Now in collection of the National Museum of Anthropology in Mexico City. MNA000218.

11. Solid Figurine Torsos: 6. Three torsos with arms crossed left over right (Figure 94a-c). Ex. A, Section 5, depth 4.25 m with Burial 17-10, probably incidental association from items in general mound fill. Two torsos with arms at their sides (Figure 94d-e; Ex. A, Section 5, depth 4.25 m), and one small figure with legs doubled up and hand clasped on the knee (Figure 94f; Ex. A, Section 6, depth 3.82 m). Escalera phase, or earlier. MRE-4565-1-6.

12. Miscellaneous Head and Extremity Fragments; 23. Assorted arms, legs, head, and torso fragments (Figure 95). Most of seated individuals. Escalera-Horcones phases.

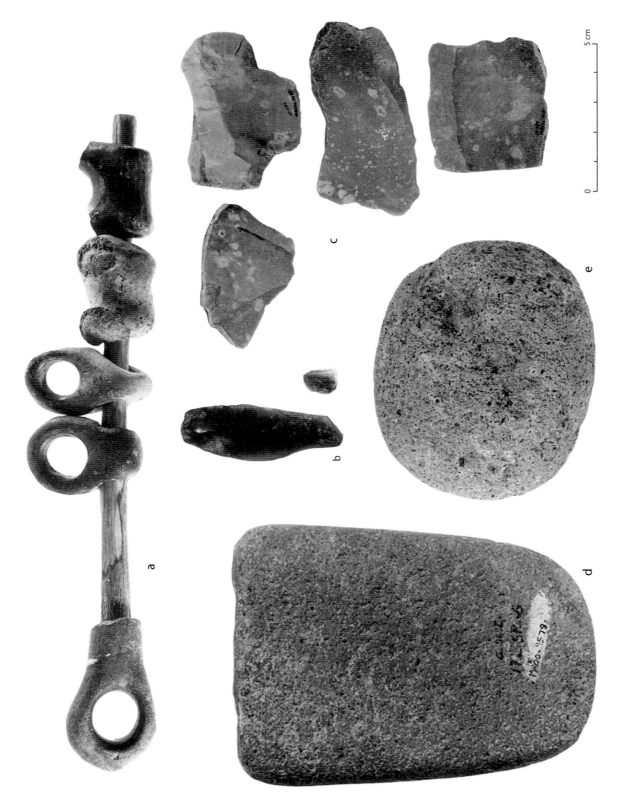

Figure 96. Miscellaneous ceramic and stone artifacts; a. Double Rings, b. Chipped Stone 1, c. Chipped Stone 1, c. Chipped Stone 2, d. Ground Stone 1, e. Ground Stone 2.

Provenience: 1, Ex. A3, depth 3.72 m; 6, Ex. A5, depth 4.25 m; 5, general backfill. MRE-4568-1-22.

### Ocarina Fragments

Three hollow bird body fragments (only one illustrated; Fig. 94g) which form the resonating chamber for an ocarina that probably had a simple mouthpiece and at least two stops. Length 3.2 cm, height 4.8 cm, thickness 3 cm. Escalera phase. Provenience: 1, Ex. B, below stairway ; 2, Ex. A5, depth 4.85 m. MRE-4569-1-3.

### Single Ring

This ring has a tubular extensión on one side which may have been inserted or hafted to the end of some kind of a small rod, or possibly a cane or hollow bone tube. The hole in the ring extension was made by forcing a tube into it while the clay was still wet (Fig. 94h). The similarity of manufacture, paste, and general surface polishing characteristics indicate that this ring was part of a double ring artifact, perhaps the loop-end of a rod on which the double rings were hung (see Figure 96a for suggested arrangement and possible function). Length 5.4 cm, diameter 3.2 cm, ring hole diameter 1.8 cm, hafting hole diameter 1.1 cm, hafting hole depth: 1.8+ cm. Late Preclassic. Provenience: Ex. A5, depth 4.25 m. MRE-4570.

### Double Rings

All nine double rings found in Mound 17 (Fig. 96a) conform to the type described for Chiapa de Corzo (Lee 1969c:71). Length 4.6 cm, width 2.5 cm, first hole diameter 1.2 cm, second hole diameter 0.9 cm. Dili through Francesa phase, probably not later. Provenience: 1, Burial 17-11; 1, Cache 17-11; 1, Ex. A8, depth 3.2 m; 1, Ex. A6, wall fill, depth 2 m; 2, A10, depth 3.2 m; 1, Ex. A5, depth 2.5 m; 1, General fill, off back dirt. MRE-4571-1-8.

### Cylindrical Stamps

1. Hollow Decorated Fragment; 1 (Fig. 94j). This stamp has narrow double bands bordering the design on one end. Next to the border is a band of isolated elements two of which are a low or recessed, negative "X" design contained in an oval cartouche, followed by a positive or salient symbol similar to a capital "H." Beyond this row of motifs is another with one small element which looks like the side profile of a cupped human hand and wrist. A 0.9 cm diameter hole pierces the center of the stamp. Length 4.2 cm, diameter 2.9 cm. Escalera phase, or earlier. Provenience: Burial 11, probably intrusive. MRE-4572.

2. Solid Decorated Fragment; 1 (Fig. 94i). A small tapered stamp with a positive spiral design beginning from a complex eye and hand (?) motif in the center and running out to the end of the stamp. Length 3 cm, diameter 1.4 cm. Escalera phase, or earlier. Provenience: Burial 11, probably intrusive. MRE-4573.

## STONE ARTIFACTS
### Ground Stone

Few fragments of groundstone artifacts were found at Mound 17, and they are poorly represented from NWAF excavations at the site as a whole (Lee 1969c). They are reported in greater frequencies for Mounds 26 and 73 (González and Cuevas 1998). At least one of these mounds was later than most of the Chiapa de Corzo excavations in the center proper. We do not think the difference in collection bias accounts for this difference because fragments of groundstone were saved and cataloged in the early NWAF excavations. Few groundstone artifacts have been reported for the Middle and Late Preclassic periods at La Libertad (Clark 1988) or Mirador (Agrinier 2000).

1. Rectangular Mano Fragment; 1 (Figure 96d). This half of a mano is roughly rectangular in plan with a slight taper toward the end. The end is only roughly rounded. In cross-section, the mano is a flattened oval. Material: Vesicular basalt with superficial red pigment on one side. Length 10.7+ cm, width 8.3 cm, thickness 4 cm. Provenience: Ex. A, Level 2 between Floors 9-10. MRE-4578.

2. Hand Grinding Stone; 1 (Fig. 96e). Small oval cobble that has one flattish surface, now secondarily pitted, and one more rounded or curved surface which has had its edges ground

off, thus leaving a smooth bevel. Material: soft andesite with superficial traces of red pigment. Provenience: Ex. A, Level 2 between Floors 9-10. MRE-4579.

## Chipped Stone

Few chipped stone artifacts were found at Mound 17, undoubtedly due to the forced, speedy excavations there coupled with the small size of these artifacts. The chert flakes are from local stone in the alluvial gravels near the site. The obsidian was imported from highland Guatemala. We have summarized elsewhere evidence for obsidian exchange and the local production of small obsidian pressure blades from small cores (Clark 1987, 1997, 2013; Clark and Lee 1980, 1984, 2007). Chiapa de Corzo was well down the line from obsidian outcrops, and this distance explains much of the scarcity

of obsidian at the site during the Preclassic period. Obsidian was abundant at La Libertad (Clark 1988) but very scarce at Mirador (Clark and Lee 2007).

1. Obsidian Blade Fragments; 2 (Fig. 96b). One blade is complete from distal end onwards, just slightly damaged on proximal end. A second piece is a flake. Both from general mound fill. MRE-4580-1, 2.

2. Large Chert Flakes; 4 (Fig. 96c). These four large primary flakes all have cortex and all are from the same core. Two have not been further worked, one only slightly, while the fourth shows considerable battering on the proximal end and both lateral edges as if to prepare it as an adze or hoe blade. Length range 9 to 14 cm, Width range 6.5 to 8 cm. Provenience: Ex. B, below stairway number 1. MRE-4581-1-4.

# CHAPTER 6

# CHIAPA DE CORZO AND MIDDLE PRECLASSIC
# CEREMONIAL ARCHITECTURE

Salvage excavations at Mound 17 obtained information on architecture, building renovations, offerings, and burials that help clarify the early history of Chiapa de Corzo. The construction history of Mound 17 provides critical data for understanding the configuration of Chiapa de Corzo as a ceremonial center, thought to have begun by Chiapa II-B times. In this chapter we describe early Chiapa de Corzo and compare its layout to those of nine contemporaneous centers in Chiapas and Tabasco. These include four sites to the north and northwest (Ocozocoautla, Mirador, San Isidro, and La Venta), two on the Pacific Coast (Tzutzuculi and Izapa), and three ancient centers located upriver to the southeast (Finca Acapulco, Santa Rosa, and La Libertad); see Figure 1. All these sites were regional centers in Chiapa II-IV times, the period when Chiapa de Corzo thrived as a regional power. Biographies of these centers varied. Chiapa de Corzo was the most long-lived; it persisted as a center from the beginning of the Middle Preclassic period through the Postclassic period. Some of its neighboring centers, namely, La Venta, Acapulco, La Libertad, and Tzutzuculi, were abandoned at the end of the Middle Preclassic. Sites considered in our interregional comparisons are thought to have shared the same ceremonial configuration and to have participated in the same Middle Preclassic interaction sphere and, perhaps, the same macro-cultural and linguistic group that included Chiapa de Corzo and its inhabitants.

Based on the most current data, we reassess these proposed relationships among Middle Preclassic centers in Tabasco and Chiapas. We consider sites in the order they would have been visited by a person traveling from Chiapa de Corzo to the Gulf Coast and then to the Pacific Coast, the headwaters of the Grijalva River, and back to the beginning. Chiapa de Corzo is located near the point on the Grijalva River where canoe traffic downriver became

impossible because of the Sumidero Canyon and its treacherous rapids. Travelers to the Gulf Coast from Chiapa de Corzo had to pass overland. The nearest center on this route was Ocozocoautla. Our imagined travel circuit goes from Chiapa de Corzo to Ocozocoautla, Mirador, San Isidro, La Venta, Tzutzuculi, Izapa, La Libertad, Santa Rosa, Finca Acapulco, and back to Chiapa de Corzo.

## PROPOSALS FOR MIDDLE PRECLASSIC SITE PATTERNING

Each site listed has been said to share the same basic Middle Preclassic pattern of arranged, specialized buildings (Clark and Lee 1984; Lowe 1977, 1982; McDonald 1974, 1983). Thus, the Middle Preclassic histories of these sites are of great importance for those interested in the spread of city life in Mesoamerica. Discussion of site patterns, and evolving claims for them, will be most understandable if we consider, in their sequential order, proposals by Andrew McDonald, Gareth Lowe, Thomas Lee, John Clark, and Michael Blake. Our differing views on site planning at Chiapas Middle Preclassic centers was the last issue we hoped to resolve in finishing this monograph. In his capacity as content editor, Clark asked Lee to upgrade his analysis of site patterning and include work published after 1987. Lee's untimely passing and Clark's subsequent assumption of authorial responsibilities obviate any ironing-out of differences. In lieu of a mutual synthesis, we present our separate views in their chronological order and context. Final observations are Clark's view of matters as of 2016.

### The McDonald Model (1974)

Different authors have proposed variant configurations for the Middle Preclassic centers of interest here. Andrew McDonald was the first, to our knowledge, to draw attention to formal similarities among Middle Preclassic Chiapas sites. In his paper presented at the International Congress of Americanists in Mexico City in 1974, he called attention to patterned "Middle Preclassic Ceremonial Centers in Southern Chiapas." His descriptors were chronological and geographical rather than formal or ethnic. Lee later labeled McDonald's model as the "Tri-Mound Complex" (TMC), a triad of architectural features shared by Middle Preclassic centers in Chiapas:

> The most striking [similarities are] the presence ... of a pyramidal platform centered on a transverse elongated platform along the central site axis ... a broad terrace supporting earthen structures situated ... northeast of the elongated platform. They exhibit a range of forms ... two of the sites, ... Chiapa de Corzo and ... Finca Acapulco, have platforms south of their axes with broad, flat tops. These shared characteristics ... indicate a definite pattern underlying the construction of the earliest platform complexes – those starting on the Escalera horizon – over much of Chiapas. (McDonald 1974)

McDonald argued that the sites of Chiapa de Corzo, Mirador, Finca Acapulco, La Libertad, Ozozocoautla, and Tzutzuculi shared this pattern. La Venta appears to have been on his list but was not described in his paper about Chiapas sites. He later added the site of Vistahermosa in Chiapas to his group (McDonald 1983:68). McDonald (ibid.) argued that the main plaza and pyramid at Tzutzuculi resembled the great pyramid on its platform at La Venta and Complex A to the north of it. This attribution shows that he imagined the ideal site pattern differently than did Lowe and others (see below). McDonald's paper forever changed the way NWAF personnel thought about the Middle Preclassic era. We publish McDonald's paper here as Appendix 2 so others will have access to the entirety of his original presentation. It was slated for publication in 1983 in an NWAF Paper to be called *Cultural Ecology and Human Geography in Southern Chiapas* (see McDonald 1983:68). We do not know what difficulties prevented the publication of this edited volume.

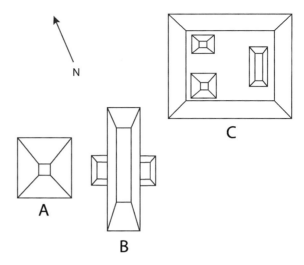

Figure 97. Lee's simplification and labeling of McDonald's site pattern.

The TMC pattern, as McDonald defined it, consisted of three mounds: a tall pyramid with a long, narrow, sometimes cruciform platform east of it, and a large, broad platform with superstructures, often referred to as an acropolis (Figure 97). For clarity in his own later analysis, Lee gave each of these kinds of mounds a letter designation so he could expand McDonald's model and include additional features. In Lee's designation, the tall pyramid of the Tri-Mound Complex is mound "A," and the long mound to the east of it is mound "B." The short, squarish platform mound or acropolis associated with these two mounds is mound "C." As described by McDonald, the long axis (that paralleling the long "B" platform) of each site – except at Mirador and Ozozocoautla – ranges between N-19°-E and N-38°-E. At Mirador this axis is almost due north. At Ozozocoautla the orientation is N-42°-W (see Appendix 2).

### The Lowe Model (1977)

Gareth Lowe (1977) popularized McDonald's unpublished model in his analysis of Mije-Soke and Maya relations in Preclassic Chiapas. Lowe described the "singular arrangement" at Chiapas sites as follows: "The emphasis is upon a [transverse] central axis crossing a pyramidal mound and a very long slender mound, with one or more broad flat platforms in close association. ... McDonald (1974) attributes [these] to a close relationship with Group A of La Venta, Tabasco" (Lowe 1977:224; see also, Lowe 1999:30-33). The long-mound-and-pyramid arrangement (mounds A and B in Lee's terminology) constitute what had long been called an "E-group" in Maya archaeology. Lowe argued that such paired mounds were observatories, perhaps for taking solstice observations (Lowe 1989b:fig. 4.10). He justified his reasoning with evidence from La Venta.

> Not noted by Heizer at La Venta was the situation, functionally important, of a small pyramid located just to the west of a long low platform south of the Stirling Acropolis; this pyramid was aligned with the massive stone Altars 4 and 5 ... placed centrally on the east and west sides of the long platform which itself had stone pillars on its surface ... This "solstice (?) observatory" at La Venta appears to have set the pattern for a series of at least 11 similar observatories at sites extending from the Chiapas Pacific coast at Tonalá [Tzutzuculi] into and throughout the Central Depression of Chiapas up to the Guatemala frontier [La Libertad], as well as into the Ocosingo Valley [Mosil C], during the "Modified Olmec" Middle Preclassic period ... This architectural pattern seems to be curiously lacking at Izapa (despite the suggestion that such a role was played by Group Ga [involving Mound 60]). The obvious explanation for this anomaly, in my opinion, is that the "ready-made" peaks of the volcanic mountain chain immediately to the east of Izapa made artificial points unnecessary. The true explanation may be more complicated, and possibly related to the unique presence (in Chiapas) of the advanced platform-building Duende culture slightly prior to the arrival or development of the Modified Olmec Escalon phase trait complex ... (Lowe 1982:278)

Lowe followed McDonald's criteria in identifying TMC sites but allowed for more variability in the location of platform mounds (mounds "C") associated with E-groups. He also identified more sites that fit the pattern. He designated these as "Modified Olmec ceremonial centers" (Lowe 1977:224), with "modified" referring to the period of the La Venta Olmec horizon that followed the Early Olmec (San Lorenzo) horizon (see Lowe 1989b, 1998b). Lowe thought that Olmecs promoted E-groups and their associated mounds. His basic idea was that Chiapas centers copied the architectural arrangement of La Venta. This has not been determined. Lowe (1989a:367) acknowledged that the direction of influence could have gone the other way; La Venta could have copied a Chiapas site. We can be certain that the peoples of these Middle Preclassic centers were in close contact and influenced one another.

Lowe did not use the implied acronym (MOCC–Modified Olmec Ceremonial Centers) for his model. Depending on the publication, Lowe identified 8 to 12 MOCC sites in Chiapas (Lowe 1977:224-226, fig. 9.3, 1982:278, 1989a, 1998a, 1999). To McDonald's list he added San Mateo, Vergel, Santa Rosa, San Isidro, and Mosil C (Figure 98). La Venta, Tabasco, was the principal MOCC site and the justification for the Olmec brand. In contrast to McDonald's proposal, Lowe saw the similarities between La Venta and Chiapas sites as concerning Groups B, C, and part of D at La Venta rather than Group A. We concur. Mounds comprising the stereotypic pattern at different sites were generally similar in size, location, and orientation. The same formal buildings were clearly constructed at many Chiapas sites and, in a modified form, also at Finca Acapulco. Lowe's most comprehensive list included the following Chiapas sites (numbers refer to sites labeled in Lowe 1977:200, fig. 9.3): (1) Acapulco, (2) San Mateo, (3) Vergel, (4) Chiapa de Corzo, (5) San Isidro, (6) Ocozocoautla, (7) Mirador, (8) Vistahermosa, (9) Tzutzuculi, (10) Santa Rosa, (11) La Libertad, and [12] Mosil C (a site near Toniná not listed by name but on Lowe's unpublished map of these centers). The principal elements at all these sites is the presence of an

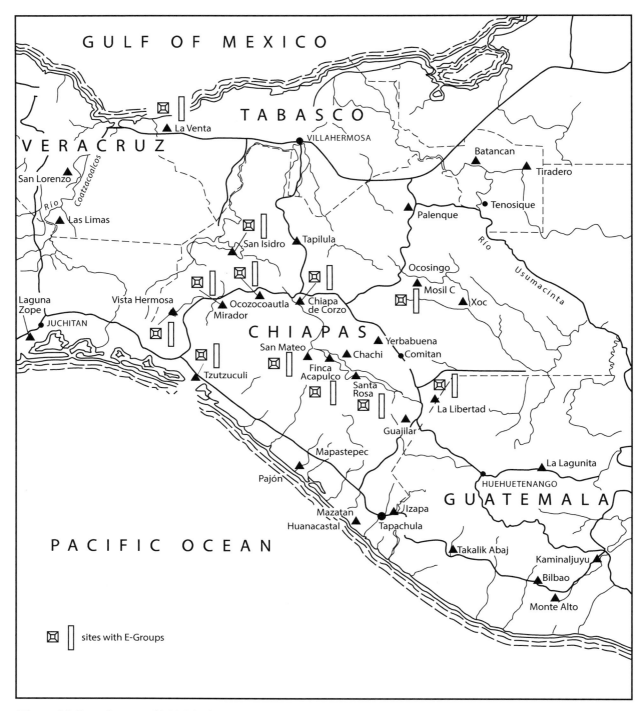

Figure 98. Lowe's map of MOCC sites.

E-group, paired mounds also known for dozens of Lowland Maya sites. Izapa did not make Lowe's list of Modified Olmec Ceremonial Centers.

## The Lee Model (1987)

In comparing the architectural characteristics of Mound 17 at Chiapa de Corzo with those of other Escalera phase mounds at Chiapas sites, Lee became aware of a more complex pattern of site organization in the core of civic-ceremonial centers that included more buildings and features than McDonald's (1974, 1977, 1983) tri-mound complex. Lee accepted McDonald's and Lowe's identifications but could not confirm a TMC pattern for Vergel or San Mateo. Lee's unpublished model, written for a draft of this monograph, combined elements of McDonald's TMC pattern and Lowe's MOCC stretching of it, as well as new elements. Adjusting Lowe's terminology, Lee christened his own configuration as the "Modified Olmec Site Core Pattern (MOSCP)" because he thought the pattern originated in the Olmec heartland, as did Lowe, and relatively late in the Olmec sequence. The term "Modified Olmec" was taken from Lowe (1977:222-228, 1982:278). An "Olmec" origin of the site pattern is very much in doubt (Inomata et al. 2013), but current evidence does support an early Middle Preclassic date for it in Chiapas and in the adjacent Maya Lowlands.

Lee argued that the MOSCP complex was present at Izapa in Chiapas and at Laguna de los Cerros (Gómez Rueda 1996b:108) and San Lorenzo Tenochtitlan (Gómez Rueda 1996b:92-4, Lam. 3.10) in Veracruz. All together he identified 15 sites with a shared pattern, adding three more sites to the growing list. A MOSCP complex consists of the A, B, and C mounds of McDonald's Tri-Mound Complex plus several other architectural units: D, E, F, and G (Figures 99-102). Previously, unrecognized architectural elements include a secondary pyramid (D) associated with A, B, and C mounds, a ballcourt (E), a northern pyramid (F), and a sunken or enclosed plaza or constructed pond or reservoir (G). Lee's "pattern" refers to the presence of mounds of supposed types rather than to a specific configuration or grouping of these mounds at any given site. For example, the location of ballcourts (E) is inconsistent among the cases for which they have been identified. Lee's site pattern is polythetic, meaning that candidate sites do not have to have all the aforementioned elements, or to have them in the same spatial configuration, to qualify for membership in his MOSCP class. The identification of different mound types and associated features allows one to analyze sites and to assess similarities and differences in the kinds of mounds present and their relative arrangement. To constitute a functional configuration, the mounds in question need to have been in use at the same time. Information on the construction histories of individual mounds is critical for determining site patterns. Lee's inclusion of sites from Veracruz and Tabasco was based on configurations alone. These are not convincing for the Veracruz sites on his list. The mounds at these sites appear to date to Classic times and conform to a site configuration described for that period by Thomas Killion and Javier Urcid (2001).

## The Clark Model (2000)

Clark's comparisons of Middle Preclassic sites began as a comparison of Chiapa de Corzo and La Venta as sister cities. He argued that these centers were built according to the same plan, a plan first evident in its full manifestation at La Venta and presumably copied by people living in Chiapas. His claims for the kinds of shared features have changed through the years, depending on which maps he used to make the comparisons. His early efforts were the most ambitious, but he later determined that the map of La Venta relied on was inaccurate and that some perceived similarities were based on poor data, and thus in error. We review these changes to clear the way for more accurate comparisons. The major articles were published in Spanish. We draw from the unpublished English versions of these texts. The first article illustrated the site cores of La Venta and Chiapa de Corzo side by side at the same scale and colored coded mound types to show significant similarities between mound sizes and placements at the two sites (Clark 2000:47). The mounds are depicted as "reconstructed" squared and rectangular

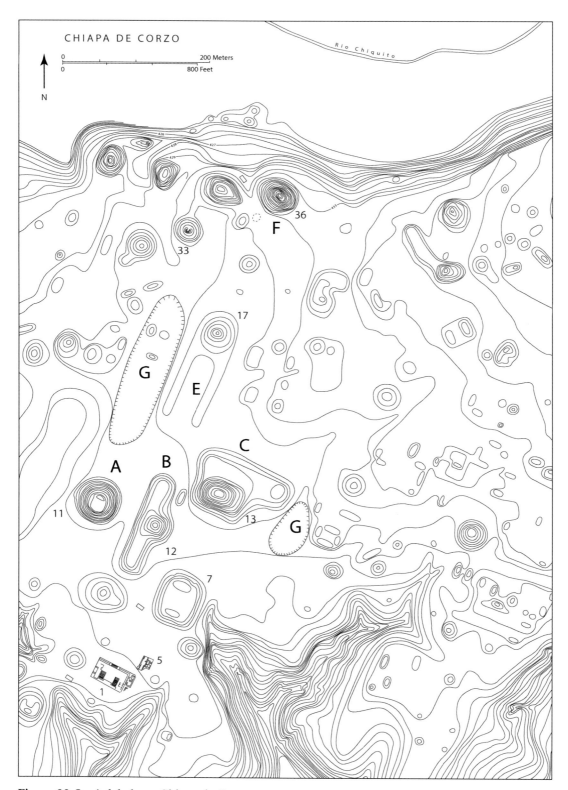

Figure 99. Lee's labels on Chiapa de Corzo map.

Figure 100. Lee's labels on Izapa map.

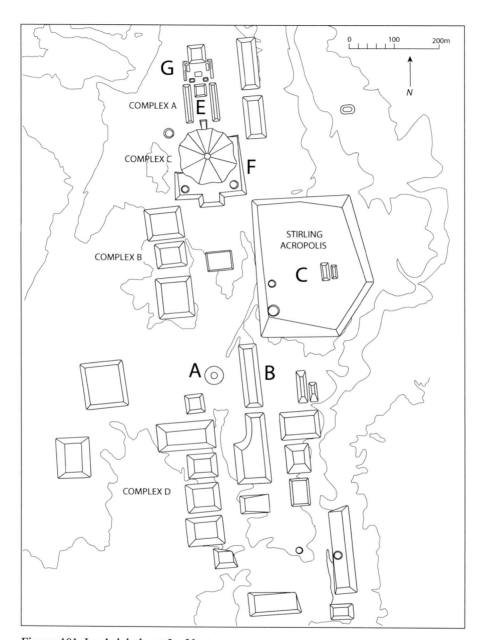

Figure 101. Lee's labels on La Venta map.

Figure 102. Lee's labels on La Libertad map.

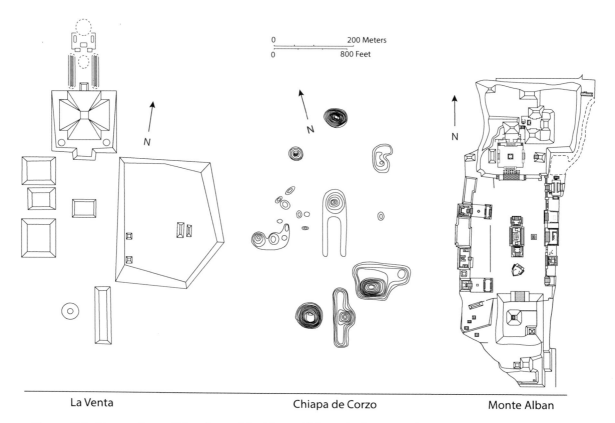

La Venta                    Chiapa de Corzo                    Monte Alban

Figure 103. Comparison of the plans of La Venta, Chiapa de Corzo, and Monte Albán.

platforms rather than as eroded, rounded mounds.

> The overall site plan of Chiapa de Corzo closely matches that of early La Venta in form and size; both must have been constructed using the same plan ... Other contemporaneous cities in the Chiapas interior were also constructed on the same plan, which consisted of a large pyramid in the north, a long plaza to the south flanked on the east and west by large residential platforms, and with a special pair of mounds on the south. These latter mounds consisted of a low, long mound on the east with a tall pyramid to the west; these are thought to have been constructed for astronomical observation. (Clark 2000:50)

No specific claims were made for this comparison because the similarities were obvious in the color illustration with regards to the sizes of mounds and their similar arrangement. Details were provided in a paper given at a conference in Spain in 2000 and published in a journal there in 2001. Discussion addressed "Ciudades Tempranas Olmecas." Clark was clearly on board with McDonald's and Lowe's arguments that the pattern of site layouts originated in the Gulf Coast lowlands and was first apparent at La Venta.

The article on early Olmec cities (Clark 2001) took a wider view and compared La Venta to Chiapa de Corzo and Monte Alban and specific features at these sites with Group E at Uaxactun. Clark argued that these and many other Middle Preclassic cities were linear and organized along a central axis and perpendicular, transverse axes (Figure 103).

Several simplifying assumptions underlay Clark's analysis concerning site histories and development. He attempted to compare the three cities as they would have appeared in Middle Preclassic times. He assumed that the central core of La Venta was the original city, that Complex A of the city was equally old but unique to La Venta, and that the city later grew southward and became less regularly organized. The main axes of these cities were roughly north-south, and each was built on a rise or bluff with natural limits. There are clear architectural differences among the cities, but their Middle Preclassic cores appear to have been the same absolute length, estimated as 640 m (Clark 2001:188, fig. 4). The mounds at each site are regularly spaced and aligned to the major and minor axes of the site. These sites have regular modules of spacing of 80 and 160 m intervals. The ceremonial cores of these sites were four modules of 160 m long. Group A at La Venta is also this length. Neither Chiapa de Corzo nor Monte Alban had a spatial equivalent to La Venta's Group A – at least not in the same position in the overall site. The large complexes in the central plazas of these two sites, however, corresponded very well to the size and proportions of La Venta's Group A. At Chiapa de Corzo, Mound 17 and its twin mound extension to the south corresponds precisely to the length and divisions of Group A (Clark 2001:192, fig. 8). The large plazas at these sites are about the same length and width. All the sites have large, broad mounds, but the Stirling Acropolis at La Venta is more than double the size of the broad platforms at Chiapa de Corzo and Monte Alban.

In his article, Clark argued for an Olmec standard unit of measure 1.54 m long and used this to translate the dimensions of La Venta into native units of distance. Planned space and space built to plan was necessarily measured space by some means, and measured space by whatever means was counted space. In terms of proposed Olmec measuring units, the 80 m module would have been a count of 52. Five such modules would have been the 260 count of the sacred almanac, and seven modules would be a 364 of the vague solar year (Figure 104). Major divisions in the architectural arrangement of La Venta show that the 260 and 364 (365) distances were clearly marked as major junctures of the site (as measured from the transverse axis of the E-group northward) (Clark 2001:205, fig. 18). The major claim was that the site of La Venta was built according to sacred calendar counts. Distances represented time intervals. These same spacings and site divisions are evident at Chiapa de Corzo and Monte Alban. The main point is that the precise distances of mounds and

buildings at Middle Preclassic cities may have been highly meaningful.

Much of Clark's analysis of La Venta concerned proportions. He argued that these were both natural and fractal. By "natural" he meant that the site proportions were the same ones used in Olmec art in portraying the human body and its proportions. Site plans could have been laid out as a human metaphor (Figure 105). By "fractal" he meant that different elements at La Venta shared the same divisions and proportions as the site core at different scales. Group A, for example, is one-fourth the length of the old part of the city and is segmented the same way. Some sculptures and axe offerings are smaller versions of Group A and La Venta proper. Some inscribed designs on individual serpentine axes also have the same relative lengths and divisions (Figure 106). Fractal relationships were not limited to La Venta. Clark (2001:203) argued that the site of Tzutzuculi on the Pacific Coast of Chiapas was built at one-half scale to La Venta. Some site divisions at La Venta and other MFC sites correspond to the golden mean, but Clark did not discuss these special proportions.

The principal weakness of Clark's analysis was that it was based on the map of La Venta published by Rebecca González Lauck (1988: fig. 1) in *Arqueología Mexicana*. This was the best map available at the time, but this nascent journal did not do justice to her original map. Later comparison of the published version with a blueprint of the original map showed that the scale in the published map was slightly off, so mound sizes and distances calculated on the basis of this scale were also off. Clark derived the 1.54 m unit of measure from an analysis of the offering pits for the massive offerings in Group A rather from the site itself. The data for these is clearly illustrated in La Venta reports (Drucker 1952; Drucker et al. 1959), and measurements given in these texts allow one to verify that scales published with drawings are correct. Information on mound sizes and distances is still not available for the site of La Venta south of Group A. The more accurate map (Figure 107) indicated that La Venta was longer than previously calculated and that the regular spacing of mounds and plazas accord better to a

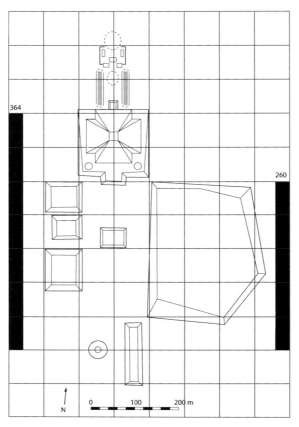

Figure 104. The plan of central La Venta and possible calendar distances. Red squares 52 units long.

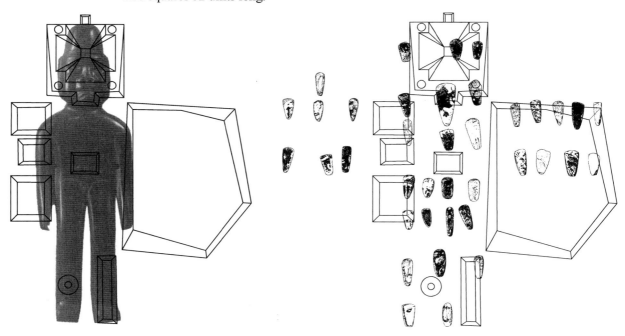

Figure 105. Fractal organization of La Venta site plan and jade figurine from tomb in Mound A-2 at La Venta.

Figure 106. Fractal organization of La Venta site plan and axe offering.

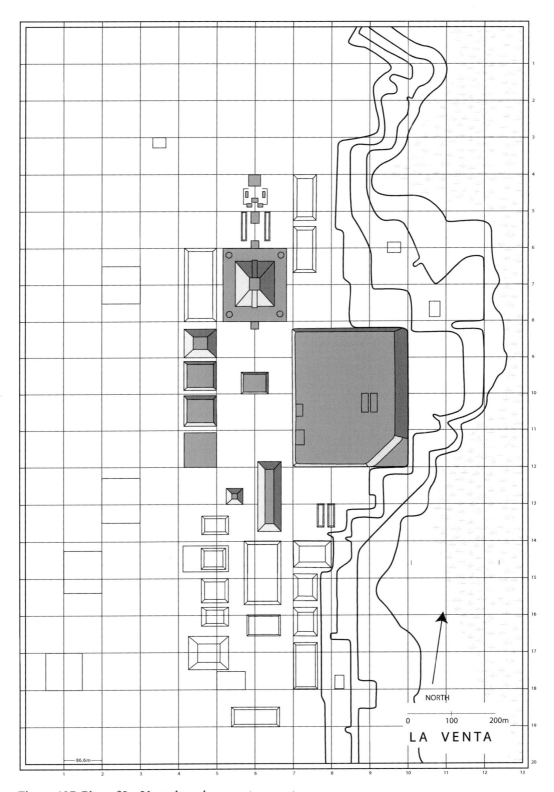

Figure 107. Plan of La Venta based on most accurate map.

measuring standard of 1.666 m rather than 1.54 m.

In his 2001 article Clark argued for measurement modules of 80 m that represented 52 units of 1.54 m each. In the 2008 revision of the earlier study, based on the better map, he argued for modules of 86.6 m, or 52 units of 1.666 m each. These estimates are overly precise, of course, and represent his best guess of the size and spacing of mounds and plazas at La Venta (and of which map is more accurate). An hypothesis of modules of 50 units each would be more appealing to Westerners used to decimal systems of counting. There is enough uncertainty in the data that a case could be made for modules of 50 units each based on the 1.666 m standard. The long length of the site, however, gives us confidence that the modules were 52 units long rather than 50. It should be kept in mind that there is some degree of error in all the estimates and numbers. Clark's revision of the scale for the La Venta map makes the site longer than he first thought. This means that the claimed similarities to Chiapa de Corzo and other sites are not as strong as thought. We address the difference this difference makes in following discussion.

**The Clark and Hansen Model (2001)**

Clark published a version of his model in a chapter on Maya royal courts co-authored with Richard Hansen (2001). The chapter is a running argument (in the endnotes) between these authors about the veracity of the Middle Preclassic site pattern and its historic and social significance. For the Chiapas sites described, Clark built on the work of McDonald and Lowe but not on Lee's unpublished proposal; he was unaware of Lee's thesis at the time. Based on his comparative analysis of Chiapa de Corzo and La Venta, Clark doubled the number of elements proposed for the TMC pattern and accorded them less wiggle room than McDonald, Lowe, and Lee allowed. Clark and Hansen (2001:4, 42, endnote 3) dubbed the pattern the "Middle Formative Chiapas" (MFC) pattern because it is known principally for Chiapas sites. The MFC pattern

> consists of a north-to-south axial arrangement of regularly spaced pyramidal platforms and plazas. The tallest platform or pyramid is located to the north, and in the south is a paired arrangement of a long, low mound flanked on the west by a tall pyramid. This latter arrangement has long been known as an "E-Group" in Maya studies because it was first identified in the 1930s at Group E at Uaxactun ... Nearly equidistantly placed between the principal northern and southern mounds of MFC sites is a smaller platform located near the center of a large, central plaza measuring about 160 by 320 meters. [There is a] large acropolis to the east of this central mound ... Other low mounds delimit the plaza on the west ... (Clark and Hansen 2001:4-5)

None of the previous models formally acknowledged the rectangular plaza as integral to the configuration of mounds (see Figure 108). Clark and Hansen (2001:42) considered calling this stereotypic arrangement of plaza and flanking mounds "the La Venta pattern," or the "Olmec pattern" but they did not because its source of origin had not been determined. They opted, as had McDonald, for more a generic label to draw attention to time period and geographic area of its popularity, but not to the Olmecs.[9]

---

[9] The benign label is due to two sources of restraint. Clark believed that the pattern came from La Venta, but his conviction was strongly resisted by Hansen (who wanted a Maya origin) and by Rebecca González Lauck (personal communication to Clark) who averred that it was equally likely that La Ventans could have borrowed from the people at Chiapa de Corzo (see also, Lowe 1989a:367). Clark described the proposed relationship as follows: "We suspect that the total configuration of mounds and alignments that constitute this [MFC] pattern first came together at La Venta about 850 B.C. and spread quickly to Chiapas, but this remains to be determined" (Clark and Hansen 2001:42-43). Takeshi Inomata and others (2013, 2014) argue that an early E-group has been found at Ceibal that dates to 1000-900 BC, earlier than any known architecture at La Venta and, thus, not derived from there. The E-group is a critical element of the MFC pattern – but not the full pattern. To Clark, early Ceibal looks like a colony from elsewhere, so he thinks the Olmec heartland is still the best place to look for the origins of the full pattern.

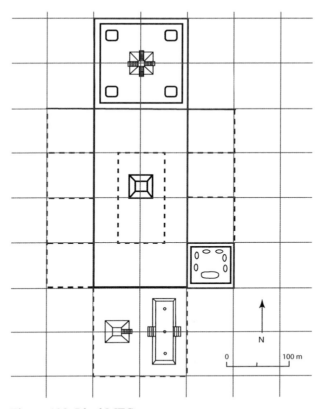

Figure 108. Ideal MFC pattern.

Lowe's and McDonald's criteria for a tri-mound complex focused on the southern half of what Clark and Hansen define as a full MFC layout. McDonald (1999) later reformed his model and described an "Early Ceremonial Platform Complex." This was essentially still an E-Group plus an acropolis. Neither McDonald nor Lowe included the rectangular plaza, its northern pyramid or western platforms. Lee's proposal retained the original three elements and also added reflecting pools or reservoirs and ballcourts, features present at only half the sites he identified as conforming to his MOSCP pattern. Given the greater number of identifying criteria, the MFC complex is more restrictive and, hence, fewer sites qualify. Lee's polythetic approach is more lenient and inclusive. Clark and Hansen (2001) discussed four sites with a clear MFC pattern: La Venta, Chiapa de Corzo, Mirador, and La Libertad. Sites that qualified but not discussed for lack of space were San Isidro, Finca Acapulco, Tzutzuculi, and Ocozocoautla (see Clark 2016). Some of these do not have all the features expected. Others appear to have the features, but a Middle Preclassic date for them has not been verified. For example, Clark never considered Santa Rosa or Izapa as qualifying as MFC sites. As discussed below, new information from Izapa makes it a good candidate for an MFC site. The case for Santa Rosa remains tenuous (see below).

**The Blake Distinction (2013)**

As described in Appendix 2 by McDonald, one feature that is not consistent among TMC sites is the orientation of their principal axis. Mirador is the only early center in Chiapas known to have had the same orientation as La Venta. The different orientations represent serious variation among sites thought to have been constructed to the same plan and for the same purposes. The differences are especially critical for E-group pairs, the one element all sites share. If these paired mounds were oriented as observatories to track solstices, then one would expect them to vary only slightly in orientation given their minor differences in latitude, rather than the more than 80 degree spread known for 10 sites in the sample. Differences in skyline could account for some of this variation, but not all. In his chapter with Hansen, Clark proposed that only the original solar observatory at the type site need have been functional. Copycat sites could have mimicked the formal arrangement of the observatory without preserving its original function (Clark and Hansen 2001:44). This ad hoc hypothesis was invoked to account for striking formal similarities in mound arrangements in light of equally blatant differences in orientation.

With new software applications available from Google-Earth, Michael Blake (2013) tested the "solar observatory" hypothesis for most E-groups proposed for Chiapas sites. He modeled solstice and equinox sunrises against the skyline associated with each site. He found that all observatories were "functional" in terms of being aligned to equinoxes or solstices, but they were not focused on the same astronomical phenomena. Based on presumed observatory functions, he found that four different kinds of E-groups are represented in the 10 Middle Preclassic centers considered here. A key idea for his evaluation comes from studies of the E-group at Uaxactun. The long mound there has three summit buildings, one in the middle and one at each end. An observer on the westward pyramid would have had three major sight lines defined by the center and two end points marked on the long mound (Ricketson 1928a, 1928b, 1930; Ruppert 1940). In Classic times buildings may have served the purpose of establishing sighting points. In Middle Preclassic times, poles or monuments may have been set atop long mounds to provide these lines of sight, as proposed by Lowe (1989b:61) for La Venta.

Blake evaluated early Chiapas E-groups according to the three-sight-lines expectation. He argued that there are five logical possibilities for functional E-groups. These are illustrated in Figure 109. All three sight lines may have been operative, or only two, or only one. E-groups with only one or two viable sight lines differed according to what was being observed, the summer or winter solstice sunrise. For a standard E-group of Type 1, the transverse

axis of the mound pair aligns to the equinoxes; winter and summer solstice sunrises can be observed with the sight lines over the two ends of the long mound. Of the sites considered here, La Venta and Mirador have E-groups of the standard type. Finca Acapulco may also qualify, but this has not been verified. Other E-groups were aligned to observe only one solstice and the equinoxes (Types 2 and 3) or just one solstice (Types 4 and 5). E-groups of Type 2 were built to observe the winter solstice over the transverse axis of the mound pair and the equinoxes along the sight line passing over the northern end of the long mound. Chiapa de Corzo, La Libertad, and Izapa have E-groups of this type. Type 3 observatories are the mirror image of Type 2, with summer solstice sunrise being the main orientation of the transverse axis and the equinoxes being aligned to the sight line over the southern end of the long mound (Fig.100). The E-groups at Ocozocoautla and San Isidro are of this type. The E-group at Tzutzuculi is Type 4; it has only one sight line for the solar phenomena in question. Winter solstice sunrise was observable over the northern end of the long mound. No example of a Type 5 observatory has been identified for a Chiapas site. E-group types have not been determined for Finca Acapulco or Santa Rosa. Given the latitudes of the sites in question, a solar observatory of the types discussed required that the transverse pyramid be spaced from the long mound according to the length of the latter so the angles between the sunrises at equinoxes and solstices could be observed from the pyramid over the middle or ends of the long mound.

Blake's analysis confirms possible utilities for E-groups at MFC sites as solar observatories and, simultaneously, indicates significant differences among them. It is worth mentioning that such "observatories" could have been used to monitor the movement of other celestial bodies, such as the moon and Venus. Given the surprising variety among the E-groups of the 10 centers considered, it seems inappropriate to lump them all together into a single type of site as all previous proposals have done. It would be more appropriate to designate them, or the sites at which they were constructed, according to type of observatory. Some sites were aligned

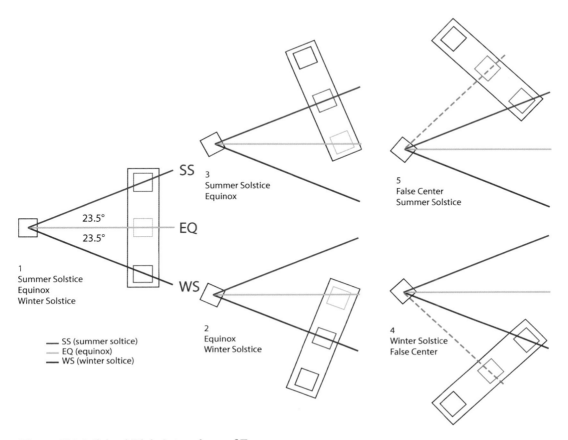

Figure 109. Michael Blake's typology of E-groups.

perpendicular to the equinoxes, the winter solstice, or the summer solstice. The minimal criteria for characterizing a Middle Preclassic center is the presence of an E-group with known orientation. In most cases considered, the long orientation of the E-group is the same as the site as a whole. The fact that each E-group was "functional" means that their designed functions were built into the design of the original ceremonial center from the very beginning. If a "functional" E-group were adopted at a site that had been constructed to a different alignment, we would expect the alignment of the E-group to differ from that of the site as a whole. Izapa may be an example of this. Its E-group has an orientation 7 degree askew from the site's principal axis (Blake 2013), which is aligned to the peak of the Tacaná volcano. For other E-groups considered here, the transverse, west-east axis of the E-group was perpendicular to the site's long axis. This orthogonal "short"

axis was actually the one that mattered more. The chosen "long" axis in these cases was a geometric permutation of aligning to the sun's path on the day of choice and then building a site using the principle of right angles.

Arguments about the function of E-groups entail notions of site planning, history, and construction. It was logically necessary that the E-group be a primary consideration in site construction if it was to be functional. Imagine the contrary, making an E-group perpendicular to the long axis of a site chosen for other reasons. The chances would not be good that the transverse axis would align to equinoxes or solstice sunrises as apparent over a mountain sky-line. The organic fit of most E-groups in the MFC sites considered here is the most compelling evidence that whole ceremonial centers were planned and built as units from scratch. The few exceptions (Santa Rosa and Izapa) prove the rule. Clark has been criticized for claiming that the E-group at La Venta was an original member of this planned site because, at the moment, there is no clear evidence of the date of the two mounds comprising it. How could it have been otherwise? His argument is from logical necessity if the E-group were a functional solar observatory. As described, the La Venta E-group is the best example of the lot and was an observatory of standard type. While on this topic, Marion Hatch's (1971:10) complex argument that the layout of La Venta was aligned to CP Ursas Majoris at midnight, June 21, 2000 BC, appears over the top. If La Venta was a star-oriented center, it is virtually impossible that its short, orthogonal axis would be aligned to the equinoxes at the site's latitude. The solar hypothesis is the more compelling explanation for the site's orientation.

Given our claim that a site oriented to the sun's passage must have been gauged to the sun's passage in the specific locale in which the site was to be built, the dependent claim that E-groups were the crucial component of the site follows. The limited historic data on site histories indicate that E-groups were constructed before the larger MFC pattern came into being. It is important to point out that these inferences are not logically necessary if one starts from other premises. Given the construction of a functional E-group at a site, such as Santa Rosa, Ceibal, or Ojo de Agua (sites only having E-groups), there would have been no logical necessity for aligning other buildings to the long or short axes of the paired mounds of the E-group. We argue that if all the mounds are aligned in the same way, and if the E-group was clearly oriented to the sun as described, then the long and short axes built into the E-group were extended to the other buildings at the site. The obverse is not necessarily true. If the E-group at a site is askew, and also functional, it could have been built earlier, later, or even contemporaneously with the other buildings at the site. At Izapa we think the E-group was added later, given what is known of the history of individual mounds there (Clark 2013:139). At Santa Rosa, the E-group was clearly the earliest complex of mounds. The same appears to be true of Ceibal (see Inomata et al. 2013). The E-group also appears to have

been the earliest buildings at La Libertad, but the core of the ceremonial center was built in the same phase, and all according to the same alignment. There is no necessary reason to align any other buildings at a site to its E-group. At most Maya sites, such as Nakbé (Clark and Hansen 2001), the other buildings clearly were not aligned. A significant feature of MFC sites is that whole sites share the same long and short orientation and appear to have been built on a Cartesian grid, much like Spanish towns after the Conquest.

## Comments

Depending on the number of elements considered for determining similar site configurations, more or fewer sites qualify as participating in the same Middle Preclassic system. The minimum criteria that fit all models are paired mounds of an E-group, or A and B mounds. To qualify, the long mound must be east of the pyramid and on its transverse axis. This is not the only way to set up sight lines between mounds, but these are the requirements for identifying an E-group in the strict sense. It is worth acknowledging that mounds are not needed to observe and track solstices or equinoxes, so the absence of an E-group at a site does not mean these celestial phenomena were not monitored or honored. The buildings of a functional complex must have been used contemporaneously; we are interested here in Middle Preclassic E-groups, the era of their popularity in Chiapas. This architectural form persisted much longer in the Maya area than it did in Chiapas (see Chase and Chase 1995). Here, we grant benefit of the doubt to unexcavated mounds at known Preclassic sites, pending archaeological investigation and dating of individual mounds. We also follow Lee's recommendation of standard labels for mound types at different sites.

Clark's (2016) analysis of Middle Preclassic kingdoms in eastern Mesoamerica supports Lee's polythetic approach. Some sites had segments of an overall ideal configuration without having the complete pattern. The lack of a complete standard configuration at a site may be indicative of its status within a settlement hierarchy. For example, San Mateo and Vergel were what Lowe (1989a:366) called "minor centers." Clark (2016) interpreted him to mean that these sites were "secondary" centers to Finca Acapulco, but this may go beyond what Lowe intended. He may have meant the sites were independent centers, but not very big ones. Both these sites had ballcourts, and San Mateo had an E-group and the full MFC pattern (for sketch map, see Lowe 1989a:381, fig. 14). The E-group at San Mateo appears to have been aligned nearly north-south like that at Mirador, so we expect it was a Type 1 observatory. We cannot find a site map for Vergel; no E-group is mentioned for it.

The "minor" centers at San Mateo and Vergel appear to have been functionally specialized and limited (i.e., many fewer mounds and fewer types of mounds) compared to Finca Acapulco. If one takes architectural complexity and formal differences of mounds as clues to functional differentiation, standard inferences in settlement pattern studies, then these three sites did not share the same set of functions. Not all sites in a settlement system can be expected to have served all functions. It is worth pointing out that site configurations discussed by different authors are minimal units that attempt to identify a core of elements shared by sites that have many other mounds and features that have not been factored into explanations. If one could identify specialized architecture qua function, it would be possible to do away with gross typologies all together and describe functional configurations of buildings at individual sites. Identifications of ballcourts, E-groups, reflecting pools, and possible royal compounds (Clark and Hansen 2001) are a step in that direction. For now, however, we follow the trail of past site typologies in our analysis of Preclassic centers. In our discussion we treat the original MFC proposal as an "ideal type" in the Max Weber sense (see 1992), meaning that no one site need have had all the features of the ideal, but the "type" is a useful heuristic for describing and comparing sites.[10]

The site of La Venta looms large in all comparisons. It was formally laid out and had a rather short history, consequently, one can be confident that the monumental architecture there dates to Middle Preclassic times. At sites with longer histories, such as San Isidro, later buildings covered earlier ones and obscured the original pattern. We do not recapitulate here all arguments made for these sites. Rather, we focus on similarities and differences in site configurations evident between Chiapa de Corzo and nine other centers. After summarizing the particulars of each case we revisit interpretations of areal distributions with an eye to understanding Chiapa de Corzo during the first half of its history.

## CHIAPA DE CORZO

Chiapa de Corzo functioned as a regional center by Chiapa II times. Timothy Sullivan (2009:83, 2015:455) estimates the site covered 71 ha at this time and had a population of about 1,100 persons. The MFC complex at Chiapa de Corzo comprises Mounds 11, 12, 13, 22, 36, and 17. Mound 36, the northern pyramid of the proposed MFC pattern, dates to Chiapa II through IV times (Figure 99). On the southern end, Mounds 11 and 12 constitute the E-Group. This E-group was a Type 2 arrangement aligned to the winter solstice sunrise. The main axis at Chiapa de Corzo is 28 degrees east of true north.

Investigations in Mound 12 uncovered a 3.5 m high platform that dates to Chiapa III times (Mason 1960a:2-3). The length of this early structure has not been determined. Recent explorations of Mound 11, excavated from the summit to bedrock, found 20 construction episodes. The earliest platform was 4 m high and was built during the Dili or Dzemba phase (Lynneth Lowe, personal communication 2012). The large offering pits found at the eastern toe of Mound 11 date to about 750 BC (Bachand 2013; Bachand and Lowe 2011:81) and represent a clear link to La Venta patterns of axe caches. In our opinion, the cruciform offering of jade

---

[10] As our brief history of proposals makes clear, the MFC type began as a descriptive type of actual sites rather than as an ideal type. Clark (2001) argued that it may have been an ideal type anciently, but this is a different issue. New data and better observations at sites show that the MFC pattern is not an accurate description of sites. But it is still very useful as an ideal type.

axes just in front of Mound 11 should date at least to Chiapa II-B times around 800 BC. In short, excavations securely date the construction of the E-Group at Chiapa de Corzo to about 850-800 BC based on ceramic associations. Radiocarbon samples have not been processed.

As discussed, Mound 17 to the north of Mounds 11 and 12 was constructed by Escalera times in the middle of the plaza as a broad low platform (Lee 1969b), as were the two 100 m long, parallel low platforms extending southward from it (Lowe 1962b:56). These 1.25 m high wings of Mound 17 may have been an early ballcourt. If so, it would have been unusually large. These structures were just north and west of the broad platform at Mound 13. This latter structure has not been extensively explored so its beginning construction date has not been ascertained. One of the earlier buildings in Mound 13, dating to 700 BC, was a stepped earthen platform 6.2 m high (Lowe and Mason 1965:212). An even earlier platform was discovered inside it (Hicks and Rozaire 1960:5).

Mound 7 was built as part of the same plaza complex. In Chiapa III times this clay mound was about 1.3 m high and had steps on its western and northern sides, and perhaps on the other two sides as well. It measured at least 15 by 15 m at the base. It was resurfaced four times during the Escalera phase. In the following Francesa phase, this platform was expanded and elevated to a height of 3.4 m. All these data indicate that the full MFC complex was in place at Chiapa de Corzo by at least 700 BC. Characteristics of site layout are compelling evidence that Chiapa de Corzo was planned, measured, and marked out by 800 BC. The southern part of Chiapa de Corzo was also leveled and extended to make a formal plaza (see Bachand et al. 2008). A small building was built at Mound 1A in Escalera times (Agrinier 1975a; Agrinier and Clark 2014:88). Buildings to flank the southern plaza were built in Chiapa IV and V times. In Chiapa II and III times the southern plaza was mostly flat, empty space, but it was deliberately prepared space.

The primary, early construction of Mound 13 appears to have been a broad platform which supported at least one low mound (Mason 1960b). This platform may have been a royal compound, a function perhaps subsequently superceded by the placement of a temple mound over it. At this time the royal compound may have moved to Mound 7 located to the south (Clark and Hansen 2001:88). At the start of the Chiapa VI phase, the royal compound was moved to the palace at Mound 5 in the southwestern sector of the site (Lowe 1962b).

## OCOZOCOAUTLA

Ocozocoautla is located in the central valley of Chiapas 40 km south of San Isidro and 40 km west of Chiapa de Corzo. It is near the southern edge of the northern Chiapas highlands on the overland route to San Isidro. As with this latter site, Ocozocoautla had a long history that spanned the early Middle Preclassic to Classic periods, with peak periods of development in the Middle Preclassic and Early Classic. Ocozocoautla appears to have first been occupied in Chiapa II-A times (McDonald 1999:61). The site is the same size as Chiapa de Corzo. Many large earthen mounds at the site were built in the Chiapa III phase and exhibit formal features also seen at La Venta and Chiapa de Corzo (Figure 110). The site is aligned 50 degrees east of north (McDonald 1999:62).

The MFC complex at Ocozocoautla comprised Mounds 5, 6, 7a, 10 and 11. Mound 18 dates to Chiapa III times but was not part of an MFC complex as strictly defined. It is evidence, however, of a significant population and architectural elaboration at the site at this early period. An unusual feature is the cruciform shape (in plan view) of the long mound in the E-Group. Excavations were undertaken at Ocozocoautla by NWAF personnel in 1972-1974 in various mounds. Mound 1 is a palace structure that dates to the Early Classic; a low platform with a Chiapa V burial was found beneath this mound (Agrinier 2014). Mound 2 also dates to the Early Classic period but was built over a Protoclassic platform dating to Chiapa VI times; a layer of Chiapa III refuse was found under this platform. Excavations showed that Mound 17 also dates to the Chiapa VI phase. Mound 15 dates to this time, too.

> Test pits in the long Mound 10 show it to be entirely a Chiapa III ... construction. As such it joins Ocozocoautla with the ranks

Figure 110. Ocozocoautla pattern.

of a great number of similar sites, from Tres Zapotes and La Venta south across Chiapas, all of which I label as part of the Modified Olmec horizon. At Ocozocoautla there are other mounds and almost surely a pyramid of this date also. Underlying Mound 10 was a deposit of Chiapa II or contemporary Late Olmec sherds. Mound 18 is a great squarish platform forming part of an even greater terrace extension crossing the center of the site. Pits in Mound 18 show it also to be almost entirely a Middle Preclassic construction. (Lowe, NWAF report, May 20, 1972)

Only one of the mounds of the conjectured MFC complex was excavated, Mound 10, and it was found to date to Chiapa III times, beginning about 750 BC. Test pits around this structure encountered deposits of the same age. McDonald found a specially constructed stone-lined basin, presumably for a reflecting pool, just to the east of Mound 10 on the axis of this E-Group. This basin or sunken court was filled in at the end of the Chiapa III phase. We can be reasonably certain that Mound 11, the companion mound of the E-Group, dates at least to Chiapa III times. The E-group is Type 3, oriented to the summer solstice sunrise.

The other remaining mounds of the proposed MFC complex, Mounds 5, 6, and 7, have not been verified as early. Clark visited these mounds in February of 2008 and found Middle Preclassic sherds on Mounds 5 and 6, and on the large platform just east of Mound 7. Most of the sherds on this last platform date to the Chiapa II phase. The sherds on the surface of Mound 7 date to the Protoclassic period, but we would not be surprised if this mound covers an earlier construction.

## MIRADOR

Mirador is the largest site located in the western end of the Central Depression, the narrow valley that runs through the middle of Chiapas. As with Ocozocoautla, Mirador was advantageously located to control travel along a natural route. Site history parallels those of sister centers at San Isidro and Ocozocoautla. During the Middle Preclassic the inhabitants of Mirador, Ocozocoautla, and Chiapa de Corzo participated in the same ceramic sphere, with the same ceramic types being found at all these sites.

Mirador was probably home to Soke speakers throughout its history. It was first occupied in the Early Preclassic (Agrinier et al. 2000; Lowe 2007), but the large pyramids and plazas at the site were not built until about 750 BC (Agrinier 1970, 1975b, 2000; Lowe 1999). This ceremonial center of 33 earthen mounds covers 1.5 km². The MFC complex at Mirador includes Mounds 10, 12, 20, 25, 27, and 33 (Figure 111). All but Mound 33 have been tested

and found to have been constructed by 750-700 BC. The main axis of the site is 8 degrees west of magnetic north, similar to the orientation of La Venta (Agrinier 2000:3). The E-Group at Mirador is Type 1, oriented to the equinoxes.

The E-Group at Mirador consists of Mound 25 flanked on the west by Mound 20, a mound 15 m tall. During its first stage of construction, Mound 20 was a 5 m high clay platform with a wattle and daub superstructure, with stairs on its eastern side facing Mound 25 (Agrinier 1970:9). During the Chiapa IV phase, this mound was elevated to 12 m in height. The flanking 100 m long Mound 25 to the east was tested with one excavation through its center. This platform was 20 m wide and 4 m high and constructed at the same time as Mound 20. "The contour of the mound [25] suggests two buried stairways: a main one to the east side and a rear one on the west side facing Mound 20" (Agrinier 2000:4).

The northern mound on the main axis is Mound 10. During Chiapa III times, this was only a 70 cm high platform (Agrinier 1975b:6). Eventually it became the second tallest mound at Mirador, but it was not a significant mound in terms of size or labor investment when the center was built. Mound 12 or Mound 33 may have been the original small platform associated with the MFC pattern at Mirador. These are nearly equally spaced from the axial line that bisects the E-Group. Mound 33 has not been tested. Mound 12 is 2 m high and 28 m in diameter. Investigations there revealed nine superimposed floors dating to 700-650 BC (Agrinier 2000:31).

Mound 27 was built on the east side of the plaza. Extensive trench explorations of this acropolis revealed a complex construction history, with platform building being limited to Chiapa III times. Agrinier (2000) describes six construction episodes for buildings discovered inside this platform. The acropolis covers earlier stages of what we presume was the same functional complex, but the earliest buildings were separate and only later elevated on the same platform. The original, separate small platforms coalesced with later expansions. All the sub-platform structures were associated with trash pits, hearths, caches, and subfloor burials, an indicator of domestic activities and overall

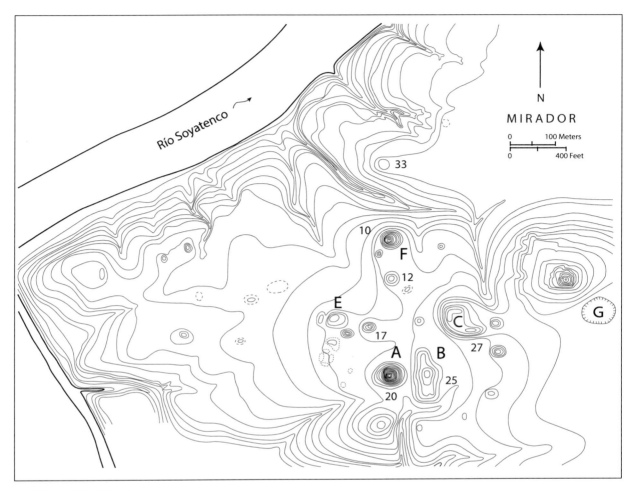

Figure 111. Mirador pattern.

function. What began as multiple platforms became a large, elevated platform, presumably with multiple, perishable buildings on top. Of particular interest is a stone drain 57.5 m long associated with this complex. It is oriented 15 degrees east of magnetic north (Agrinier 2000:24). Portions of another, parallel drain were also recovered. Agrinier suggests that water drained from the Mound 27 complex ran off to the north to a prepared reservoir. Another reservoir was located 200 m east of Mound 27 (Agrinier 2000:3). Reflecting pools or reservoirs have also been reported for Ocozocoautla and Izapa (Gómez Rueda 1995, 1996a; Lowe et al. 1982).

## SAN ISIDRO

San Isidro is located about 135 km southwest of La Venta near the northern edge of the rugged northern highlands of Chiapas in the Middle Grijalva region (Lowe 1998a, 1999). San Isidro is the northernmost Preclassic center in Chiapas and one of the closest regional centers to La Venta. San Isidro extended over a 100 ha and was a regional center in early Olmec times closely aligned with San Lorenzo (Lowe 1998a, 1988b). The site was nearly continuously occupied until Late Classic times and was a locus of occasional pilgrimage and offerings into Early Postclassic times (Lee 1974a; Lowe 1999). Limited excavations were undertaken at the site from March to June in 1966 as part of salvage

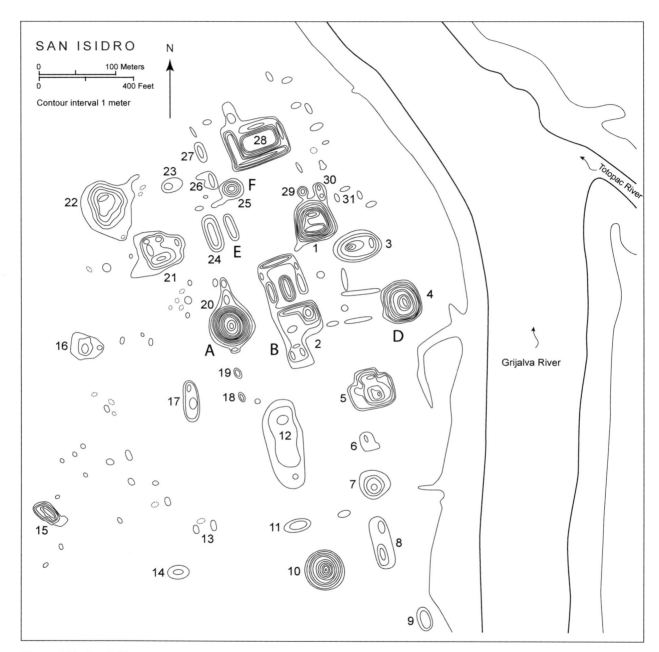

Figure 112. San Isidro pattern.

operations for the Malpaso reservoir (Lee 1974b; Lee et al. 2015; Lowe 1967, 1981).

The main mounds at San Isidro were constructed mostly during the Middle Preclassic. Some were erected over low clay platforms built about 1200 BC. Of the numerous large

mounds at the site, only six were somewhat adequately tested in the few months available for exploration (Figure 112). Test excavations were carried out at Mounds 20 (Lowe 1981, 1998a, 1999), 4 (Lee 1974a, b), 1, 2, 3, 29 (Lowe 1998a), and near other mounds (Lowe 1999). Rising water prevented excavation to sterile layers in the tallest mounds, so the available information for these mounds concerns the latest stages of their construction. Many of these mounds are presumed to be older than the periods verified by excavation.

The major building efforts at San Isidro were contemporaneous with those at La Venta, but with different results. Based on Lowe's (1981, 1998a) observations of early clay platforms under Middle Preclassic mounds, we suggest that a possible reason for the differences in layouts of these two centers may be that the Middle Preclassic occupants at San Isidro deliberately erected their pyramids over earlier platforms (Clark 2016). Among the centers described here, San Isidro is one of two that had relic mounds on its future cityscape by Middle Preclassic times (Finca Acapulco was the other). San Isidro exhibits evidence of planning along major and minor axes and of large platforms clustered around north-south trending plazas (see, Lowe 1999:30-33).

San Isidro does not conform to the full MFC pattern. It lacks a large northern pyramid. Lowe (1998a:85, 1999:31) argued that Mounds 20 and 2 at San Isidro comprise a solstice observatory or astronomic complex. It is a Type 3 E-Group like the one at Ocozocoautla, its nearest neighboring center. An E-Group is only half of the proposed MFC pattern. The east-west axis appears to have been the primary one at San Isidro; the placement of offerings there conveys this impression, too. Future research may reveal that another critical component of the MFC complex is architectural techniques. Lowe (1967:136) observed that at San Isidro "Platform floors and walls were of clay, frequently highly polished and fired and having inset stairways." In his final synthesis on San Isidro, Lowe provided the following summary observations.

At the close of the Dzewa phase [Chiapa II-B], surely before 600 BC, the proto-Zoque Olmecs of the Middle Grijalva had established their regional center and community, the most important in the San Isidro region. During this time, in Mound 20, we find a pyramidal platform 7-8 m tall. This same architectural development is also evident in the large acropolis-like platforms at Mounds 1 and 4 during the Felisa phase [IV], both constructed on top of occupations of the Cacahuanó [I] and Dombi [II-A] phases. Other platforms at the site that were not explored probably have similar sequences of growth. The locations of structures along axial lines, leaving open places for plazas, suggests planning and probably a division of tasks and ranks among the population. It is important to note that Mound 20 at San Isidro, along with the elongated platform at Mound 2, would form part of an astronomical commemoration complex, emphasized in the Equipac [III] or Felisa [IV] phase, if not before (Lowe 1989a:365). (Lowe 1998a:85, JEC translation)

The second half of the Middle Preclassic is well represented in Mounds 1, 4, and 29. Mounds 1 and 4 would cover acropolis-like platforms and become 8 and 10 m high, respectively, dating to the Felisa phase. Surely their centers or cores consisted of lower platforms of the Equipac and Dzewa phases, as was the case in Mound 20. Pyramids 5 and 10, also over 10 m tall, were not explored but they probably had their own sequence of development starting in the Middle Preclassic. (Lowe 1998a:50, JEC translation)

## LA VENTA

La Venta is the best known Olmec city in Mesoamerica. Information for this site comes mostly from excavations carried out in the 1940s and 1950s in its northern sector (Drucker 1952; Drucker et al. 1959). La Venta was constructed along a centerline oriented 8 degrees west of north (Drucker et al. 1959:fig. 4). Clark (2008) proposed that the original city center was segmented into intervals 86.6 m in length, or simple fractions and multiples of this length. Early La Venta was 10 of these intervals long and 8 wide. Subsequent platform additions to the city center respected the original orientation and measurement interval. Later mounds encroached on early mounds in the north. The city center eventually extended 1,482 m north-south. Towards the end of La Venta's history, large stone monuments were set up as boundary markers. Three basalt, colossal stone heads were placed at the northern edge of the city, and they faced the sea to the north. Three even larger sandstone heads were placed near the southern end; two faced south and one faced north (González Lauck 1995:39, 1996:fig. 1, 2004: fig. 1, 2010b; Grove 1999:fig.6; Stirling 1968). These northern and southern lines of monuments were 1300 m apart.

La Venta appears to have been partitioned and arranged according to function. The original layout shows a 346 m long, 6 ha plaza with mounds flanking it in each cardinal direction. This plaza was probably for public ceremonies and for viewing rituals performed on the platforms surrounding it. Looking north, a spectator standing in the plaza during the city's heyday would have seen the 32 m high, stepped pyramid made of about 90,000 cubic meters of dirt and clay (Heizer 1968:17). A temple of perishable materials probably graced the summit of this artificial mountain. The temple was accessed from stairs on the south and north faces and maybe on the other two sides as well (González Lauck 1997, 2006).

East of the plaza lay a broad, 8 ha, low platform (Stirling Acropolis) that required nearly twice as much earth and clay to construct as the main pyramid (Figure 101). This platform probably supported the residence of the king, his courtiers, and servants (Clark and Hansen 2001; Reilly 1990). A small ballcourt and an elaborate system of subterranean stone drains have been identified there (Heizer et al. 1968). The eastern edge of the platform and of the site proper show evidence of deliberate sculpting and terracing. Evidence suggests that many buildings rested atop this acropolis and were occupied for the full duration of the site, 900-400 BC (Heizer et al. 1968:152).

Just south of the main plaza lay an E-group comprised of a long mound (D-8) flanked on the west by a short pyramid (Mound D-1). This was an E-group of standard type, or Type 1, oriented to equinox sunrises (Blake 2013; Lowe 1982:278). To the west of the main plaza at La Venta was a row of low platforms (Mounds B-1, B-2, and B-3), probably special residences or temples. Axial asymmetry is evident in the placement of platforms at La Venta. Buildings around the plaza were complementary sets: the central pyramid and observatory formed N-S sets, and the eastern acropolis and western platforms E-W sets.

North of the tallest pyramid, Complex A was built at one-fourth the scale of the original plaza arrangement (Clark 2001; Drucker et al. 1959). The northern half of Complex A was five low mounds surrounded by a 2 m high and rectangular palisade of upright, natural basalt pillars. This compound arrangement appears to have been a novel architectural feature first seen at La Venta. Spectacular jade and serpentine offerings, and royal tombs, were found in this sector along the principal axis, and in mirror symmetry on both sides of it. At least one of these offerings had more than 1000 tons of serpentine (Drucker et al. 1959:97).

In its final form the central and monumental part of La Venta was about 58 ha in extent. With its residential neighborhoods, the city covered at least 200 ha (González Lauck 1996:75, 2001) and could have accommodated several thousand people. Rebecca González Lauck (2010a:74) estimates that the 200 ha of La Venta currently preserved represents about half of the city's original extent.

## TZUTZUCULI

This 35 ha site is located on the northwest end of the Chiapas coast and 12 km inland from the Pacific Ocean. Of particular interest, this is the only site in Chiapas with Middle Preclassic sculptures found in association with public architecture. The bas relief sculptures date to 600-500 BC (McDonald 1983:16). They flank each side of a 4 m wide southern stairway of Mound 4.

Tzutzuculi was built on a broad terrace on the south margin of the Zanatenco River. Some of the site's tight configuration was dictated by local hills and topography. Even so, the main features of the MFC pattern are clear, especially when the dates of the different mounds are considered. Basic components of the MFC pattern include Mounds 4, 5, 6, 7, Enclosure B, and possibly Mounds 8 and 10 (Figure 113). Of these, Mounds 4, 5, 7, and 8 have been tested and determined to have been

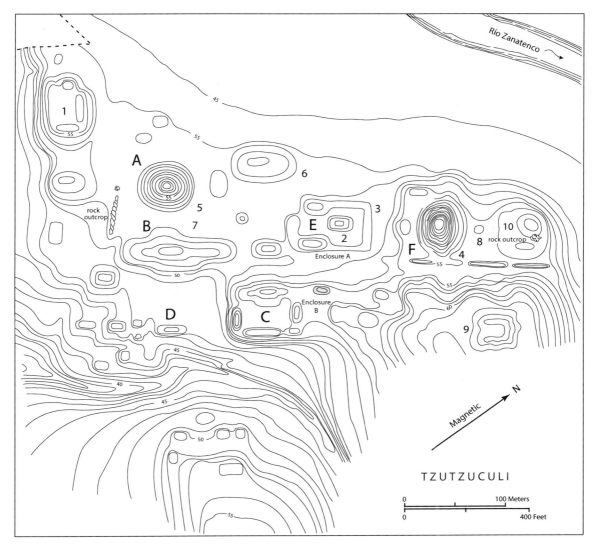

Figure 113. Tzutzuculi pattern.

built in Chiapa II-B times about 850-750 BC
(McDonald 1983:10, 16, 32, 33). Mound 4 was
enlarged until it was 8 m tall by 500 BC. When
first constructed, it was less than 4.5 m high
(McDonald 1974). It rests upon a broad, low
platform, like its larger counterparts at La Venta
and Chiapa de Corzo.

The main plaza at Tzutzuculi is complicated
by the presence of Enclosure A. Excavations
there show that this enclosure was built in
Chiapa IV times, long after the original site,
so the main plaza was originally open. Mound
6 and Enclosure B were not tested, but they
conform to the MFC pattern known from

other Chiapa III sites and probably date to that
time period. The main axis of Tzutzuculi is 38
degrees east of magnetic north, an axis which
aligns the site with Tres Picos, a prominent peak
of the Sierra Madre range (McDonald 1977:561).
The sculpture and architecture at Tzutzuculi
point to strong ties to La Venta. These sites had
parallel histories as well. Both were established
about 900-850 BC and abandoned about 400
BC.

The E-group at Tzutzuculi is of Type 4 and
is the only example of this type identified for
Middle Preclassic Chiapas (Blake 2013).

## IZAPA

Izapa is situated about 240 m above sea level in the piedmont zone of the southern Soconusco in an area of evergreen tropical forest, a locale ideal for growing cacao. The apogee of Izapa was in the Late Preclassic, but its history extended a millennium in both directions to the Postclassic and Early Preclassic. At its height in the Late Preclassic, Izapa extended over 400 ha and had at least eight plaza groups, each surrounded on three or four sides by small pyramids. Of particular interest are the numerous stelae and altars set up along the edges of some of the larger plaza groups.

The first pyramid at Izapa was constructed in Chiapa II-B (Duende) times. Mound 30a at Izapa was built and enlarged half a dozen times in this phase until it was 12 m high and 45 m wide at the base by 750 BC (Ekholm 1969; Lowe et al. 1982:123; cf. Clark and Lowe 2013:76). Lowe argued that Izapa extended 25 ha at this time and that the early mound complex likely included Mounds 25, 47, and 50 (Figure 100). The Duende settlement seems "to have been concentrated upon the restricted Group B terrace overlooking the Río Izapa" (Lowe et al. 1982:127). This arrangement may have been Izapa's earliest plaza. Izapa was a large center or town by Chiapa III times. Pottery of this phase is found all across the central zone of the site (Ekholm 1989:335; Lowe et al. 2013; Lowe et al. 1982:127). Ironically, very little construction has been detected at Izapa for Chiapa III times beyond a few thin layers added to the Duende mound in Group B (Lowe et al. 1982:127) and a small platform under Mound 60 (Clark and Lee 2013:89-93). By Chiapa IV times, Mound 30a was 16 m high, and there were also large platforms at Mounds 9, 25, 56, and 60.

Of the various models considered here, Lee's is the only one to propose Izapa as a member of patterned Middle Preclassic centers, likely because of his added criterion of reflecting pools and his polythetic approach. Other investigators did not include Izapa because it lacks an obvious E-group. Clark (2016) considered Izapa as an exception to the MFC pattern, and he took its deviant site pattern as evidence of different cultural practices and likely different cultural affiliations of the inhabitants of Izapa. He could not find a good candidate for an E-group at Izapa. This changed in 2012 with the LIDAR image of Izapa taken by Robert Rosenwig and others (2013). The LIDAR image shows that the NWAF map of Mounds 71 and 73 in southern Izapa did not do them justice. On the LIDAR image these mounds look like good candidates for an E-group in terms of size, orientation, location, and age (see Clark 2013:139). The long mound at Izapa is not as long as those of other sites considered here, but it still well qualifies as such. Blake's (2013) analysis shows that the Izapa E-group has the same winter solstice orientation as seen at Chiapa de Corzo and La Libertad.

## LA LIBERTAD

La Libertad is the easternmost early pyramid center on the Grijalva River; it was advantageously located at the headwaters of the Grijalva River, perhaps so its rulers could regulate trade coming from the Guatemala highlands and down river. La Libertad lies at the edge of the Cuchumatan Mountains and occupies a flat peninsula between four rivers. Evidence of its regional center status comes from excavations undertaken at the site in 1975-1976. Its large earthen mounds were built about 700 BC and enlarged several times in the ensuing centuries. The site was founded in a region sparsely populated at the time, and it was abandoned about 400-300 BC (Clark 1988; Lowe 1977; Miller 2014; Miller et al. 2005). La Libertad's large mounds are spread over 45 ha and conform to the MFC pattern.

> The site center is dominated by a long cruciform platform mound flanked by 12 m high pyramids on both the east and west sides. A multi-plaza group is located just north of the line of three mounds. The entire plaza group – divided into four or five plazas surrounded by 1.5-2.5 m high mounds – is elevated 1-2 m above the surrounding surface. This area appears to have been an elite residential area or palace ... All mounds and elevated plazas were constructed with earth fill. (Miller et al. 2005:141-42)

The cruciform mound and its flanking pyramids constitute the E-Group at La Libertad (Figure 102). These mounds were tested and found to have been mostly constructed during the Enub or Chiapa III phase and enlarged very little in the following phase (Miller 2014). The western pyramid of the E-Group (Mound 5) was 9.5 m high at the end of the Enub phase. The rest of the MFC pattern at La Libertad is constituted by the northern pyramid, Mound 36, and the eastern acropolis.

As mentioned, in terms of orientation the E-group at La Libertad is most like that at Chiapa de Corzo, with both functional equivalents aligned to winter solstice sunrise (Blake 2013). Formally, however, the La Libertad E-group is most like that at Ocozocoautla, with ramps on each side of the center of its long mound, giving it a cruciform shape in plan view. Also, the long mounds at both sites are flanked by tall pyramids both to the west and to the east.

The acropolis at La Libertad was extensively tested by Donald Miller in 1975-1976 and found to have been built at the same time as the large pyramids – with substantial enlargements in Chiapa IV times. This broad, 3 m high platform supported four large and two low mounds. Stairways to the plaza were found on three sides of the acropolis. The largest structure excavated was a stone-veneer base of a building that measured 15 by 21 m (Miller 2014), perhaps an elite residence. In size and form it is most similar to the acropolis at Mirador. Two elite house mounds at La Libertad were excavated by Gareth Lowe and Glenna Nielson at the southern edge of the site; these measured 24 by 18 m and 15 by 18 m (Clark 1988; Miller 2014). Significant differences among elite domestic structures at different Middle Preclassic centers were their location and relative elevation on special platforms rather than their basal dimensions. The eastern raised compounds at Chiapa de Corzo and La Libertad both measure about 80 m square at their bases and are about three meters high, an order of magnitude smaller than the Sterling Acropolis at La Venta, but probably the same idea and for similar purposes. Noteworthy features of the Chiapas compounds are the numerous individual

buildings involved. We think these were palace complexes or royal compounds (Clark and Hansen 2001). The good state of preservation at La Libertad provides the best evidence of the arrangement of one of these compounds.

## SANTA ROSA

We consider Santa Rosa here among the planned Middle Preclassic centers because Lowe and Lee both included it on their short lists of such sites, an attribution that appears at odds with the published evidence. The apogee of Santa Rosa was during the Protoclassic period, and most of its mounds appear to have been built then. The site was also extensively occupied during the late Early Preclassic and early Middle Preclassic period (Chiapa I-B and II-A), but no mounds of these ages were identified in the two seasons of NWAF explorations at the site. Only one mound was identified securely as dating to the Chiapa III phase, the period when most of the sites described here were built as bona fide ceremonial centers. The chronology of Santa Rosa and its mounds, and the arrangement of the mounds, would seem to disqualify it as an important Middle Preclassic center.

Santa Rosa does not fit the MFC pattern described by Clark and Hansen (2001), but the ways in which it deviates from the pattern are instructive. The largest mounds at this site are aligned east-west (Figure 114). In this sense, it is most similar to San Isidro. None of the excavators who reported on Santa Rosa detected much planning among the structures at the core of the site. In his brief summary of the 1956 excavations, Lowe (1959b:52) reported that the site "consists of approximately thirty earthen mounds arranged informally at the base of a broad goose-neck of the river." In his monograph on the 1958 excavations, Agustín Delgado (1965:6) reported that the "Santa Rosa structures may have been laid out upon a general east-west axis, but there is little evidence of formal grouping." Also, there is "no overall designed plan ... in the placement of mounds and platforms at Santa Rosa" (Delgado 1965:9). At a finer scale of detail, however, he observed "that the specific orientation of both individual structures and groups where present is 21 degrees east of present magnetic

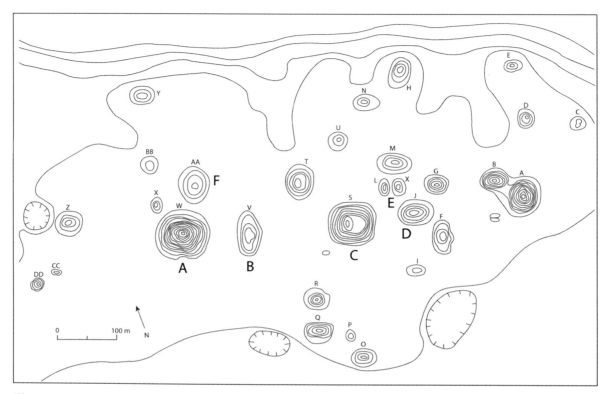

Figure 114. Santa Rosa pattern.

north" (Delgado 1965:7). These opinions were repeated by Donald Brockington in his study of the ceramics at the site: "Other than three or possibly four irregular courts and the general east-west alignment of structures, no order can be discerned in mound placement" (Brockington 1967:1).

As summarized above, Lowe's and Lee's site "patterns" concerned the types of mounds present, with the only set arrangement being an E-group and a large platform or acropolis close by. Santa Rosa might fit these relaxed requirements, but there is insufficient evidence for it. The only mound identified as dating to the Middle Preclassic period is Mound V (Brockington 1967:53, 60; Delgado 1965:33). This could qualify as a long, low mound. It is flanked on the west by the tallest pyramid at the site, Mound W. Excavations in the apex of this 14 m high pyramid in 1956 and 1958 only went down a few meters. The upper levels of this mound date to Chiapa IV-V times ("Phase 3" in the local chronology; Brockington 1967:37, 54, 60; Delgado 1965:33), hence it is highly probable

that the core of this pyramid dates to Chiapa III and even earlier. Most of the pyramids of Chiapas E-groups were accorded a major remodeling and elevation in height in Chiapa IV times. We think it nearly certain that Mound W underwent such renovation and that Mounds V and W at Santa Rosa were an E-group in Chiapa III and IV times. Its long axis was about 20 degrees east of north, an orientation virtually identical to those at Chiapa de Corzo and La Libertad, consequently, our best guess is that Santa Rosa had a Type 2 E-group. No other mounds are known to have been built at Santa Rosa during Chiapa III times. As evident in Figure 114, there is no obvious plaza north of Mounds V and W, and certainly no large pyramid or acropolis – or even much space on the river terrace to have built them. The mounds north of Mounds V and W were not aligned with them and most likely post-date them.

The broad mound identified by Lowe and Lee as a possible acropolis at Santa Rosa is Mound S, located just over 200 m to the east of Mound V. It has the proper basal dimensions to qualify as an acropolis. Mound S is 6 m high and measures 74 by 80 m at its base. Excavations there detected four construction phases; the upper levels date to the Classic period (Delgado 1965:29). Brockington's (1967:61) analysis of ceramics suggests that the lower levels of Mound S were constructed in Protoclassic times. It is not clear whether test pits reached sterile layers under the mound or even the earliest stages of construction. If not, there could be a Late Preclassic mound underneath the later constructions. Otherwise, the late date for Mound S would mean that Santa Rosa lacked a mound C of the three Middle Preclassic mounds expected for McDonald's triadic model or Lowe's or Lee's modifications of it. Nonetheless, there is little doubt that it has an E-group. Of our sample of sites, Santa Rosa is the only Middle Preclassic site that had an E-group but lacked other Chiapa III mounds.

The incomplete MFC pattern at Santa Rosa raises important questions about this proposed pattern and its significance. We already described San Isidro as an exception that may have been a truncated version of the full plan due to site history. We doubt this for Santa Rosa. Two obvious solutions present themselves for explaining the incompleteness of a MFC configuration there: age and socio-political position.[11] Age is shorthand for chronology. There surely was a time before the full MFC pattern came together. Perhaps the Santa Rosa E-group is an example of a proto-MFC site that lacked an acropolis. The Maya site of Ceibal appears to have been an early site with an E-group sans acropolis (Inomata et al. 2013). Alternatively, an "incomplete" pattern may have signaled the sociopolitical status of a site in a settlement hierarchy. A site-hierarchy explanation may be appropriate for Santa Rosa because it was nearly as proximate to Finca Acapulco as was San Mateo and Vergel, possible secondary centers to Finca Acapulco. All these sites were located on the south side of the Grijalva River near the junctures of major

tributaries (see Clark 2016:fig. 1). San Mateo and Santa Rosa were about the same distance by canoe to Finca Acapulco. By land, San Mateo was 22 km from Finca Acapulco and Santa Rosa 28 km distant.

The excavations at Santa Rosa, and analyses of materials recovered, are insufficient for resolving questions of site planning. The site now lies beneath the waters of the Angostura reservoir, so one is limited to the published descriptions. The publications concern the first years of NWAF work, and it was not the best. Five test pits were excavated at the site in 1973 during salvage work, but these have not been reported, and the critical notes on the placement and findings of the excavations are missing. NWAF analyses of the 1956 and 1958 materials were completed before the ceramic sequence for the region had been refined, thus, the loose "Phase 1-6" chronology. The following remarks are based on Clark's close reading of the published monographs. The possibility that the Santa Rosa E-group dates to Chiapa II-A times seems plausible. Brockington mentioned that only Phase 1 and 2 sherds were found in the excavations in Mound V (our only concrete evidence); according to his analysis, these loosely relate, respectively, to the Chiapa II (Dili) and Chiapa III (Escalera) phases at Chiapa de Corzo (Brockington 1967:63-64).

What is reported as secure is that the upper levels of Mound V date to Chiapa III times. Information is lacking for the lowest levels. Ceramics from surface collections indicate a large population in the Santa Rosa locale in Phase 1 (Chiapa II) times (see Brockington 1967:58, fig. 46; also, Lowe 1959b:49-52). Occupation stretched for several kilometers along the river and its tributary. Some of the ceramics and vessels Brockington illustrates for Santa Rosa for Phase 1 appear to date to Chiapa I-B times rather than to Chiapa II times. For instance, Cache 4 at this site (Delgado 1965:42), found beneath a Protoclassic ballcourt, is a vase with incised Olmec motifs (Brockington

---

[11] Other options are possible that we do not consider because they seem less plausible, namely, that early buildings in the pattern were destroyed by later peoples or even eroded away by changes in the river course. From the map it appears that the gooseneck in the Grijalva River by Santa Rosa was moving away from the site. The site was built on high ground, so it may have been out of harm's way.

1967:22, figs. 27 and 28). Brockington classifies this as Phase 1 and thus Chiapa II; Clark considers it a Chiapa I-B artifact and related to the Jocotal horizon. The vase is the oldest offering known for central Chiapas, but it has never been discussed. Some of the human burials at the site date to this same time period (ca. 1100-900 BC), including Burial 7 found next to Cache 4 (see Delgado 1965:25, 39). If the Santa Rosa E-group dates to the time of these other indicators of ceremonial activity, then the E-group at this site could be the oldest in central Chiapas. Underwater archaeology may be the only way to confirm or falsify this possibility as long as the reservoir waters stand. The settlement data for the Santa Rosa region indicate this was a very important spot on the Grijalva River in Chiapa II-A times, but it does not appear to have been a major center in Chiapa III times, the period when the largest ceremonial centers were built in this region. Santa Rosa again rose to prominence in Protoclassic times. The E-group at Santa Rosa (Mounds V and W) might be evidence that the Middle Preclassic pattern of ceremonial centers started as E-groups. The history of mound construction at Ceibal might also indicate this. At the moment a good candidate for the earliest E-group in Mesoamerica is Ojo de Agua on the Pacific coast (Inomata et al. 2013). There are no acropolis-like mounds at this site.

## FINCA ACAPULCO

Finca Acapulco is located about 100 km upstream from Chiapa de Corzo following the twists and turns of the Grijalva River. As are San Isidro and Santa Rosa, Finca Acapulco is now buried beneath the dammed-up waters of the Grijalva River. Limited information was obtained during a three-month salvage operation there in 1971 as part of the "Angostura Project, 1970-74" (Gussinyer 1972; Martínez Muriel and Navarrete 1978). Located about midway between Chiapa de Corzo and La Libertad, Finca Acapulco was built as a pyramid center before either of these neighbors. It was the largest Preclassic site in its region and the earliest city in central Chiapas. It was also the first to be abandoned, an event that occurred by 500 BC (Lowe 2007:89). "The site is an extensive one

consisting principally of many stone-bordered platform mounds, some long and rectangular, others smaller and squarish, with several taller pyramidal mounds with complex adjoining platform features" (Lowe 1959b:42).

Finca Acapulco appears to have been the primary capital of three closely-spaced centers and other sites in the center of the upper Grijalva River Valley. Each had broad platforms and an earthen ballcourt that date to Chiapa III times (Con Uribe 1976:176; Gussinyer 1972:10; Lowe 1977:226; Martínez Muriel and Navarrete 1978:234). The mounds of the E-Group were also tested (see Lowe 1977:225, fig. 9.4 for the location of excavations) and date to Chiapa II-III times (Figure 115). Based on size and architectural elaboration, Finca Acapulco with its more than 50 mounds was the primary center, and San Mateo and Vergel were secondary centers. These latter two sites had ballcourts. The ballcourt at Vergel was of the same proportions, size, and construction as that at Finca Acapulco (Gussinyer 1972:10). The San Mateo ballcourt was smaller, but this site appears to have had an E-group and most of the mounds of the MFC pattern. The long mounds at Chiapa de Corzo south of Mound 17 may have framed the playing ally of a ballcourt. San Isidro probably also had a ballcourt in Chiapa III times (Lowe 1999:113), and La Libertad definitely did (Lowe 1977). These ballcourts were placed in different locations at all these sites and were not part of a standard arrangement.

The salvage work at Finca Acapulco has not been published. Lowe drew attention to Finca Acapulco in all his later works.

> Finca Acapulco was without doubt the best example known of a Middle Preclassic city of the Escalera horizon [Chiapa III]. It is clear that it has the basic pattern of a large mound, pyramid, and large and wide platforms in perfect order. It also had a ballcourt. A burial with an offering of a polished orange plate and a jade axe were found ["at the foot of a pyramid"; Lowe 1991:115; illustrated in Gussinyer 1972:13]. Much could be said of the planning of this regional center of first order and the possible reasons for its early abandonment [by 500 BC]. The mounds were

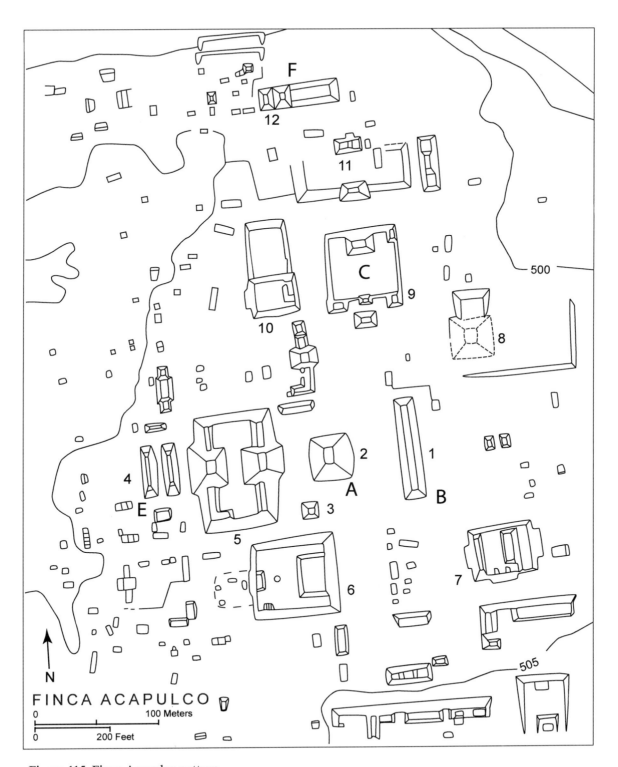

Figure 115. Finca Acapulco pattern.

constructed with large quantities of fill that contained Early Preclassic and early Middle Preclassic ceramics, but polished orange ceramics [Chiapa III] constitute between 10 to 20 percent of all sherds. Salvage of the site was undertaken by the New World Archaeological Foundation and the National Institute of Anthropology and History, but there was not time to do more than trench a few platforms. (Lowe 1989a:366, JEC translation)

The platforms were made of earth, or earth and rubble fill, with carefully laid stone veneers of natural stone covered with a thick layer of clay (Gussinyer 1972:8-10). The preceding translation preserves a grammatical ambiguity that becomes apparent only in reading fieldnotes. Lowe appears to claim, and actually may have, that a burial at Acapulco had a polished orange offering plate and an axe. These were two different deposits and events. Both were buried on the axial line of the E-Group constituted by Mounds 1 and 2. Mound 1 at Acapulco, the long eastern mound of the E-Group, was about 90 m long, 15 m wide, and 2 m tall. The axial pyramid to the west across the plaza was 5.5 m high and about 20 m square at the base (smaller than the map in Figure 115 implies). Two elite burials dating to early Chiapa III times were found on the E-Group axis in front of Mound 1 (western face). Blake (2013) did not analyze the E-group at this site, thus its type has not been specified. In terms of orientation, based on the available map, Finca Acapulco was oriented about 7 degrees west of north, virtually the orientation of La Venta. We surmise that both had a Type 1 E-group.

The MFC pattern is not very clear at Finca Acapulco (Figure 115); it becomes lost in the proliferation of stone-faced platforms at this urban center. The sites of Chiapa de Corzo (Figure 99) and La Venta (Figure 101) share more formal features of site layout with each other than either does with Finca Acapulco. It is possible that Finca Acapulco was established as a regional center with monumental buildings before either of these other centers. Finca Acapulco certainly had a deeper and more continuous history. Lowe (2007:89) argues that Finca Acapulco was established to control

trade, the reason for its having been built in a place with relatively poor agricultural potential. If superior control points for trade were subsequently established up and down river, this new distribution of population could have led to instability in the Finca Acapulco kingdom. Finca Acapulco is the only MFC site thought to have had one or more secondary centers with E-groups and ballcourts. This may have been because it was older and more developed than the other MFC centers.

## ARCHITECTURE, SITE PLANNING, AND IDENTITY

Comparisons of the architectural layouts of Middle Preclassic sites in southern Mesoamerica have been undertaken at various levels of detail and for different reasons, most of them geared to promoting better interpretations. Comparisons of similarities and differences have not begun to exhaust possibilities, nor have interpretations of perceived patterns. Comparisons have focused on the kinds of mounds present at a site, their relative and absolute sizes, the relative positions of mounds at various kinds at sites, site orientations, absolute measurements, measuring units, and proportional arrangements of mounds. Chiapa de Corzo and La Venta have been the main players in all these comparisons, with other sites considered because they were similar in some way to these principal centers. Sites can be similar or different in numerous ways, so we expect comparative analysis to continue as more is learned about the age and histories of individual mounds and sites. An overriding objective of these comparisons is better understanding of ancient sites in their historic settings. For most studies, the goal has been rather simple: to identify the people who built a site, whether Olmecs, Mayas, Sokes, or others. Lowe's various analyses sought to compare whole herds of people living in adjacent territories, the Sokes of Chiapas versus lowland Mayas living to the north and east. Site layouts were interpreted as large artifacts, one element in cultural inventories indicative of certain cultures and thus markers for peoples of these cultures.

Lowe identified the MFC pattern as La Venta Olmec in authorship. This presented an immediate paradox for his analysis – San Lorenzo and Tres Zapotes, the two other famous Olmec cities, did not qualify. San Lorenzo was explained away, by implication, as being too early; it was part of the Early Olmec Horizon. Tres Zapotes has no such excuse since it was obviously a center with colossal sculpture coeval with La Venta. Lowe did not pursue the implications of Tres Zapote's failure to make the list of his MOCC sites. He clearly included Tres Zapotes in his ceramic study as the westernmost site in the Olmec area with splotchy-orange resist pottery. At the time of his study there was no good map of Tres Zapotes as a whole, only maps of its various groups (Stirling 1943:9, fig. 2; Weiant 1943:5, map 3). But the fact the site is organized in small clusters of mounds is a significant departure from the logic of site organization for MFC sites. Christopher Pool's (2003, 2007, 2010) map of the site shows that Tres Zapotes was very differently arranged than Middle Preclassic La Venta. The upshot of all this is that La Venta – in terms of architecture and site configuration – is much more similar to sites in Chiapas than to any sites in the Gulf Coast lowlands. In terms of architecture, the Olmec heartland was phenomenal but not a singular phenomenon; it consisted of divergent patterns rather than one single one. Thinking about the Olmec heartland as a unitary and singular phenomenon has had adverse consequences. Middle Preclassic sites in this region were diverse, both in time and space. The diversity of the Olmec region is becoming more and more apparent with more study. The same is true of the supposed unity of Middle Preclassic Chiapas centers.

Clark's early studies started from Lowe's premise of an "Olmec" pattern and attempted to extract more precise information on the kinds of relationships uniting the peoples at Chiapa de Corzo, presumed Sokes, and the Olmecs at La Venta, inferred to be Sokes because of the close similarities between these two centers in terms of architecture, offerings, and artifacts. He argued that these sites were built on the same blueprint and developed historically in parallel. The initial assessment was that the MFC buildings marking the northern and southern boundaries of the original centers were the same

absolute distance, that the principal buildings were placed in the same arrangements, and that they were nearly the same size when first built (Clark 2001). Clark further argued that builders of these sites used the same measurement standards, measurement cords, measured increments, proportions, and construction geometry. Some of these claims are more secure than others, and some have since been shown to be improbable. Given different levels of precision in different maps, all such proposals should be considered preliminary and requiring testing.

Most studies to date have searched for similarities among sites to identify the distributions of peoples. We are only beginning to understand the diversity among these sites. To start with the obvious, comparisons of MFC sites show significant differences in sizes and orientations. Blake's (2013) study of orientations of E-groups provides a plausible functional explanation for these signal differences. Consider Chiapa de Corzo. If it were indeed built according to the same plan used for building La Venta, why did the builders of Chiapa de Corzo not align its mounds and plazas to the same celestial phenomena? Laying out precise alignments according to the heavens should have been one of the easier engineering tasks in constructing a city from scratch. The sites of Mirador, Finca Acapulco, and San Mateo appear to follow the basic La Venta alignment, so why not Chiapa de Corzo and other MFC centers? We do not know. But given the formal similarities among the 10 sites considered, the orientation differences were surely intentional. For the MFC sites with orientations similar to that at La Venta (Mirador, San Mateo, Finca Acapulco), the sites are not the same size as La Venta or have major mounds arranged in the same configuration (Finca Acapulco). What do the differences and similarities among these sites in a range of attributes mean? There are more differences between close neighbors than between distant ones, beginning with La Venta versus Tres Zapotes. For any single attribute, we do not see the expected core-periphery pattern of old-time cultural geography in which a trait diffused from a center and moved outward like ripples on a pond. A repeated pattern for all of the MFC sites of the sample is that all of the traits are spotty and discontinuous. This is also true of pottery and figurine types when one considers details rather than sweeping similarities.

We will not consider in detail Clark's thesis of measurement units or implied native counts. The main claims are that measurement units can be determined inductively for individual sites and objects, and ought to be; one should not presume the presence of a particular standard at a site, or for all features at a site. A 1.54-1.55 m unit was inferred for La Venta based on an analysis of the massive serpentine offerings there. The overall site, however, appears to have been constructed according to the 1.666 m unit (Clark 2008; Clark and Colman 2012). Both systems are actually related in an interesting way; 13 units of the short measure equal 12 units of the longer measure. We recommend that measurement standards and their applications at sites be considered separately, just as both are independent of issues of site orientation. In assessing a site plan, the analysis should determine its orientation, modular regularities, measurement units, and native counts independently. For example, it should have been possible to construct sites of the same size with different measuring units. Such dimensional identity between sites would not relate to cultural similarities because, in actual fact, the sites would have had different "counted" dimensions. Clark's different proposals for La Venta provide a ready example. His early study claimed the site was laid out in 80 m intervals and multiples thereof, with each module representing 52 native counts in the 1.54 m system. In the 1.666 m system, each square would have been 48 units on a side. The difference is that of counting by twelves or by thirteens. In the first system, five modules of 80 m would have represented 260 native units of measure of 1.54 m each but only 240 units in the 1.666 m system. Which, if either, represents the number of units actually counted out by the builders?

Such questions may not interest everyone, but we find phenomenological issues appropriate. The caution behind our example is that something that may look like a virtually identical feature at different sites, such as a plaza 400 m long, may actually have represented a significant difference. Did the distance we count as 400 m or 1,312 feet long represent 260 native units (at 1.54 m), 250 units (at 1.60 m), or 240 units (at 1.666 m)? Did the natives employ calendar counts (260) or straight decimal or vigesimal counts (250)? All of this is to say that raw data of absolute distances cannot resolve the question. The same absolute distances can be phenomenologically distinct (represent different counts), and vice versa. Different absolute distances can represent the same counts (using different measurement standards). To consider the three measurement units mentioned, a numeric distance of 260 in native units could appear to an archaeologist as 400 m (1.54 m units), 416 m (1.60 m units), or 433 m (1.666 m units). In analyzing MFC sites, we have focused on the junctures of major segmentation to identify measurement modules and, hence, the base unit.

As evident in preceding site maps, none of the MFC centers were the exact same size; Clark's (2001) claims to the contrary were invalidated when he determined that the map of La Venta he had used had an improper scale.[12] Of course, we do not know how accurate the map we are currently using is. LIDAR images of La Venta could resolve this problem. Our discussion here presumes that the second map is more accurate than the first (Figure 107). On the second map the distance from the transverse axis of the La Venta E-group to the center point of the northern pyramid is 514 m. These are measuring points that should not have been affected by subsequent enlargements to the mounds in question. The distance between the same measuring points at Chiapa de Corzo is 500 m. Given the quality of the maps grounding our analysis and sundry sources of measurement error, these two measures are very close. In

---

[12] The error is the width of a pen stroke in copying the scale, but given the small scale and site size, the difference becomes significant. A few published distances between major points at the site would allow one to verify any scale. We have been told by others that the La Venta map we are currently using is still distorted. Clearly, our proposals for the various sites requires better maps and verified distances between points.

1.666 m units, the distance at La Venta would have been 309 units and at Chiapa de Corzo 300 units. We consider the Chiapa de Corzo map the more accurate because mapping conditions were much better.

The forgoing measurements are encouraging so we will attempt another of particular relevance for Mound 17 at Chiapa de Corzo. As noted, this mound occupied the center of the main plaza between the E-group to the south and the northern pyramid. From the center of Mound 17 to the transverse axis of the E-group (Mounds 11 and 12) is 283 m (Figure 116). The analogous measure at La Venta from the midpoint of the small mound in the center of the plaza (B4) to the transverse axis of the E-group (Mounds D1 and D8) is 279 m (Figure 117). These measures are virtually identical given measuring and mapping errors. This distance would be 167-170 units (of 1.666 m) or 181-184 units (of 1.54 m). The latter number looks more like one a Mesoamerican native would be interested in because it is a half count of the solar year (i.e., 182.5). An equal distance from the center of Mound 17 northward, however, would land one in the bottom of the ravine north of Mound 36, so Mound 17 was clearly not the center point of a site a solar year long (in the 1.54 m system). So what of the position of Mound 17 in the early ceremonial center at Chiapa de Corzo?

From the southern edge of the long mound of the Chiapa de Corzo E-group to the northern edge of the basal platform underlying its northern pyramid – the total length of the Chiapa II-B ceremonial center – is about 609 m (Figure 116). In the system of short units (1.54 m, red line), this is 396 units, within one-percent error of 400, a baktun count and great calendar number. The ideal number for completeness in a vigesimal system (20 by 20). The same distance in the 1.666 m system (blue line), however, is 365.5, the count of the vague solar year, another fabulous number. It appears that the original Chiapa de Corzo was a year long after all. Which number was intended? Were both intended? Was this particular distance of special significance because of how it converged so closely to these two different counts in two different measuring systems?

Of the two possibilities, the 365 count appears the more precise, but other evidence at the site indicates that the shorter measurement unit was the principal one used in laying out the site.

In its final form, La Venta was longer than Chiapa de Corzo. From the southern edge of the long mound of its E-group to the northern edge of the basal platform under its northern pyramid was about 678 m (Figure 117). In the 1.54 m system this would have been 440 units, 40 units longer than Chiapa de Corzo, a distance well beyond measurement error from string stretch. In the 1.666 m system, however, the La Venta distance would have been 407 units, within one percent measuring error of 400, the same baktun count seen at Chiapa de Corzo. The 400 unit distance appears intended at both sites. Other information presented by Clark (2008) indicates that La Venta was laid out in the 1.666 m system. If validated by future analysis, we will have a concrete example of the hypothetical scenario proposed of two sites of different lengths that may have been the same "counted" distance in different measurement standards. The significant difference was the measuring cords and marked units on them used at different sites. A measuring cord 20 units long in the 1.666 m system would have been 33.3 m long; a 20 unit cord in the 1.54 m system would have been 30.8 m long. Imagine someone coming to Chiapa de Corzo from La Venta with the basic specifications of the city built there: make it 40 cords long and 20 cords wide. Building Chiapa de Corzo to the proper specifications, but with a different cord, would account for the absolute differences in site dimensions and numerical identity in native units.

Clark (2013:144) argues that the original center at Izapa was 608 m long and represented a solar count in the 1.666 m system (Figure 118, blue lines). Izapa's configuration differed significantly from that at Chiapa de Corzo, but both sites were the same length when first laid out and may have shared some native counts. Other MFC sites varied significantly from La Venta and Chiapa de Corzo. Tzutzuculi appears to have been built at half the scale as La Venta (Figure 119), so some of the counts would have been maintained at half the scale (e.g., from 1.666 m to 83 cm). Mirador is also a short site,

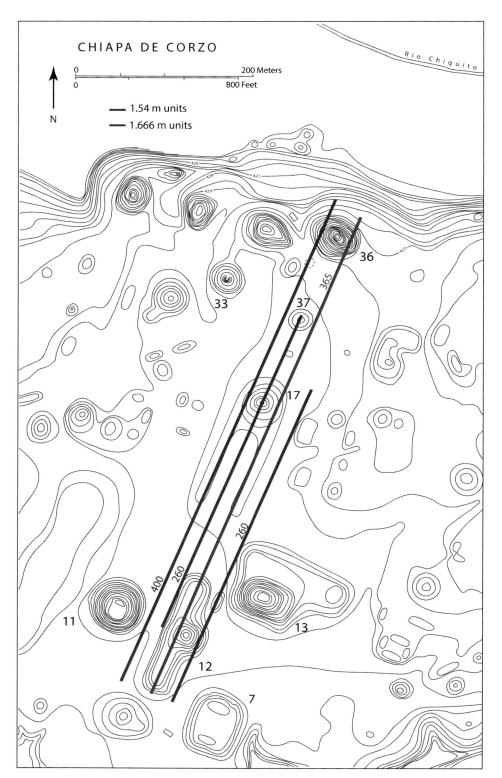

Figure 116. Plan of Chiapa de Corzo and counts of possible measurement units.

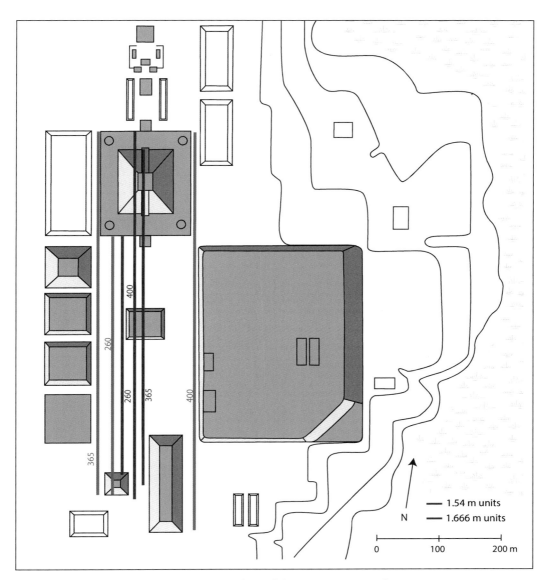

Figure 117. Plan of La Venta and counts of possible measurement units.

depending how one interprets its layout. If the northern mound were Mound 10 (rather than the short Mound 33), then the site would have been 407 m long from bluff edge to bluff edge. In the 1.666 m system, it would have been 244 arm spans (*brazadas* or fathoms); in the 1.54 m system, this would have been 264 *brazadas* (Figure 120). The latter looks like a promising number. It is within one percent measuring error of 260. If that was the desired distance, Mirador was built by engineers who used cords marked in intervals of 1.54 m.

The Mirador case highlights the complicated variety among MFC sites. Orientation at Mirador is like that at La Venta; both have Type 1 E-Groups. The measuring units used to lay out Mirador were the same as used at Chiapa de Corzo. Unlike this site, however, the total length of Mirador was a 260 count of the sacred almanac rather than the baktun count evident at Chiapa de Corzo and La Venta. The Mirador count is well short of a 400 count. Counts of 260 units are well marked at these other sites, however. At Chiapa de Corzo

Figure 118. Plan of Izapa and counts of possible measurement units.

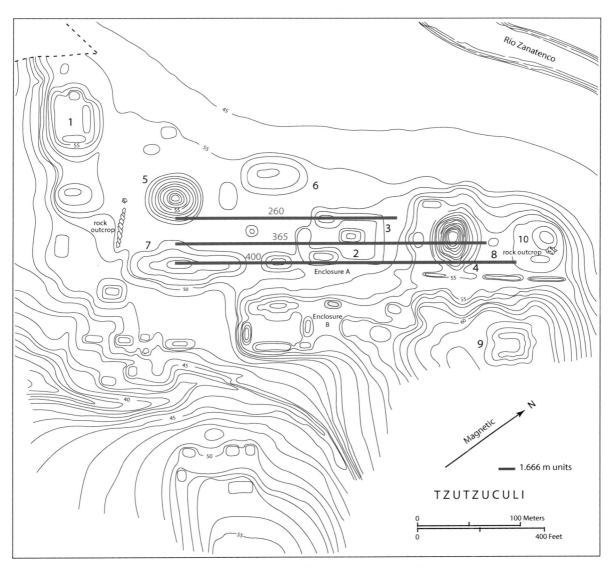

Figure 119. Plan of Tzutzuculi and counts of possible measurement units.

the 260 modular count is the distance from the southern edge of the long mound of its E-group to the northern edge of Mound 17. In fact, Chiapa de Corzo is a precise parallel of Mirador in this respect. Mirador Mound 10 is analogous to Chiapa de Corzo Mound 17. Mirador looks like it was patterned after this part of Chiapa de Corzo. In previous analyses, Clark (Clark and Hansen 2001) considered Mound 33 at Mirador as the northern "pyramid" at Mirador. It never grew to pyramidal stature, but it is an aligned mound in the right place. It is well to remember

that the height of the northern pyramids at MFC sites attained their stature near the end of the Middle Preclassic period (Chiapa IV times). We do not know the heights of the original mounds under these pyramids. The original platform under Mound 36 at Chiapa de Corzo was only a few meters tall. We have no information for La Venta. The large northern pyramid at Izapa probably preceded the installment of the MFC pattern at that site. The low Mound 33 at Mirador may be an example of an original mound that was not subsequently exalted. If so,

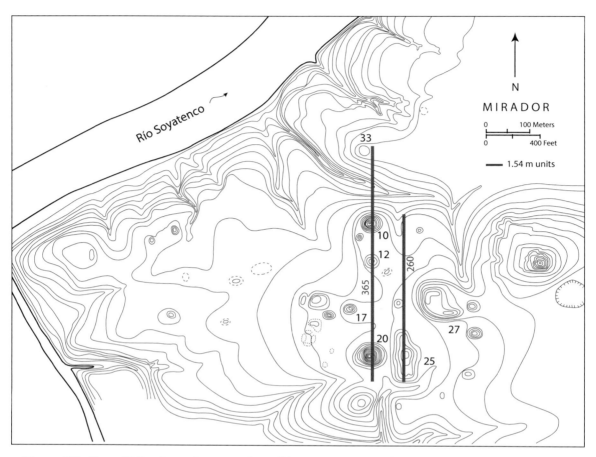

Figure 120. Plan of Mirador and counts of possible measurement units.

the difference would not be in how these centers were laid out but in the subsequent growth histories of individual mounds. If Mound 33 were the northern mound, then Mirador would have been 566 m long, or 367 *brazadas* in the 1.54 system. This would have been the solar year count seen at Chiapa de Corzo and Izapa. The main segmentation at Mirador was at 260 and 365 units. Izapa had the same segmentation, but in units of 1.666 m each. In sum, Mirador was shorter than Chiapa de Corzo, Izapa, and La Venta but had the same general layout, form, and some of the same native counts. Mirador and Chiapa de Corzo were built according to the 1.54 m standard, and Izapa and La Venta were built according the 1.666 m standard.

Similar features show up at these sites but not in the same ways. What is one to make of this diversity? The original analyses of Middle

Preclassic ceremonial centers were grounded in the logic of culture history, as best exemplified in Mesoamerica by ceramic analysis. Archaeological cultures were identified by their special configuration of artifacts, including ceramic wares, figurines, architecture, sculpture, and other objects. These all related to culture practices and traditions, some of them thought to be distinct to ethnic, culture, or linguistic groups. The innovative move by McDonald and Lowe was to view site layout (community pattern) as a possible diagnostic trait of Olmec-related peoples – a diagnostic that differentiated their communities from those of Maya and Sapotec neighbors. When considered with other cultural diagnostics, such as pottery and sculpture, the distribution of MFC sites appears to have mapped out the limits of a culture group. The evidence brought to bear on this hypothesis had the immediate consequence of destroying the traditional meaning of "Olmec" because Tres Zapotes did not make the grade. The obvious solution, to which Lowe came to slowly, was that all of the Chiapas sites on his list were "Olmec" (see Lowe 1991, 1998b, 1999, 2007; Pye and Clark 2006). Nonetheless, any solution made mincemeat of "Olmec" as a useful label for a people. More appropriate labels were traditional language/culture labels from culture history, thus Lowe's exegesis on "Mije-Soke," his synonym for lowland Olmec. This still left Tres Zapotes out. Clark's (2016) solution was to argue that Tres Zapotes was a Mije community. The old "Mije-Soke" Olmec (i.e., San Lorenzo) split into its two daughter languages in the Middle Preclassic.

The differences among MFC centers complicated Lowe's interpretation of a homogeneous, continuous block of peoples of the same culture and language who acted in sync as a social unit. Lowe counterpoised them to a Maya block with similar monolithic propensities. This was a gross simplification, as we are sure he was aware. His was a first attempt to get at the cultural and historical significance of the major differences in site layouts and distributions of different ceramic wares. The core premises of Lowe's interpretation appear sound, but they were overdone. Our brief analysis here shows that the supposed homogeneity of the Soke culture block was another gross simplification. Clark (2016) proposed that different MFC sites be viewed as seats of individual kingdoms that competed as much with each other as with foreign kingdoms. He argued for competition between Soke kingdoms (e.g., Chiapa de Corzo vs. Finca Acapulco) as well as cooperation between distant kingdoms (e.g., Chiapa de Corzo and La Venta). We suppose that some MFC centers were aligned to Maya communities such as Ceibal (e.g., La Libertad), but we lack good evidence for Middle Preclassic Maya sites and their connections to Chiapas sites. The important point Clark makes is that peoples in culture blocks did not act in unison or necessarily cooperatively. It is well to keep in mind that the Olmec origins of this pattern have not been established, and one must specify the

meaning of "Olmec" in any case. Lowe extended the term to include Chiapas, or Mije-Soke, and we followed his lead. It would be just as easy to characterize people by major sites, such as the people from La Venta or Chiapa de Corzo rather than guess their ancient language.

The grand patterns of culture objects that Lowe attributed to Sokes (vs. Mayas) exist and likely marked cultural territories. It does not follow, however, that peoples who shared a mother tongue and culture acted in concert or were natural allies or friends (see Demarest 2011). Just judging from the uneven distribution of elements of the ideal MFC pattern, the communities involved appear to have been bound together in a complex web of relationships which extended well beyond the limits of peoples of the same culture and language. Designating all MFC sites as "Soke" does not really explain anything about the people of individual kingdoms, the Sokes, or their neighbors. The so-called Mije-Soke block of sites no longer appears so homogeneous or to have had such clear boundaries. For any given trait, distributions overrun proposed frontiers between Sokes, Mayas, Sapotecs, and Olmecs. For example, Lowe (1977:223) argued that the distribution of splotchy-orange resist pottery goes all the way to Tres Zapotes. We see no evidence of an MFC pattern at this Olmec site (Clark 2016), hence two traits of this Mije-Soke pattern do not co-occur there. In earlier work Clark argued that the MFC pattern did not occur at Izapa, another site with splotchy-orange resist pottery. Partly on the basis of this negative evidence he posited that the people of Izapa were not Sokes but were Mijes (Clark 2000, 2016; Clark and Pye 2011). Finding the MFC pattern at Izapa requires that his argument be adjusted.

The great surprise of our more detailed look at Lowe's Modified Olmec pattern is that only one site in the Olmec heartland of the Gulf Coast lowlands has the pattern: La Venta. Comparisons of La Venta and Chiapa de Corzo bring this out. There are multiple ironies here, the primary one arises from labels. The term "Olmec" does not have parallel meaning with language-culture labels such as Soke, Maya, or Sapotec. Clark (2016) argued that the MFC pattern was a Soke marker, that Chiapa de Corzo was at the center of the distribution of this pattern, and that, by logical extension, La Venta was a Soke city. But the concordances are inconsistent. Of all the sites considered here, La Venta is the only one that did not have splotchy-orange resist pottery. The coeval figurines at La Venta for Chiapa III times also differed significantly from those in Chiapas. And there is the profound difference of stone sculpture – abundant at La Venta but nowhere in evidence in central Chiapas in the Middle Preclassic. Some polished red and orange pottery was used at La Venta, but it appears to date to Chiapa IV times and to have been imported mostly from the Maya area rather than from central Chiapas (Andrews 1990). The pottery wares at La Venta were white-rim black pots and white and gray wares (von Nagy 2003). Traded vessels of these types from La Venta show up in all the Chiapas MFC centers in Chiapa III assemblages, so the strongest connections to La Venta date to Chiapa II-B and III times. The Chiapa IV period represents a divergence of all the centers considered here (Clark 2014; Lowe 1977).

Did the relations go beyond trade and the sharing of some ideas? For any such questions one must specify the "when." The similarities and differences between the sites of La Venta and Chiapa de Corzo varied through time, as most apparent from the evidence from Mound 17. Clark and Lee (1984) argued that the closest ties between these communities were near the beginning of the Middle Preclassic period. Clark (2016) argued that the earliest elite burial in Mound 17, Burial 17-11, was a royal woman from La Venta who married into a line at Chiapa de Corzo to establish a cadet royal line linked to La Venta. All subsequent elite adult burials in Mound 17 were of males, presumed descendants of this queen mother. The same burial analysis argued that the trappings of rulership at Chiapa de Corzo shifted in Chiapa V and VI times from Olmec to Maya. That the kingdom of La Venta had just been abandoned or conquered at this time is of more than passing interest (Clark et al. 2000). The new royal burials found in Mound 11 require that this proposal be reconsidered.

As a ceremonial center, Chiapa de Corzo shared more traits with the centers of La Venta and La Libertad than with any other MFC sites. Both these allied centers ceased to be occupied about 400 BC, but Chiapa de Corzo persisted (Clark 2016; Clark et al. 2000). Part of its survival appears to have involved a shift in loyalties from Olmecs to Mayas. These are claims about past history meriting extensive research. More important is the claim that ethnic or culture identity was another trait that could be adopted or abandoned by people living at MFC centers. Cultural affiliations and natal language were not biological destiny. Bringing cultural identity into play undercuts Lowe's original project of mapping ethnic borders between Soke and Maya speakers. Such sweeping claims no longer appear appropriate or useful. The histories of individual kingdoms were complicated. The Mound 17 data provide critical pieces for understanding the history of Chiapa de Corzo. Of all the postulated MFC kingdoms, it is the one for which we have the most and best information. It is appropriate to close our analysis of Mound 17 with a precis of the early history of this site.

## CHIAPA DE CORZO IN THE TIMES OF MOUND 17

Mound 17 saw use from about 800 BC to AD 200, the millennium of Chiapa de Corzo's greatest influence as a regional capital and center under Soke rule. During this time Chiapa de Corzo was the capital of an ancient kingdom and perhaps eventually a small state, as evident in its building histories, caches, and burials. We think the Preclassic people who lived there were Sokes. Early on they were influenced by Gulf Coast Olmecs and, towards the end of this millennium, they may have come under the sway of lowland Maya kings, some of whom may have resided at Chiapa de Corzo and have been buried there. The artifacts and features found in Mound 17 concern mostly the early part of the site's history and connections with Lowland Olmecs rather than with Mayas. Evidence of cultural connections comes mostly from ceramic vessels, figurines, other artifacts, and burial practices.

No Middle Preclassic stone sculptures are known for Chiapa de Corzo, but there are some for the Late Preclassic or Protoclassic, including Stela 2, a monument with a long-count date of December 7, 36 BC, the oldest attested longcount date in Mesoamerica thus far (Coe 2005:64; Lee 1969c:105). A jade Olmec figurine head was found in the northern sector of Chiapa de Corzo (Lee 1989:fig. 9.8c, 1993; Lowe 1995:fig. 7.1; Martínez Espinosa 1971; Paillés 1980:fig. 14). A small serpentine axe with an incised Olmec frontal face was found in 2008 above a large offering pit with over 100 pseudo-axes made of limestone and andesite (Bachand and Lowe 2011); these were laid out in patterns at different levels of the offering pit dug into soft bedrock. A cruciform axe cache laid out horizontally was found at the eastern edge of Mound 11 on its east-west axis, also in a shallow pit dug into bedrock. These La Venta-like axe offerings may date to late Chiapa II-B times, or about 800 BC. They were contemporaneous with axe offerings at La Venta, San Isidro, and Ceibal.

Whether or not our speculations about Chiapa de Corzo's queen mother and subsequent cadet kings prove correct (Clark et al. 2000; Clark and Lee 1984), the Chiapa de Corzo data for the early Middle Preclassic show exceptionally strong ties to the La Venta kingdom in terms of ceramic vessel types and forms, hand-modeled figurines, site layouts, massive offerings of pseudo-axes, and incised iconography on cached objects (see Cheetham and Lee 2005). Given these connections, the absence of carved stone monuments at Chiapa de Corzo is a remarkable difference that must have been intentional, meaningful, and significant. This absence could have signaled in some significant sense Chiapa de Corzo's secondary status to, or deference to, La Venta. The few busted stelae fragments found at Chiapa de Corzo (Lee 1969c:105-109; Lowe 1962a) date to the Chiapa V or VI phases and postdate La Venta's demise. This was the period of the strongest Maya influence in central Chiapas, as also recognized for San Isidro, Ocozocoautla, and Mirador (Lowe and Mason 1965:217; cf. Clark 2016).

The best evidence for foreign relations and changes therein is obsidian, pottery, burial practices, and architecture. Not much obsidian is available from dated contexts at Chiapa de Corzo. Most imported obsidian came from two sources in highland Guatemala. During the Middle Preclassic, obsidian arrived as roughed-out blade cores from San Martín Jilotepeque, a source located near Chimaltenango (Clark 1988; Clark and Lee 2007:214; Nelson and Clark 1998). These cores were broken down into fine blades locally (Clark 1987). During the Late Preclassic and Protoclassic periods (Chiapa V-VI), most obsidian came from El Chayal, a source located 30 km east of Kaminaljuyu and presumably under the loose control of the state society there (Clark and Lee 2007). Obsidian was imported into central Chiapas during this era as ready-made fine blades. The increased importance of El Chayal blades in Chiapas beginning about 300 BC corresponded to a lowland Maya intrusion and occupation in the upper Grijalva River Valley (Bryant and Clark 1983, 2005a, 2005b; Clark and Lee 2007; Clark et al. 2005) as well as the mayanization of Chiapa de Corzo (Lowe 1995).

Changes in pottery styles corroborate the noted shifts in obsidian trade. Ceramic wares during the Chiapa II phase were a clear continuation from the tecomate and gray plate tradition of the preceding phase. The Chiapa III phase witnessed abrupt changes all across Chiapas (Brockington 1967:67; Warren 1978). This era of city building in Chiapas was marked by different ceramic wares and forms that appear to have been inspired by earlier ceramic vessels from the Maya Lowlands. The diagnostic ceramics of Chiapas in Chiapas III times were slipped, waxy orange-resist wares, black and brown burnished monochromes, and a shift to plain, necked jars instead of tecomates. There was also a change in figurine styles and other new vessel forms, such as double-chamber whistling pots, chamfered cylinders, and cuspidor-shaped bowls. This era also saw the first ballcourts constructed in central Chiapas (at Finca Acapulco, San Mateo, Vergel, and La Libertad). These changes were so extensive and pervasive that Bruce Warren (1964:294, 1978:45) argued they represented a new group of people, perhaps from the Gulf Coast. Lowe and Mason (1965:212) were in accord that the "Chiapa III occupation seems to be intrusive at Chiapa de Corzo." Most imported pottery found at Chiapa de Corzo for this era is fine-paste black and white pottery from either Tres Zapotes or La Venta, an observation made by Anna Shepherd to Warren in 1958 (1978:60) and more recently corroborated by Cheetham and Lee (2005). These differences in pottery usage indicate important changes beginning about 750 BC, but wholesale migration from the Gulf Coast cannot account for them. Central Chiapas had more population in Chiapa II times than is known for any other region of Mesoamerica (see Sullivan 2009). These people did not leave, therefore the dramatic changes in cooking and serving pots were due to processes other than migration by which local Chiapas peoples adopted foreign styles and made them their own.

Lowe (1977, 1978, 2007) interpreted the changes in ceramic inventories at the beginning of the Chiapa III phase as evidence of a stable, local population of Mije-Sokes that adopted new forms and styles of vessels – both utilitarian and service wares. The distribution of orange, cloudy-resist pottery across Chiapas and into the Isthmus of Tehuantepec, and all the way to Tres Zapotes, was the key marker of Mije-Soke identity (Lowe 1977). The irony of Lowe's proposal is that this marker of Mije-Soke identity was adopted and adapted from Maya neighbors. Their polished red bowls were earlier than those made in central Chiapas.

Ceramic complexes in Chiapa IV times were a clear continuation of the monochromes adopted earlier, and also clearly similar to late Mamom pottery in the Maya lowlands. Chiapa IV times represented an era of great uniformity in the types of ceramic wares used in Chiapas and the beginning of regional differences (Miller et al. 2005:263; Warren 1978:54). The main diagnostics were slipped, highly burnished red monochromes and the popularity of flat-bottomed plates with wide-everted rims. This distribution "represents the zenith of Zoquean cultural developments (Lowe 1977:226-27). This cultural fluorescence, in a period of pre-Maya dominance, was perhaps also the time when Zoquean influence was felt the most strongly in adjacent areas" (Miller et al. 2005:263).

The little evidence for trade from Francesa phase areas indicates a changing pattern of external contacts. The earlier Escalera phase had pottery traded in from the Olmec area of southern Veracruz and Western Tabasco, but the only identified trade items in the Francesa phase seem to be from the Oaxaca Valley. (Warren 1978:54)

The story of the following Guanacaste phase (300-100 BC) in Chiapa de Corzo is of particular interest because it represents the post-La Venta era in Mesoamerica. Sullivan (2009:197, 2015:466) estimates a reduction in the size of Chiapa de Corzo from 69 ha to 61 ha. To judge from the mortuary offerings in Tomb 7 at Chiapa de Corzo, it was a time of heightened international trade and commerce. One of the remarkable changes was the cessation of the manufacture and use of human figurines, an avoidance shared with lowland Maya societies at that time.

> Tomb 7 in Mound 1 ... had 34 ceramic offerings. Several of the tomb's bridged-spout face-necked jars (Cuilapa Slipped group) were brought in from the Oaxaca area. Other large red slipped florero-shaped vessels (Sierra Slipped group) were from somewhere in the Highlands of Guatemala or adjacent areas, some Usulutan (Sartenejo Slipped group) from El Salvador and still other vessels were from southern Veracruz (Cueva Grande Slipped group). All of these vessels were traded in from distant regions and none were of the local ceramic tradition at Chiapa de Corzo. In the case of the Tomb 7 burial we have evidence of a very important person being honored at his death with elaborate sophisticated pottery transported from a radius of some 600 miles. (Warren 1978:59)

Ceramic modes and styles paralleled those of Chicanel pottery in the Maya lowlands, and some trade wares are apparent – including those in Tomb 7 (see Lowe 1995) that Warren attributed to the Guatemala highlands. The importation of pottery from many distant neighboring regions continued at Chiapa de Corzo through the Horcones or Chiapa VI phase. There was also pervasive experimentation locally in forms and decorations.

During Guanacaste times Chiapa de Corzo underwent what Clark calls "mayanization," as best seen in the distribution of imported Maya pottery and local copies of it. These special wares were mostly for elite usage (Lowe 1977:230, 1995), perhaps overt symbols of paraded identity.[13] At the same time, there was clear continuity in the local population, and the utilitarian wares that remained were those of long tradition. Only traditional Soke pottery was interred with commoners as mortuary offerings (Lowe 1977:230, 1995:329). The kings buried in the newly constructed Mound 1 were accompanied with elaborate imported pottery (Lowe 1995:324). Lowe (1977:230, 1995:329) argued that the use of imported lowland Maya pots ceased at the beginning of the Horcones phase (Chiapa VI). During this phase

> the previously abundant Chicanel-like types [Sierra Red] are notably absent. This pattern is characteristic for the length of the Chiapa VI occupation during which the rudimentary Maya modes are mostly lacking in the five tomb offerings and many dedicatory caches and ceremonial dumps of the period found at Chiapa de Corzo. Chiapa VI seems to have had its closest affiliations with the Arenal phase of sites such as Kaminaljuyu in the highlands of Guatemala, but both its architecture and its ceramics show local development or manufacture with the exception of certain finer vessels which appear to be imports from southern Veracruz, Oaxaca, and El Salvador. (Lowe and Mason 1965:218)

Chiapa de Corzo experienced a renaissance of sorts in Chiapa VI times as old clay and adobe brick platforms were covered over with veneers of cut limestone blocks and covered with stucco and red paint (Lowe 1960b:6; Warren 1978). A new palace was constructed at Mound 5 in the south plaza of Chiapa de Corzo at this time to accompany the temple at Mound 1; both appear inspired by lowland Maya prototypes. Sullivan (2015:464) argues that the very configuration of the southern plaza was borrowed from Lowland

Maya centers. This Maya influence was rather short-lived and ended about AD 100.

> When we look at the ceramic vessels with Guanacaste phase [Chiapa V] burials of commoners at Chiapa de Corzo (Agrinier 1964:figs. 57-66), we see the general absence of Chicanel ceramics. And, if we examine the vessels of the Istmo phase [Chiapa VII] burials of the same site (Agrinier 1964: figs. 68-117) we see that the differences in ceramics are even more marked .... The content of two Guanacaste phase tombs ... included a good percentage of vessel forms and slips typical of Chicanel ceramics (Lowe and Agrinier 1960b:fig. 53, plates 27b-h, q, s, 28a-c, I; Lowe 1962b:fig. 22a-g). And in a similar manner, we see three Sierra Red floreros ... in the great tomb of Burial 11 of the Guañoma phase at San Isidro ... Definitely, imported Maya ceramics were luxury wares in western Chiapas and were not used – or accessible – for everyday uses. (Lowe 1999:124, translation JEC)

Warren (1978:65) interpreted the Horcones phase as the climax of Chiapa de Corzo, and he estimated that the site covered over 3 km² and had 7,000 inhabitants (Warren 1978:199). Sullivan (2009:199, 2015:466) infers a contrary pattern and argues that the site actually became smaller. He estimates the site was 56 ha in extent at this time and housed 1,450 people; many former residents left the center for the countryside. The demographic trend thus represented a further reduction in the size of this center, according to his analysis. Chiapa de Corzo sloughed population at the same time that the number of inhabitants in its hinterland increased. This era ended in the general destruction of major buildings at Chiapa de Corzo and in another pervasive shift in cultural practices. The palace at Mound 5, erected at the beginning of this phase, was burned. Architectural styles, pottery traditions, and burial practices were terminated (Warren 1978:66). We suspect the carved stelae at Chiapa de Corzo were broken at this time and

---

[13] This was our understanding of Lowe's argument up until 2016. Clark reviews and critiques all the evidence for Maya influence at Chiapa de Corzo in the report of the salvage excavations at Mound 15 (see Glauner, Herman, and Clark in press).

that the royal tombs in Mound 1 were looted. Agrinier and Lowe (1960:39) date the looting of Tomb 1 to the beginning of the Chiapa VII phase. During this Istmo phase, the residents who remained at Chiapa de Corzo started using white-rim black smudged pottery and became closely and permanently affiliated with the Sokes of western Chiapas. They distanced themselves from any Maya connections. These changes in the Protoclassic period are important because they cast light on the earlier changes at the beginning of the Late Preclassic.

Clark, Hansen, and Tomás Pérez (2000; also, Clark and Hansen 2001) proposed that Late Preclassic Kings at Chiapa de Corzo (beginning in Chiapa V times) were Maya regents affiliated with and subject to those at El Mirador. Gareth Lowe (personal communication to Clark, 1989) believed at one time that there was a lowland Maya enclave at Chiapa de Corzo residing at Mound 3 just west of the temple at Mound 1 (see Lowe 1995). Chiapa de Corzo's Maya interlude came to an end by AD 100 when the palace at Mound 5 was burned and torn down and its inhabitants presumably killed or run out of town. These are interpretations that will benefit from DNA and isotopic analyses of human remains to determine genetic relationships and possible movements of nobles between kingdoms. The larger fact is that Chiapa de Corzo during the Late Preclassic cast off its Olmec ways and adopted Maya ones. These claims of ethnic and cultural identity of kings may have been real or fictive. It may be that kings were of the local populace but presented themselves as "stranger kings" as part of their political strategy for ruling at Chiapa de Corzo (Sullivan 2015:469). If nothing else, these major shifts in vogue practices and symbols indicate changes in the balance of power and global politics. Burial practices evident at Chiapa de Corzo for this era clearly show that the resident population at Chiapa de Corzo remained the same, with the major changes being confined to the governing elites.

This era of Chiapa de Corzo's history carries us to the end of the active refurbishing (and functioning?) of Mound 17 and well past the Middle Preclassic era of its glory. This part of the site's history shows that the rulers and residents of Chiapa de Corzo adopted trappings of Maya identity, both lowland and highland in turn, at the beginning of the Late Preclassic (300-200 BC) only to discard them three or four centuries later. There is much to do to verify this history and understand it. Lowe discussed the different uses of pottery in mortuary rituals rather than in everyday use, with the implication being that elites had exclusive access to these symbols. Consideration of everyday practices suggests that commoners as well as elites used "Maya" pottery, so a critical distinction may have been between imported pots and local copies of foreign wares. Thus, the distinction Lowe describes for burial goods may have been between expensive and cheaper pots. Sullivan's (2009) survey of the Chiapa de Corzo region indicates the widespread use of Maya-like ceramics at Chiapa de Corzo and its immediate political hinterland in Chiapa V times. Maya-style pottery was in common use in domestic settings – but not as mortuary offerings. This pattern of selective use of imported Maya pots and locally made Maya-style vessels suggests a role in signaling identity and cultural practices and, most importantly, some long-lived tensions in the identities of commoners and elites at Chiapa de Corzo that eventuated in a return to traditional Soke values and material symbols about AD 100. This coincided with the collapse of the El Mirador state in the Petén (Clark et al. 2000) and presumably to the loss of foreign muscle to support the kings at Chiapa de Corzo. The rapidity of this change, and the reversals in domestic symbolism (ceramic wares) that accompanied it, indicate that the base population at Chiapa de Corzo during the Late Preclassic and Protoclassic had maintained its Soke identity all along. If so, the major changes at the end of the Middle Preclassic would have concerned more the trappings of rulership and its overt identity rather than changes in the base population. The destruction of the few stone monuments at Chiapa de Corzo may have been part of the repudiation of foreign kings or "stranger kings," and visible markers thereof.

Chiapa de Corzo persisted as a local center well past the Spanish Conquest (see Navarrete 1966). The last millennium of indigenous occupation appears to have been as dramatic as the first two millennia, but it postdates the biography of Mound 17. Two changes – both likely manifestations of the same event – occurred. Chiapa de Corzo (it would have had a different name) was conquered by Chiapanecs, probably in Late Classic times, and the ceremonial center was moved from the bluff to the river levee land below it. The relocation of the ceremonial core of Chiapa de Corzo a few hundred meters downslope turned the old mounds into relics located at the northern margin of the new town, perhaps a version of urban renewal. The old mounds and plazas were left to go feral, and this was their

condition when first described and mapped in 1868 by D. Julian Grajales (Navarrete 1966:3). Ironically, the new Chiapa de Corzo became a Colonial town under Spanish rule, thus all of its pre-Hispanic architecture has since been throughly destroyed or buried by nearly five centuries of Colonial and modern occupation. The ceremonial center that survived was that of old town, a relic of the Chiapanec Conquest of this place. Fortunately for us, the Chiapanecs did not erase the memory or monuments of their predecessors, the Sokes and Mayas who lived at Chiapa de Corzo in earlier centuries.

# THE HUMAN SKELETAL REMAINS FROM MOUND 17 AT CHIAPA DE CORZO

## by Phillip Walker

The remains of at least 18 individuals were recovered during the excavation of Mound 17 at Chiapa de Corzo. These burials were highly fragmented and in a poor state of preservation. An additional burial from Mound 17 has been previously reported (Agrinier 1964:4) and will not be considered further here.

## DEMOGRAPHICS

A relatively large portion (35 percent) of the burials from Mound 17 were younger than twenty years of age at death (Table 7). The proportion of sub-adults to adults is similar in two other mounds (Table 8) previously studied at this site. In the Francesa phase burials at Mound 1 and the Istmo phase at Mound 5 reported by Agrinier (1964), the proportion of sub-adults to adults do not differ significantly from those found at Mound 17 (x2= 0.862, d.f.= 2, p= 0.656). Considering the poor conditions of preservation, the actual proportion of children and infants in these mounds may have been slightly underestimated since the remains of immature individuals are less likely to be preserved than are those of adults.

The age structure of the skeletal population recovered from Mound 17 appears to correspond to the rates of mortality found in some modern developing countries. For example, mortality statistics reported for Guatemala in 1950 (Dorn 1962) predicted that 30 percent of the females born in that year would die during the first twenty years of life.

One out of the seven burials from Mound 17 which could be sexed was a female (Table 9). A similar sexual bias is present in burials from Mound 1 and Mound 5 (Table 8). The predominance of males in the skeletal population recovered at Chiapa de Corzo could be the result of series of different cultural factors. It is possible that male-female differences in status resulted in the exclusion of most females from burials in the mounds at Chiapa de Corzo. Implicit in this interpretation is the assumption that the majority of the burials of infants and children at Chiapa de Corzo are males. Unfortunately this assumption can not be tested due to the lack of reliable criteria for sexing the skeletal remains of infants and children. The relatively low frequency of female burials could also be the result of restricting burial in the mounds at Chiapa de Corzo to members of a single patrilineage (B. Voorhies, personal communication). Since lineages are characteristically exogamous, married females would normally not be in residence at the time of death and thus would not have access to their lineage's burial site.

## PATHOLOGICAL CONDITIONS

Although no postcranial pathologies were identified in the skeletons from Mound 17, little significance can be attached to this apparent lack of disease since the majority of the burials consisted of teeth and only a few fragments of long bone. Oral pathologies are prevalent in the burials afflicting slightly more than 40 percent of the individuals examined (Table 10). The teeth of four burials exhibited caries. Caries were most frequently located on the lingual and interproximal surfaces of the anterior teeth. The teeth of Burial 17-7a, for example, exhibit ten caries, most of which are located on the interproximal surfaces of the incisors and canines (Table 10). An alveolar abscess is present near the second and third mandibular molars of Burial 17-12.

The crown of the right maxillary central incisor of Burial 17-9 is encircled by an extremely deep hypoplastic line. This line indicates an interference in the deposition of enamel when the individual was between three and four years of age. Although hypoplastic lines in the dentition can result from a variety of environmental and genetic factors, they are often associated with infectious diseases and nutritional stress (Shafer et al. 1974).

## DENTAL MUTILATION

At least two of the individuals that were designated as burial number six during the excavation of Mound 17 possessed filed maxillary lateral incisors. Since none of the four filed maxillary lateral incisors from the burial were associated with alveolar bone, it was impossible to ascertain which of the teeth came from the same dentition. Two of the incisors were filed on both their mesial and distal borders, producing a pointed occlusal surface which corresponds to Romero's 3C category of dental mutilation (Romero 1970). The other two incisors are filed only along their mesial borders. These teeth correspond most closely to Romero's B1 category. Dental filing and inlay has previously been reported for several individuals excavated from late Classic and Early Classic components of mounds at Chiapa de Corzo (Agrinier 1964).

Table 7. Estimates of age at death of individuals from Chiapa de Corzo Mound 17.

| Burial Number(s) | Age Assigned | Criteria Used in Age Determination |
|---|---|---|
| 1 | CHILD; 6 months | Calcification of the central maxillary permanent incisor crown is complete. Two-thirds of the second maxillary permanent molar crown is calcified. |
| 2a | CHILD; 6-7 years | Roots of first mandibular permanent molar approximately two-thirds complete, crown of second mandibular permanent molar is complete. |
| 2b | CHILD; 5-10 years | One half of maxillary permanent molar is calcified. |
| 3 | ADULT; 25+ years | Dentine on three cusps of mandibular first molar is exposed, the third mandibular molar is only slightly worn. |
| 6 a, b, c | ADULT; 25+ years | The commingled teeth of at least three individuals are represented in this burial. The molars present have a degree of which is consistent with an age of young adult. |
| 7a | ADULT; 40+ years | Mandibular molar posses dentine exposures on the tips of all cusps, and two dentine exposures have fused together. |
| 7b | CHILD; 4-6 years | Complete maxillary deciduous dentition present, approximately two-thirds of the central maxillary permanent incisors crowns are calcified. Mandibular first and second permanent molars crowns are complete. |
| 8a | Adult | Male (?) |
| 8b | CHILD; 6 years | Calcification of the central maxillary permanent incisor crown is complete. Two-thirds of the second maxillary permanent molar crown is calcified. |
| 9 | CHILD; 11 years | Fourth mandibular premolar just erupting, second deciduous mandibular molar is still in place although its roots are partially resorbed. Distal articular epiphysis on right humerus is unfused. |
| 10a | ADULT | Maxillary third molar is unworn, maxillary first molar possesses one dentine exposure. |
| 10b | ADULT | Maxillary incisor and canine crowns are moderately worn, maxillary third premolar possesses two dentine exposures. |
| 11 | ADULT; 40+ years | First and second maxillary molar completely lack occlusal enamel, two dentine exposures on third maxillary molar have fused together. |
| 12 | ADULT | Third mandibular molar is unworn, two dentine exposures on a first mandibular molar have fused together. |
| 13 | ADULT | Mandibular molar (M2 ?) is slightly worn. |
| 14 | ADULT | First mandibular molar has three dentine exposures, third mandibular molar is unworn. |

Table 8. Age and sex distributions of burials from mounds at Chiapa de Corzo.

| Mound | Period | Subadults | Adults | Males | Females | Unknown |
|---|---|---|---|---|---|---|
| Mound 1* | Late Preclassic | 13 | 31 | 2 | 1 | 28 |
| Moune 5* | Late Protoclassic (Istmos Phase Burials) | 10 | 32 | 13 | 5 | 14 |
| Mound 17 |  | 6 | 11 | 6 | 1 | 4 |

*data from Agrinier (1964)

Table 9. Sexual identification of adult skeletal remains from Chiapa de Corzo Mound 17.

| Burial Number(s) | Sex Assigned | Criteria Used in Sex Determination |
|---|---|---|
| 6 a, b, c | Male(s) | Robusticity of long bone fragments suggested that at least one male is represented. |
| 7 | Female | Information not available |
| 8 | Male? | Information not available |
| 9 | Male? | Size of mastoid process and robusticity of mental area. |
| 10a or b | Male | Maxillary third molar is unworn, maxillary first molar possesses one dentine exposure. |
| 11 | Female | Sharp supraorbital margin, gracile zygomatic process, cranial vault fragments are relatively thin and lack heavily developed areas for muscle attachment. |
| 12 | Male? | Rounded supraorbital margin, mental eminence is well developed, a distinct temporal line is present. |
| 13 | Male | Prominent mental eminence, robust humeral fragment. |
| 14 | Male | Large mastoid process, general robusticity of cranial fragments. |

Table 10. Dental pathology in individuals from Chiapa de Corzo Mound 17.

| Burial Number(s) | Pathological Condition |
|---|---|
| 2b | Two small caries present on lingual side of mandibular molars. |
| 7a | Carious molar (?) root which lost its crown prior to death. Mandibular incisors possess three interproximal caries, one mandibular canine exhibits caries on both mesial and distal surfaces, the other is carious only on its distal side. Approximately one half of one maxillary canine has been destroyed by caries. Interproximal caries are present between one pair of maxillary molars. |
| 7b | Large caries are present on the lingual surfaces of both deciduous maxillary incisors. |
| 9 | Severe linear hypoplasia is present on the right maxillary central incisor. The hypoplastic area passes around the entire circumference of the tooth and has a depth of approximately one millimeter. The lingual portion of this line is the site of a small caries. |
| 10b | Horizontal ramus of the mandible exhibits moderate alveolar reabsorption. All mandibular teeth distal to the third premolars were lost prior to death. |
| 12 | An alveolar abscess is present on the area of the left mandibular molars. Both central mandibular incisors were lost prior to death. |
| 14 | Small occlusal caries are present on the mandibular third molar. |

# MIDDLE PRECLASSIC CEREMONIAL CENTERS IN SOUTHERN CHIAPAS [14]

### by Andrew J. McDonald

It has been said that "the appearance of plazas, temples, and other public buildings in any local or regional Mesoamerican sequence is the most reasonable point at which to postulate the beginnings of changes leading from relatively undifferentiated to relatively highly differentiated societies" (Willey et al. 1964:489). In Southern Chiapas, platform and plaza complexes were first constructed during the Middle Preclassic period, following the Dili horizon.

In this report I examine briefly some of these first ceremonial complexes and note a consistent formal arrangement reflecting the standardized sociocultural development of the time in the Chiapas area.

The earliest earthen platforms, presumably at least partially ceremonial in function, appear at 700 BC on the Pacific Coast; the best known example is the series of superimposed platforms constructed within Mound 30a at Izapa (Ekholm 1969) situated near the Guatemala border (Figure 1).

Starting with a low elevation cleared of refuse for a base, the Duende phase occupants of Izapa began the construction of a small, 2 m high, clay and rubble platform with slopping sides. Subsequently, before the end of the period some 150 years later at about 550 BC, four major additions, each essentially a larger version of the original, brought the structure to the imposing height of 10.5 m with a front-to-back length of about 47 m. Postmolds, indicating a modest temple built of poles, and a small round "altar" were uncovered on the upper surface of the final Duende phase platform. Nothing is known of the associated plaza.

Tzutzuculi (McDonald 1971), in the northwestern sector of the coastal plain (Figure 1), is another site with earthen constructions associated with a phase between Dili-like and Escalera-like phases (the Tzutzuculi II phase), noted on the map (Figures 119 and 121) as Mound 1 and Mound 4. Mound 1 is basically a natural hillock with superficial alterations made during the Tzutzuculi II phase. Mound 4 lies atop a broad artificial terrace constructed over a slight rise, also of the Tzutzuculi II phase. The fill material of the terrace, which is approximately 1.5 m thick, appears to be a construction mix. It is overlain by a layer of rough, river-worn stones, and, at least in front of the mound, a burned clay floor was placed over that.

At least the upper 3.5 m of the 8 m high Mound 4, as well as its external features in general, correspond to the Escalera-like Tzutzuculi III phase. These features include an ovate base and a central, 4 m wide stairway of unworked, river-worn stones flanked on each side by an engraved monument (Monuments 1 and 2). One of these depicts a stylized serpent's head in profile, the other a were-jaguar in the late Olmec style. A Tzutzuculi II phase substructure is expected, although the central portion of the mound's interior is still untested. Apparently prior to the site's abandonment near the end of the Francesa-like Tzutzuculi IV phase, Mound 4 fell into disrepair and possibly disuse.

Also at Tzutzuculi, Mound 7, an elongated platform about 110 m in length, seems to be another Tzutzuculi III structure. Other structures were built during the succeeding Francesa-like Tzutzuculi IV phase. Among them was the mound enclosure in front of Mound 4. A somewhat similar platform arrangement at the side of Mound 7 is uninvestigated.

---

[14] This paper was presented at the 1974 International Congress of Americanists in Mexico City. The papers of this session were slated for an NWAF Papers volume edited by Gareth W. Lowe and Susanna M. Ekholm. This is the version edited by Lowe and Ekholm. We have not upgraded the facts or references.

One of the last platforms to be built prior to the site's abandonment was Mound 5. Its construction seems generally to coincide with the above noted lapse of Mound 4 into disrepair and possibly disuse. Perhaps the center of ceremonial activities had shifted from the Mound 4 area to the vicinity of Mounds 5 and 7. Regardless, judging from positioning and comparative data to be discussed below, Mound 4 and the northernmost mound enclosure may have been the primary constituents of one ceremonial unit, while Mounds 5 and 7 and the other mound enclosure may have been core elements of another.

Turning inland, an important early platform complex is found at Mirador in the Central Depression (Figures 120 and 121). Like Izapa and Tzutzuculi, Mirador has a post-Dili pre-Escalera occupation (Early Quequepac). In contrast, however, platform construction at Mirador apparently did not begin until the succeeding, Escalera-like, Late Quequepac facet.

Late Quequepac platforms have so far been uncovered at Mounds 20 and 27. To date, only the excavation results from Mound 20 have been reported (Agrinier 1970). They show the Late Quequepac substructure to have been a 5 m high platform with a stone-based wattle-and-daub superstructure. There is more information on the additions during the next phase, a Francesa phase equivalent, which brought the platform to a height of about 13 m. The sides were at least partially terraced, a clay stairway with balustrades ascended the east side, and a protective, compacted coating confected from clay, lime, and sand was applied to the surface.

Unfortunately, Mound 25, the elongated platform adjacent to Mound 20, remains uninvestigated, for the pattern it makes with Mound 20, a pyramidal platform, and Mound 27, a broad topped platform with wall-like mounds, is seemingly duplicated at Tzutzuculi (Figure 121).

One of the premier sites in Chiapas from Early Preclassic times to the Conquest was Chiapa de Corzo. It is situated on the Grijalva River in the Central Depression at the eastern edge of the Sumidero Canyon (Figure 1). It was during the Escalera phase that the long Chiapa de Corzo tradition of ceremonial architecture began.

The initial platform complex seems to have been centered around Mounds 7, 12, and 13 (Figures 99, 116 and 121). Mound 7 (Lowe 1962b), presently distinguished by its broad, level surface, began in the Escalera phase as an earthen platform approximately 1.5 m high. It featured retaining walls of rough stones and a fired construction mix finish. Steps were found on the two sides investigated, the north and the west.

The following Francesa phase saw additions raising the platform's height to about 3.5 m. Cellular fill walls of rough stones and of poor quality lime plaster surfacing were important Francesa phase innovations.

The elongated Mound 12 (Mason 1962a) acquired much of its present size during the Escalera phase. Other than the presence in places of retaining walls of unworked stones, little remains to indicate the construction techniques employed on the exterior of the Escalera phase platform. The Francesa phase additions are similarly eroded. During the Istmo phase (AD 100-200) – and possibly earlier – a superstructure was erected over a pyramidal base extending eastward from the mound's center.

Mound 13 (Hicks and Rozaire 1960; Mason 1960b) originated as a terrace-pyramidal platform combination, a smaller version of its present-day arrangement. During the Escalera phase, the pyramidal portion reached approximately 6 m above the level of the plaza, rising to about 7 m during the Francesa phase. The Escalera phase pyramidal platform was surfaced with a yellowish coating of smoothed mud or adobe. Surfacing during the Francesa phase was indistinct. Steps ascended the south and east sides of the pyramidal platform in both phases. In the case of the Escalera phase structure, the steps were molded from a construction mix.

Standing back and looking at the complex as a whole, the question arises, "What about Mound 11?" Certainly its placement in relation to Mounds 7, 12, and 13 fits the pattern noted for platform complexes originating during the

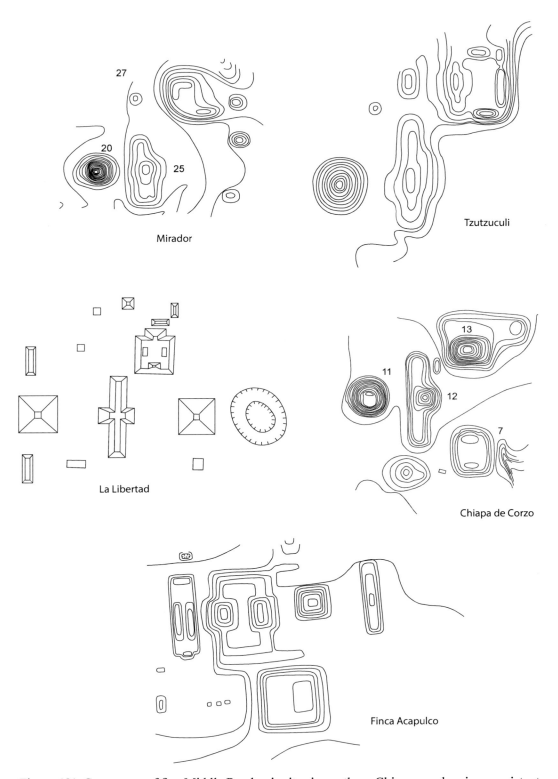

Figure 121. Core zones of five Middle Preclassic sites in southern Chiapas as showing consistent pyramidal and platform relationships.

Escalera phase horizon. Unfortunately, a study of Mound 11 has been hampered by its modern use as a base for a water tank. A superficial examination, however, has provided evidence of Francesa phase construction near the surface, and an earlier, Escalera phase substructure is likely.

The largest of the known Escalera horizon platform complexes is at Finca Acapulco (Gussinyer 1972), upriver from Chiapa de Corzo in the Angostura Basin (Figure 1). This remarkable complex (Figures 115 and 121) was constructed and abandoned all during a single Escalera related phase. As a reflection of the sociocultural character of its builders, it is striking evidence of considerable complexity.

Like the other Escalera horizon structures discussed above, those at Finca Acapulco have exteriors of unworked stones coated with clay. Among the complex members, the broad platform south of the central axis and three of the four structures alongside it, the pyramidal platform, the elongated platform, and the terrace with the superimposed platforms and wall-like rim, have counterparts (although differently arranged) at the other Escalera horizon sites. A notable addition to the Finca Acapulco complex, as yet unrecognized at contemporary sites elsewhere in Chiapas – and more broadly, Mesoamerica – is the fourth centrally aligned structure, identified as a ball court.

Still farther upstream on the Grijalva at its headwaters by the Guatemala border is La Libertad (Lowe 1959a), another site with a large platform complex which, judging from surface collections, was built up and partly abandoned during the Middle Preclassic. The site layout (Figures 102 and 121), consisting in part of a pyramidal platform and an elongated platform along the site axis and a platform-supporting terrace to one side, is typical of the pattern observed for Middle Preclassic platform complexes in the Chiapas area. Also along the alignment another platform and a curious depression reminiscent of a peculiar feature of the Escalera horizon platform complex at Ocozocoautla (the sunken patio) to be described below. To date no excavating has been done at La Libertad.

Comparing the different platform complexes originating during the Escalera horizon, a number of important similarities are noted (Figure 121). The most striking is the presence in every case (assuming that Mound 25 of Mirador is a Middle Preclassic structure) of a pyramidal platform centered on a transverse elongated platform along the central site axis. Moreover, measuring the site alignment from the pyramidal structure toward the elongate one, all axes but one are oriented around S-60-E. The exception, the Mirador axis, is not far off at nearly due east. Also, all examples have a broad terrace supporting earthen structures situated in every case but at Finca Acapulco northeast of the elongated platform. They exhibit a range of forms, varying from the Chiapa de Corzo example with its single superimposed pyramidal platform through the example from Finca Acapulco with a pair of superimposed platforms of lesser height and a wall-like mound enclosure to the examples from Tzutzuculi, Mirador, and La Libertad with only mounds rimming the terrace tops. Finally, two of the sites, the two largest, Chiapa de Corzo and that at Finca Acapulco, have platforms south of their axes with broad, flat tops. These shared characteristics, then, indicate a definite pattern underlying the construction of the earliest platform complexes – those starting on the Escalera horizon – over much of Chiapas.

In general it seems that the natural topography played an important part in the location of the sites and the arrangement of their features. To a degree, this is probably the reason for differences in site layouts and orientations.

Recently, investigations were made by the NWAF in a platform complex at the site of Ocozocoautla that conforms to the Middle Preclassic pattern. The site is located on the outskirts of the town whose name it takes, between the sites of Mirador and Chiapa de Corzo (Figure 1). Complex features in the Middle Preclassic mold are Mound 18, a broad, flat-topped platform south of the central axis, and on the axis, Mound 11, a pyramidal platform, Mound 10, an elongated platform, and a sub-complex consisting of Mounds 2 and 3 and a wall-like enclosure (Figure 110). The mound in front of the northern extremity of Mound 10 is largely a natural hill.

Like the site alignments of the other related complexes, that at Ocozocoautla is easternly directed, but at N-50-E it differs somewhat from the norm. Also, an Escalera-related phase (Ocozocoautla III) marks the beginning of construction on the platform complex.

The initial complex constructed during the Ocozocoautla III phase includes platforms making up the bulk of Mounds 18, 10, and 3 and an unusual feature east of Mound 10 referred to as the "sunken patio." Another platform of the same date is postulated at Mound 11 because of the likelihood of earlier substructures underlying the structure dating to the early part of the Ocozocoautla IV phase, a Francesa phase equivalent, which was uncovered near the surface in limited excavations. Also, while platforms constructed shortly after the start of the Ocozocoautla IV phase were oriented slightly differently that earlier ones, the base of Mound 11 appears to follow the original alignment.

Surfacing techniques for the platforms, consisting of walls and floors of rough stones coated with clay and occasionally fired, were in keeping with those employed elsewhere in Chiapas at this time.

The sunken patio was a rectangular depression, measuring about 11 by 14 m and initially a little over a meter deep, with walls of stacked rough stones over a base of vertical slabs. It received a series of floors, first of rough stones, then of cobblestones, and last of fired clay rising to near the surface, where a layer of fill was finally added, leveling it. Fossil stream beds, as well as a modern one, in use intermittently, cross the patio from south to north near its eastern edge. These and hints of an inlet and outlet on the same path and interior

riverine sediments, indicate that the so-called "sunken patio" functioned as an impoundment for water. Possibly the whole platform complex had been purposely laid out perpendicular to the existing stream with the sunken patio in mind, thereby explaining the marked deviation of the general site alignment from the Middle Preclassic norm. The exact orientation of the initial complex axis was N-48-E.

Near the end of the Ocozocoautla III phase the remainder of the sunken patio above the last floor was filled in. Slightly later, at the beginning of the Ocozocoautla IV phase, a platform with a burned clay top (a Mound 10a substructure) was built just west of the covered sunken patio in front of Mound 10, possibly as a replacement.

Subsequently, still during the early part of the Ocozocoautla IV phase, the platforms were resurfaced with cut stone masonry and plaster. This dramatic change in surfacing techniques is all the more remarkable for the high quality of the finish, not at all a rudimentary beginning. As presently known, the Ocozocoautla example of this type of construction is as early as any known in Chiapas. Comparable examples on the same time horizon have been reported for San Agustín (Navarrete 1959) about 20 km east of Ocozocoautla and at Mound 17 of Chiapa de Corzo (Lee 1969b).

To summarize, a consistent early ceremonial center pattern has been observed, apparently originating in Chiapas on the Escalera horizon, which is distinguished by a nearly east-west axis crossing a pyramidal structure and a long north-south platform. The rapid and wide spread of a formalized ceremonial system apparently witnessed the arrival of a more complex way of life in Chiapas; this began a broader cultural reaching east and west and serving eventually as an ancestral type for the "Classic" cultures.

Figure 122. Picture of Tom Lee crossing the river near Mango Amate in his 1974 survey of the upper Grijalva River Basin.

# THE ANTHROPOLOGICAL WORK OF THOMAS A. LEE JR.

## MY LAST CONVERSATION WITH THOMAS ARVOL LEE, SCHOLAR OF CHIAPA VIEJO[15]

**Víctor Manuel Esponda Jimeno**
Cuerpo Académico Patrimonio Sociocultural
CESMECA-UNICACH

### INTRODUCTION

Since his arrival long ago to Chiapas (June of 1962), Tom had a special interest in the history and culture of the Chiapeños (now referred to as "Chiapacorceños, a curious demonym[16]") and to them he dedicated a good part of his studies and life's experiences; he loved the chocolate pozol, cochito al horno, tasajo with or without pepita, as well as meringue cookies.[17] While learning to communicate better in Castilian Spanish—something which he was never completely successful at, given his carelessness, mischievousness, and impulsive use of popular slang—he dedicated his time to the exploration of the surroundings and readings of the legendary places that gave our province its name. Lee knew many people in Chiapa de Corzo, was himself popular, and it was there he learned the bad manners he would imitate in his own peculiar style. In fact, he spent time with the workers from his archaeological projects from whom he learned to communicate in "Chiapaneco," using its idioms, regional expressions, and his unique sly humor. There he made his first regional linguistic contact. I have many colorful anecdotes about him, and I will share two of them with the audience here today.

During one of the numerous occasions that he was invited to present at a conference, Tom was speaking of the ingenuity and bravery of the ancient Chiapanecos, and while reading that part of the text, he made a mistake and immediately corrected himself, saying "Hou perdón me pendejé" or in much less colorful English, "I made a fool of myself" (repeating a hybridization of what he had been hearing many times from the mouths of the workmen when they were reprimanded by him for doing something incorrect during fieldwork), and everyone in the audience began to laugh and some applauded; he was shocked by this and in a low voice he asked me, "What did I just say?", to which I replied, "Continue and I'll explain later."

On another occasion he asked me if I would accompany him to Tuxtla Gutiérrez to take care of errands and go with him to his dentist by the name of Culebro. We arrived at his office and immediately the receptionist had him enter the interior room where he was to be attended. The odontologist anesthetized the area in his mouth that he would be working on, and then

---

[15] This work was presented at the 3er Congreso Internacional de la Región Chiapaneca: Evolución Histórica y Cultural, Homenaje a Thomas Arvol Lee, held on October 11, 2013, Chiapa de Corzo. English translation and editing by Mary E. Pye.

[16] Demonym refers to a word that identifies the natives of a particular place that is derived from the name of that place. In this case the place is Chiapa de Corzo, hence "Chiapacorceños." Chiapa de Corzo was first christened Chiapa de Indios by the Spaniards after the Conquest.

[17] The author is poetic in his phrasing here. First, he lists regional dishes of Chiapas that Tom was partial to, including chocolate pozol, which is a beverage of chocolate and maize, cochito al horno, which is suckling pig traditionally cooked in a large earthen oven, tasajo, which is dried beef served grilled or in a pumpkin seed sauce, and finally "suspiros." Here, he plays on the double meaning of the word "suspiros," being "meringue cookies" or "sighs," preferably from a woman, equating love of food with love of women.

as the dentist was about to start drilling, he said, "If you feel pain, let me know;" he began working and Tom was stoically gesticulating without saying anything, when the receptionist interrupted, telling the doctor he had a phone call; he stopped what he was doing and went to take it. In the interim Tom asked me, "What is destemplar [to cause pain]?" I explained it to him and when the doctor returned to his work and again said "If you feel pain, let me know," Tom replied, "Yes, I felt pain since you started"—a painful lesson for integrating another word into his unique vocabulary.[18]

Apart from his numerous experiences and friendships, Tom bequeathed to the Chiapa de Corzo people the following works:

"Instrumentos musicales de viento de cerámica de Chiapa de Corzo", Kikiriki, año 1, nos. 1/2, 1966, Tuxtla Gutiérrez, Chiapas.

Una exploración del cañón del Sumidero, Boletín No. 8, 1966, editado por la sección 37 del Sindicato de Trabajadores de la Educación, Tuxtla Gutiérrez.
[This first limited and modest piece was published by the "Venustiano Carranza" press in 1966 thanks to the good offices of the now deceased Gaspar Jiménez Pozo, then Secretary General of Section 37 of SNTE[19]; the second edition was corrected and expanded and was published by UNICACH[20] through the Centro de Estudios Superiores de México y Centro América in its Separata del Anuario 1995 [1996] upon the occasion of the creation of the Premio de Chiapas; in 2010 the third edition was published by the state government of Chiapas through the State Secretary of Public Education in its series "Colección Premios Chiapas."]

 "Figurillas antropomorfas de Chiapa de Corzo", Estudios de Cultura Maya, 6, pp. 199-214, 1967. Centro de Estudios Mayas, UNAM.

"Salvamento arqueológico en Chiapa de Corzo", Boletín del INAH, 38, pp. 17-22, 1969. Instituto Nacional de Antropología e Historia, Mexico.

The Artifacts of Chiapa de Corzo, Chiapas, Mexico, Papers of the New World Archaeological Foundation, No. 26, 1969, Brigham Young University, Provo.

"Fiesta del niño florero", Renovación, hebdomadario, comentarista y crítico, época 3, no. 1, 1970, Tuxtla Gutiérrez, Chiapas.

"Época prehispánica," Acala. Un pueblo y un municipio de Chiapas, pp. 48-55, 1988. H. Ayuntamiento del Municipio de Acala; Patronato Fray Bartolomé de las Casas; Centro de Investigaciones Humanísticas de Mesoamérica y el Estado de Chiapas-UNAM y Programa Cultural de las Fronteras.

"Evidencia olmeca en el dominio de Chiapa de Corzo", Segundo y tercer foro de arqueología de Chiapas, pp. 228-235, 1993. Gobierno del Estado de Chiapas, Instituto Chiapaneco de Cultura, Tuxtla Gutiérrez.

"El niño florero. Una tradición chiapaneca", Anuario 2001, Centro de Estudios Superiores de México y Centro América, pp. 161-179, 2003. Universidad de Ciencias y Artes de Chiapas.

Archaeological Salvage at Chiapa de Corzo, Mound 17, Papers of the New World Archaeological Foundation, No. 80, 2016, Brigham Young University, Provo.

## PENDING WORKS

Tom and I spoke almost daily, mostly by phone, since his work in Chiapa de Corzo and Tuxtla Gutiérrez always kept him busy and

---

[18] There is also a bit of word play here. The doctor says "Si destiempla, me avisas;" the word "si" means "if." Tom responds, "Sí destiempla y desde que empezaste;" here the word "sí" means "yes." In both instances, si and sí are pronounced the same.

[19] SNTE is the acronym for Sindicato Nacional de Trabajadores de la Educación

[20] UNICACH is Universidad de Ciencias y Artes de Chiapas

rushed. We spoke of pending items we had planned and those about to be finished.

Of the many things we were planning, I recall the "Sacred Spaces" Project, the geographic coverage for which we had expanded to include methodological approaches, as a needed requirement for proving some hypotheses that we had outlined around "sacredness" and its validity having derived from its remote antecedents as a fundamental practice in the spheres of what the Marxists call "superstructures."

The "Camino Real" Project that he was working on with diligence and resolution for many years was a constant topic in our discussions; we had agreed to expand his spatial coverage and I told Tom that he needed to explore the section of the road from the border with Oaxaca, through long and difficult passes, to some of the haciendas in the ancient valley of the Xiquipilas [today Jiquipilas]. This he agreed with and said he would communicate with Mario Uvence, then Director of CONECULTA, that this section of the road had not been sufficiently considered.

We had pending—a matter always in the forefront of our interests—the completion of the Magna Bibliografía Chiapaneca de Ciencias Sociales, which currently contains 16,000 references, classified by ethnicity, region, topic and subtopic, organized chronologically and by name. We had announced and argued in a modest work some years ago that it would be a magnificent tool for planning and doing documentary studies, as well as a formidable guide for launching various types of projects, given that one would have basic references (what had been done, who had done it, with what focuses, in which places, time periods, areas, etc.) to begin new directions, signaling what was still missing and should be pursued, as well as act as an index to avoid plagiarism and reiteration.

We were planning to investigate some archaeological sites in Cintalapa and Jiquipilas, which for some reason were not covered in our earlier survey.

We outlined a project on ancient industries in Chiapas, emphasizing mining, textiles, dyes and fibers, tobacco and distilleries, and logging as important branches of the state economy in the 18th-19th centuries; we had only worked on the mining component, suspending the project for lack of a budget and institutional support.

I had the satisfaction of checking the pdf version of what would be published as "Música vernácula de Chiapas," which took us some years to finish; the latest version of it was presented at the II Congreso de Etnomusicología in Tuxtla Gutiérrez, November of 2012.

For the Anuario 2010 of CESMECA, an original contribution by Elizabeth Paris, Eric Taladoire, and Tom was published on the singular archaeological site of Moxviquil in the foothills near Ojo de Agua, northwest of San Cristóbal de Las Casas.

We were working on a new volume that would complement two previous works that focused on investigations by some members of the group, Patrimonio Sociocultural del CESMECA-UNICACH; this work would comprise new information on the archaeology, ethnology, history, linguistics, and speleology in the valley of Cintalapa and Jiquipilas

Tom was always restless and looking to keep himself occupied and active, and this, combined with his dispersion, would often lead to him sketching out projects that he would not stick with. He was captivated and delved into various topics: vernacular architecture, ancient communication routes, iconography, ceramic styles, rites and funerary customs, linguistics, in particular the Zoque language, and recently he had become interested in the extinct Chiapanec language which he wanted to rescue and teach in the language programs at UNICACH. Ambar and Maya codices powerfully called his attention. Among his various projects he wanted to establish site museums at key locations.

His intense activity was one of the causes of his physical and emotional deterioration (ultimately manifested in his exhaustion and anxiety); almost daily he was driving down to Chiapa de Corzo and Tuxtla Gutiérrez from San Cristóbal de Las Casas. The fledging Archaeology program at UNICACH based in Chiapa de Corzo took a great deal of his efforts and health; besides de facto directing the program, he was teaching on a variety of topics. In the history program of the same university he was also giving some classes; in addition, he was in charge of a number of thesis committees and responsible for providing academic advice to students; and if that were not enough, he accepted many invitations to lecture and present at conferences. As a consequence, he was all over the place: one day in Copainalá, the next in Tzimol, Tecpatan, Ocosingo, Tonalá, Comitan, Chicomuselo, Pijijiapan, Las Margaritas, La Concordia, Simojovel, San Fernando, Chachihuitán, Jiquipilas, Tila, Tapachula, etc.

Tom left an infinity of outlines, notes, and projects that should have been taken up and worked on by teams. The valuable legacy of his varied and extensive academic production was complemented by his wide-ranging library, which he created over many years and was made possible by his great efforts and costly expenditure.

### TWILIGHT

The last time I spoke with Tom, he was in my cubicle at CESMECA, Thursday, January 31, 2013; after reaching some agreements and prioritizing some pending issues, he said he was going to Palenque on Friday to accompany the secretary of the School of Archaeology to the funeral of her grandfather. I said that perhaps it wasn't convenient for him to go since we had various standing commitments, and we had to present ourselves on February 4th at a meeting in La Candelaria. He told me he would return on time, and I insisted that he shouldn't go to Palenque; but his decision was set and his date with an ungrateful destiny was confirmed.

I have said to my friends that Tom died doing what he liked to do, his habitual intrepidity led to his death on Monday, the 18th of February, 2013. Tom or Thomas Arvol Lee Whiting came into this world on December 23, 1933, in St. Johns, Arizona; his parents were Thomas Lee Wilkens and Monita [Anita] Whiting Johnson. His life was intense and turbulent; he married a number of times and brought three children into the world: Marc (United States), Anita Hipólita (Chiapas) and Juan Tomás (Chiapas), and he adopted María de Lourdes, sister of Juan Tomás, Gerardo, son of María Lourdes, and Dyane Estefanía, daughter of his last spouse.

Tom summed up his life in Chiapas in the following manner: "…it has given me much, I was given the Premio de Chiapas, even though I didn't deserve it. I am a blessed individual because some institutions have paid me throughout my life to do what I most wanted to do in my life, trying to put name and history to the unknown. However, I do not consider my personal life a total success because I have not been able to answer all of the questions that I have pending. Unfortunately, as a man, I have weaknesses, but I have not failed that much. I have not fulfilled [my word] all the times that I should have, but I feel inside that overall mine was a full and successful life."

His last wish was that at the end of his life, after he was cremated, his ashes be scattered from the Cahuaré quay so that the waters of the majestic Grijalva River would carry him by the ancient and transformed places where his successful Chiapan path had been launched.

# PUBLISHED WORK OF THOMAS A. LEE WHITING, JR.
## compiled by John E. Clark and Mary E. Pye

BYU: Brigham Young University

CESMECA: Centro de Estudios Superiores de Mesoamérica y Centroamérica
(academic unit of UNICACH)

CIHMECH: Centro de Investigaciones Humanísticas de Mesoamérica y el Estado de Chiapas
(academic unit of UNAM which became PROIMMSE in 1998)

CIMSUR: Centro de Investigaciones Multidisciplinarias sobre Chiapas y la Frontera Sur
(academic unit of UNAM based in San Cristóbal de las Casas)

CONACULTA: Consejo Nacional para la Cultura y el Arte
(subsumed into the Secretaría de Cultura, 2015)

CONECULTA: Consejo Estatal para las Culturas y las Artes (of Chiapas)

INAH: Instituto Nacional de Antropología e Historia

NWAF: New World Archaeological Foundation
(also known by its Mexican name Fundación Arqueológico Nuevo Mundo)

PROIMMSE: Programa de Investigaciones Multidisciplinarias sobre Mesoamérica y el Sureste
(academic unit of UNAM which became CIMSUR in 2015)

UNACH: Universidad Autónoma de Chiapas

UNAM: Universidad Nacional Autónoma de México

UNICACH: Universidad de Ciencias y Artes de Chiapas

## I. Works by Thomas A. Lee, Jr., as sole author

LEE, THOMAS A., JR.

1962     The Beals Saddle Site: A Nonconformity. *Plateau* 34(4):113-127.

1964     NA 7696, a Stratified Site in Three Turkey Canyon, Northeastern Arizona. *Plateau* 36(3):73-82.

1966a     Una exploración del cañón del Sumidero. *Boletín* No. 8 de la Sec. 37 of S.N.T.E., Tuxtla Gutiérrez.

1966b     Instrumentos musicales de viento de céramica de Chiapa de Corzo. *Kikiriki* 1(2/3). Tuxtla Gutiérrez.

1967a     Excavation in a Rock Shelter. *Katunob* 6(3):4.

1967b     Figurillas antropomorfas de Chiapa de Corzo. *Estudios de Cultura Maya* 6:199-214.

1968     Fast Acculturation of the Zoque in Chiapas, Tabasco, and Oaxaca. *Bulletin of the International Committee on Urgent Anthropological and Ethnological Research* No. 10:123.

1969a     Apuntes sobre el trabajo del ámbar en Simojovel, Chiapas. *Boletín del INAH* 35:13-19.

1969b     Archaeological Salvage at Chiapa de Corzo, Chiapas, Mexico. Preliminary Report submitted to the Instituto Nacional de Antropología y Historia, Mexico.

1969c     *The Artifacts of Chiapa de Corzo, Chiapas, Mexico.* Papers of the New World Archaeological Foundation, No. 26. BYU, Provo.

1969d     Cuevas secas del Río La Venta, Chiapas (informe preliminar). *Antropología e Historia de Guatemala*, Año 21, 21 (1-2): 23-37. (Expanded and edited in 1985 and published in *Revista de la UNACH*, época 2, No. 1:30-42, Tuxtla Gutiérrez).

1969e     Salvamento Arqueológico en Chiapa de Corzo. *Boletín del INAH* 38 (dic):17-22.

1970     Fiesta del niño floreros. *Renovación, Hebdomadario, Comentarista y Crítico* (3 época) Núm. 1. Tuxtla Gutiérrez.

Figure 123. Tom Lee on an archaeological expedition in 1963 that navigated the Usumacinta River on a rubber raft. Here he is reading one of Teobert Maler's early 1900s research reports on the Usumacinta Valley while exploring San Pablo Cave.

1971    Review of *Bilbao, Guatemala: An Archaeological Study of the Pacific Coast Cotzumalhuapa Region* by Lee A. Parsons. *American Anthropologist* 73(2); 421-422.

1972    *Jme'tik Lubton: Some Modern and Pre-Hispanic Maya Ceremonial Customs in the Highlands of Chiapas, Mexico.* Papers of the New World Archaeological Foundation, No. 29. BYU, Provo.

1973    Secuencia de fases postformativas en Izapa, Chiapas, México. *Estudios de Cultura Maya* 9:75-84.

1974a   The Middle Grijalva Chronology and Ceramic Relationships: A Preliminary Report. In *Mesoamerican Archaeology: New Approaches*, edited by Norman Hammond, pp. 3-20. University of Texas Press, Austin.

1974b   *Mound 4 Excavations at San Isidro, Chiapas, Mexico.* Papers of the New World Archaeological Foundation, No. 34. BYU, Provo.

1974c   Preliminary Report of the 2nd and Final Reconnaissance Season of the Upper Grijalva Basin Maya Project (Jan.-May, 1974). Unpublished manuscript on file with the New World Archaeological Foundation, San Cristóbal de las Casas.

1974d   Terminal Late Classic Settlement Patterns Responses to Demographic and Ecological Pressures in Southern Chiapas: A Sociopolitical Model. Paper presented at the XLI International Congress of Americanists, Mexico City, Mexico.

1975a    The Postclassic People of Chiapas, Mexico. Paper presented at the "BYU Centennial Social Science Symposium, No. 1: Uncovering Mesoamerican Civilization." BYU, Provo.

1975b    The Uppermost Grijalva Basin: A Preliminary Report of a New Archaeological Project. In *Balance y perspectiva de la antropología de Mesoamérica y del norte de México, XIII Mesa Redonda, Vol.2: Arqueología*, pp. 35-47. Sociedad Mexicana de Antropología, Mexico.

1976a    The Coxoh Colonial Project and Coneta, Chiapas, Mexico: A Provincial Maya Village under the Spanish Conquest. *Abstracts of Papers Presented at the Ninth Annual Meeting, Society for Historic Archaeology*, p. 14. The University Museum, Philadelphia.

1976b    The Historical Routes of Northern Chiapas and Tabasco: Hypotheses of their Effect on Cultural Contact. *Atti del XL Congresso Internazionale degli Americanisti, Roma-Genova, 3-10 settembre 1972*. Vol. 4:185-191. Tilgher, Geneva.

1976c    A Preliminary Report of the First Phase of Excavations at Guajilar, Chiapas, Mexico. Unpublished manuscript on file with the New World Archaeological Foundation in Chiapas, Mexico.

1977    El origen del lago Jécameyá, Mescalapa, Chiapas. *Tlalocan* 7(1):367-370.

1978a    The Historical Routes of Tabasco and Northern Chiapas and their Relationship to Early Cultural Developments in Central Chiapas. In *Mesoamerican Communication Routes and Cultural Contacts*, edited by Thomas A. Lee, Jr. and Carlos Navarrete, pp. 49-66. Papers of the New World Archaeological Foundation, No. 40. BYU, Provo.

1978b    Informe Preliminar de la 2a Temporada de Campo, febrero-junio, 1978, del Proyecto de la Zona Guajilar-Niagara.

Reported submitted to Instituto Nacional de Antropología e Historia, Mexico.

1978c    The Origin and Development of Plumbate Ware. *Revista Mexicana de Estudios Antropológicos* 24 (3):287-300.

1979a    Algunos aspectos antropológicos del pueblo Coxoh. Paper presented at the XVI Mesa Redonda of the Sociedad Mexicana de Antropología, Saltillo, Mexico.

1979b    Coapa, Chiapas: A Sixteenth Century Coxoh Maya Village on the Camino Real. In *Maya Archaeology and Ethnohistory*, edited by Norman Hammond and Gordon R. Willey, pp. 202-222. University of Texas Press, Austin.

1979c    Coapa, Municipio de Trinitaria, Chiapas (Tr-162). Report of the second season of excavation submitted to the Instituto Nacional de Antropología e Historia, Mexico.

1979d    Domestic Patterns of the Colonial Coxoh. Paper presented at the XVI Mesa Redonda of the Sociedad Mexicana de Antropología, Saltillo, Mexico.

1979e    Early Colonial Coxoh Maya Syncretism in Chiapas, Mexico. *Estudios de Cultura Maya* 12:93-109.

1980a    Algunos aspectos antropológicos del pueblo coxoh. In *Sociedad Mexicana de Antropología, XVI Reunión de Mesa Redonda, Saltillo, Coahuila, del 9 al 14 de septiembre de 1979*. Vol. 2: 415-428. Sociedad Mexicana de Antropología, Saltillo.

1980b    Comment on "Precolumbian Old World Coins in America" by Jeremiah Epstein. *Current Anthropology* 21(1):15.

1980c    Commentary on the symposium "Intercambio y rutas comerciales prehispánicas en la zona Maya." In *Sociedad Mexicana de Antropología, XVI Reunión de Mesa Redonda,*

*Saltillo, Coahuila, del 9 al 14 de septiembre de 1979*, Vol. 1:317-323. Sociedad Mexicana de Antropología, Saltillo.

1980d    The Long Path to Extinction: Colonial Coxoh Maya of Chiapas, Mexico. *Mexikon* 11(2):21-24.

1980e    *Tuxtla-Montebello: Una antigua ruta de comunicación.* UNACH, Tuxtla Gutiérrez.

1981      *New World Archaeological Foundation Obra: 1952-1980.* NWAF, Provo and San Cristóbal de las Casas, Chiapas.

1982a    Dos esculturas olmecas del valle del río Grijalva. *Revista Mexicana de Estudios Antropológicos* 28:67-77.

1982b    Review of *Bibliografía sumaria para el estudio de vidrio (Colección Científica)* by Gonzalo López Cervantes. *Historical Archaeology* 17(1):109.

1982c    Review of *The Quiche Maya of Utatlán: The Evolution of a Highland Guatemalan Kingdom*, by Robert Carmack. *American Antiquity* 47(3):690-692.

1983a    Frans Blom y la antropología contemporánea de los mixe-zoques y mayas. In *Antropología e historia de los mixe-zoques y mayas: Homenaje a Frans Blom*, edited by Lorenzo Ochoa and Thomas A. Lee, Jr., pp. 87-95. UNAM and NWAF, Mexico.

1983b    Informe preliminar de la John Geddings Gray Memorial Expedición a America llevado a cabo por la Tulane Universidad de New Orléans, Louisiana, 1928 (translation). In *Antropología e historia de los mixe-zoques y mayas: Homenaje a Frans Blom*, edited by Lorenzo Ochoa and Thomas A. Lee, Jr., pp. 103-128. UNAM and NWAF, Mexico.

1983c    Prologue. In *Antropología e historia de los mixe-zoques y mayas: Homenaje a Frans Blom*, edited by Lorenzo Ochoa and Thomas A. Lee, Jr. UNAM and NWAF, Mexico.

1984a    Arqueología chiapaneca: Cuna y encrucijada. *Numero Uno.* Tuxtla Gutiérrez.

1984b    La arqueología histórica maya en Chiapas: Un inicio. In *Sociedad Mexicana de Antropología, XVII Mesa Redonda, Investigaciones Recientes en el Área Maya.* Vol. 2:195-205. Sociedad Mexicana de Antropología, San Cristóbal de las Casas.

1984c    El asentamiento humano precolombino del valle de Hueyzacatlán. In *San Cristóbal y sus alrededores*, Vol. 2:151-159. Gobierno del estado de Chiapas, Tuxtla Gutiérrez.

1984d    Investigaciones arqueológicas recientes del clásico, postclásico y colonial Maya en Chiapas: Resumen e implicaciones. In *Sociedad Mexicana de Antropología, XVII Mesa Redonda, Investigaciones Recientes en el Área Maya.* Vol. 2:113-130. Sociedad Mexicana de Antropología, San Cristóbal de las Casas.

1985a    *Los codices mayas.* Introduction and Bibliography. UNACH, Tuxtla Gutiérrez.

1985b    Cuevas secas del río La Venta, Chiapas *Revista de la UNACH*, época 2, 1:30-42 (expanded version of Lee 1969).

1985c    Ramifications of the Colonial Coxoh Maya Household Group. In *Estudios del reino de Guatemala: Homenaje a S. D. Markman*, edited by D. T. Kinkead, pp. 61-76. Escuela de Estudios Hispano-americanos de Sevilla, Seville.

1986a    En el sendero de la escritura maya. *Anuario 1*, pp. 159-170. Centro de Estudios Indígenas, UNACH, Tuxtla Gutiérrez.

1986b    La lingüística histórica y la arqueología de los zoque-mixe-popolucas. In *Memorias de la Primera Reunión de Investigadores del Área Zoque*, pp. 7-36. Centro de Estudios Indígenas, UNACH, Tuxtla Gutiérrez.

1988a    Época prehispánica. In *Acala: un pueblo y un municipio de Chiapas*. H. Ayuntamiento Municipal de Acala, Patronato Fray Bartolomé de Las Casas, CIHMECH, and el Gobierno del estado de Chiapas, Tuxtla Gutiérrez.

1988b    Preface. In *Introduction to the Ethnoarchaeology of the Chiapas Maya*, edited by Thomas A. Lee, Jr, and Brian Hayden, pp. iii-iv. Papers of the New World Archaeological Foundation, No. 56. BYU, Provo.

1989a    La arqueología de los altos de Chiapas: Un estudio contextual. *Mesoamérica* 18:257-293.

1989b    Chiapas and the Olmec. In *Regional Perspectives on the Olmec*, edited by Robert J. Sharer and David C. Grove, pp. 198-226. Cambridge University Press, Cambridge.

1989c    Rearticulación del Camino Real de Chiapas a Guatemala. *Ancorasur: Revista del Instituto Chiapaneco de Cultura*, suplemento 1(2): iii-x. Tuxtla Gutiérrez.

1989d    Rutas históricas de Tabasco y el norte de Chiapas y su relación con los desarrollos culturales tempranos de Chiapas Central. In *Comercio, comerciantes y rutas de intercambio en el México antiguo*, edited by Lorenzo Ochoa, pp. 149-178. Secretaría de Comercio y Fomento Industrial, Mexico.

1990a    Un nuevo complejo de escultura en la planicie costera de Chiapas. *Arqueología* época 2a, 3:57-66.

1990b    El proyecto de reintegración del Camino Real de Chiapas y Guatemala: Marco teórico y estrategias. In *Memorias del Encuentro de Intelectuales: Chiapas-Guatemala*, pp. 35-39. Gobierno del Estado de Chiapas, Tuxtla Gutiérrez.

1990c    Relaciones extra-regionales del complejo cerámico Nichim de Guajilar, Chiapas. Revista de Difusión Científica/Tecnológica y Humanística 1(1):32-36.

1991a    El carnaval de San Fernando, Chiapas: Los motivos de continuidad milenaria. *Anuario 1990*, pp. 119-154. Instituto Chiapaneco de Cultura, Tuxtla Gutiérrez.

1991b    Los cazadores-recolectores y agricultores tempranos en el Alto Grijalva. *Primer Foro de Arqueología de Chiapas*, pp. 131-140. Instituto Chiapaneco de Cultura, Tuxtla Gutiérrez.

1991c    Tres mil años de artesanía en Totolapa, Chiapas. *Anuario 1990*, pp. 204-217. Instituto Chiapaneco de Cultura, Tuxtla Gutiérrez.

1992a    Alberto Ruz Lhuillier: Arqueólogo antropológico. In *Homenaje al Dr. Alberto Ruz Lhuillier en el décimo aniversario de su muerte. Memorias de la Primera Congreso Internacional de Mayistas*, pp. 38-41. UNAM, Mexico.

1992b    La arqueología como ciencia y tecnología al servicio de la cultura. *Tierra y Agua: La antropología de Tabasco* 3:57-63. Villahermosa.

1992c    Los olmecas en Chiapas. In *Encuentro de Intelectuales, Chiapas-Centroamérica*, pp. 131-138. Instituto Chiapaneco de Cultura, Gobierno del Estado de Chiapas, Tuxtla Gutiérrez.

1992d    La vida y la muerte en Copanaguastla. *Revista del Consejo Estatal de Fomento a la Investigación y Difusión de la Cultura* 6:18-21 (febrero-marzo). Tuxtla Gutiérrez.

1993a    Bonampak: Pueblo de muros pintados. *Revista del Consejo Estatal de Fomento a la Investigación y Difusión de la Cultura* 10:17-21 (diciembre). Tuxtla Gutiérrez.

1993b    El Camino Real de Chiapas: Un enlace entre dos pueblos. *Revista de CIHMECH* 3(2):91-102. Tuxtla Gutierrez.

1993c   Evidencia olmeca en el dominio de
Chiapa de Corzo. In *Segundo y Tercer
Foro de Arqueología de Chiapas*,
pp. 228-235. Instituto Chiapaneco
de Cultura, Gobierno del Estado de
Chiapas, Tuxtla Gutiérrez.

1993d   Introducción al Segundo Foro de
Arqueología de Chiapas, In *Segundo
y Tercer Foro de Arqueología
de Chiapas*, pp. 11-12. Instituto
Chiapaneco de Cultura, Gobierno del
Estado de Chiapas, Tuxtla Gutiérrez.

1993e   El Protoclásico: Un problema de
definición. In *Segundo y Tercer Foro
de Arqueología de Chiapas*, pp. 119-
125. Instituto Chiapaneco de Cultura,
Gobierno del Estado de Chiapas, Tuxtla
Gutiérrez.

1993f   Tipos de arqueología vernácula en
Chiapas: Perspectiva histórica cultural.
*Anuario 1992*, pp. 303-324. Instituto
Chiapaneco de Cultura, Tuxtla
Gutiérrez.

1994a   "Arquitectura y Urbanización en el
Chiapas Colonial" de Sidney Markman.
*Revista de CIHMECH* 4(1-2): 203-207.
Tuxtla Gutiérrez.

1994b   La antigua historia de las etnias de
Chiapas. In *Chiapas, una radiografía*,
edited by María Luisa Armendáriz, pp.
55-69. Fondo de Cultura Económico,
Mexico.

1994c   Copanaguastla: Enlace étnico con el
pasado. *Arqueología Mexicana* 8:39-44.

1994d   Los coxoh. In *La población de Chiapas*,
edited by Víctor Manuel Esponda,
pp. 321-341. Instituto Chiapaneca
de Cultura, Gobierno del estado de
Chiapas, Tuxtla Gutiérrez.

1994e   Fronteras arqueológicas y realidades
étnicas en Chiapas. *Sociedad Mexicana
de Antropología, Memorias de la XXII
Mesa Redonda, 11-16 agosto, 1991*,
pp. 41-55. Instituto Chiapaneco de
Cultura, Tuxtla Gutiérrez.

1994f   Investigación antropológica en los
Altos de Chiapas: El caso del proyecto

"El Hombre en la Naturaleza." In
*Homenaje al Profesor Prudencio
Moscoso Pastrana (1913-1991)*,
pp. 149-157. CIHMECH, San Cristóbal
de las Casas.

1994g   *Patrimonio arquitectónico monumental
del pueblo: Preservación para el futuro
del arte religioso colonial de Chiapas.*
Instituto Chiapaneca de Cultura, Tuxtla
Gutiérrez.

1994h   La perspectiva diacrónica y resistencia
étnica en Chiapas. In *El arreglo de los
pueblos indios: La incansable tarea
de reconstitución (Tyi ichajpäntyel
Ityejklumob Lakpi'älob)*, edited
by Jacinto Arias Pérez, pp. 19-
106. Gobierno del estado, Instituto
Chiapaneco de Cultura and Unidad
de Escritores Mayas Zoques, Tuxtla
Gutiérrez.

1994i   Las relaciones extra-regionales del
complejo cerámico Nichim de Guajilar,
Chiapas. *Anuario 1993*, pp. 276-289.
Instituto Chiapaneco de Cultura, Tuxtla
Gutiérrez.

1995    Probabilidades de expansión del
turismo arqueológico y la demanda
de servicios turísticas. *Anuario 1994,
CESMECA*, pp. 302-330. Tuxtla
Gutiérrez.

1996a   Educación formal prehispánica
en Mesoamérica. *Comunidad
Universitaria*, Año 1(3):5-8. Tuxtla
Gutiérrez.

1996b   *Una exploración del cañón del
Sumidero.* Separate issue of *Anuario
1995, CESMECA.* Tuxtla Gutiérrez.

1996c   Introducción a la historia arqueológica
del Soconusco. In *Tapachula: La perla
del Soconusco*, edited by Roberto
Ramos Maza, pp. 40-65. Gobierno del
estado de Chiapas, Tuxtla Gutiérrez.

1996d   Introducción. *Quinto Foro de
Arqueología del Estado de Chiapas*, pp.
11-13. CESMECA, Tuxtla Gutiérrez.

1996e   El parque ecoturístico e histórico de
Coapa: Conservación y producción.

*Cuadernos de Arquitectura y Urbanismo* 2:121-131.

1996f    El patrón de asentamiento del Clásico Tardío en la cuenca superior del río Grijalva: Comentarios en la presentación del libro. *Patrón de asentamiento rural en la región de San Gregorio, Chiapas, para el Clásico Tardío* por Sonia Rivero Torres. In *Quinto Foro de Arqueología del Estado de Chiapas*, pp. 229-232. CESMECA, Tuxtla Gutiérrez.

1996h    Sincretismo coxoh: Resistencia maya colonial en la cuenca superior del río Grijalva. In *Quinto Foro de Arqueología del Estado de Chiapas*, pp. 175-190. CESMECA, Tuxtla Gutiérrez.

1997a    El proyecto arqueológico río La Venta–1997. In *Memorias de la VIII Semana de Investigación Científica*, edited by Pedro de Jesús Ovalle Muños, pp. 11-33. Universidad Autónoma de Chiapas, Tuxtla Gutiérrez.

1997b    Resistencia étnica ante las instituciones coloniales en Chiapas: la selva Lacandona y la cuenca superior del río Grijalva. *Anuario 1996, CESMECA*, pp. 481-497. Tuxtla Gutiérrez.

1998a    Algunas reflexiones sobre el comercio antiguo entre Chiapas y el resto de Mesoamérica. *Antropológicas* 14:38-43.

1998b    Algunas tareas arqueológicas pendientes en la cuenca del río Usumacinta. *Anuario 1997, CESMECA*, pp. 150-154. Tuxtla Gutiérrez.

1998c    El camino real Chiapas a Guatemala como estrategia teórico y práctico para rescatar el patrimonial cultural del centro de Chiapas. *Primer Congreso Nacional de Arqueología Histórica, Memoria, Oaxaca*, edited by Enrique Fernández Dávila y Susana Gómez Serafín, pp. 294-302. INAH, Mexico.

1998d    El cañón río La Venta en la historia zoque. In *Cultura y etnicidad zoque: Nuevos enfoques en la investigación social de Chiapas*, edited by Dolores Aramoni, Thomas A. Lee, and Miguel Lisbona, pp. 47-61. UNICACAH and UNACH, Tuxtla Gutiérrez.

1998e    Instrumentos musicales prehispánicos en Chiapas. In *Fin de siglo: Arte, ciencia, literatura*. Año 1 (1):14-25 (abril-mayo) Tuxtla Gutierrez.

1998f    The Maya Codices. In *The Mayas: 3000 Years of Civilization*, edited by Mercedes de la Garza, pp. 206-215. Monclem Ediciones and Bonechi, Mexico and Florence.

1998g    Popol Vuh: Literatura maya congruente con su tiempo y lugar. In *Lecturas*, No. 3, pp. 17-20. Tuxtla Gutiérrez.

1998h    El Proyecto Arqueológico Río La Venta –1997. In *Memoria de la VIII Semana de Investigación Científica*, edited by Pedro de Jesús Ovalle Muñoz, pp. 11-33. UNACH, Tuxtla Gutiérrez.

1998i    Telas antiguas de Chiapas. *Textiles de Chiapas. Arte de México* 19. Mexico.

1998j    Veredas, caminos reales y vías fluviales: Rutas antiguas de comunicación en Chiapas. In *Rutas de intercambio en Mesoamérica. III Coloquio Pedro Bosch Gimpera*, edited by Evelyn C. Rattray, pp. 239-258. UNAM, Mexico.

1999a    Algunas tareas arqueológicas pendientes en la cuenca del río Usumacinta. In *Fin de Siglo: Arte, Ciencia, Literatura*. Año 2, 1 (4):43-46. Tuxtla Gutiérrez.

1999b    La cerámica del río La Venta. In *Río La Venta, Tesoro de Chiapas*, edited by Giovanni Badino, Alvise Belotti, Tullio Bernabei, Antonio De Vivo, and Italo Giulivo, pp. 175-178. Associazione La Venta, CONECULTA, and Tipografía Turra, Padua.

1999c    Los codices mayas. In *Los mayas: 3000 años de civilización*, edited by Mercedes de la Garza, pp. 207-215. Monclem Ediciones and Bonechi, Mexico and Florence.

1999d    Don Faustino Miranda y "La Vegetación de Chiapas." *Fin de Siglo: Arte, Ciencia, Literatura* Año 2, 1(6):3-4. Tuxtla Gutiérrez.

1999e    Fray Francisco Ximénez y su obra "Historia de la Provincia de San Vicente de Chiapas y Guatemala de la Orden de Predicadores." *Cartelera, La Ruta Cultural* 8(mayo):15. Tuxtla Gutiérrez.

1999f    Historia de la investigación arqueológica. In *Río La Venta, Tesoro de Chiapas*, edited by Giovanni Badino, Alvise Belotti, Tullio Bernabei, Antonio De Vivo, and Italo Giulivo, pp. 149-152. Associazione La Venta, CONECULTA, and Tipografía Turra, Padua.

1999g    History of the Archaeological Research. In *Río La Venta, Treasure of Chiapas*, edited by Giovanni Badino, Alvise Belotti, Tullio Bernabei, Antonio De Vivo, and Italo Giulivo, pp. 149-152. Associazione La Venta, CONECULTA, and Tipografía Turra, Padua.

1999h    Parques estatales y recorridas arqueológicas: Protección y producción del patrimonial cultural. *Cartelera, La Ruta Cultural* 9:13-15.

1999i    Prólogo. In *Viaje de Fray Alonso Ponce por tierras de Chiapas, Siglo XVI*, by Antonio de Ciudad Real. Gobierno del estado de Chiapas and CONACULTA, Tuxtla Gutiérrez.

1999j    Prólogo. In *Los zoques antiguos de San Isidro*, by Gareth W. Lowe. Serie de Libros de Chiapas. Consejo Estatal para la Cultura y las Artes, Tuxtla Gutiérrez.

1999k    El proyecto arqueológico. In *Río La Venta, Tesoro de Chiapas*, edited by Giovanni Badino, Alvise Belotti, Tullio Bernabei, Antonio De Vivo, and Italo Giulivo, pp. 143-144. Associazione La Venta, CONECULTA, and Tipografía Turra, Padua.

1999l    Río La Venta y la cultura zoque. In *Río La Venta, Treasure of Chiapas*, edited by Giovanni Badino, Alvise Belotti, Tullio Bernabei, Antonio De Vivo, and Italo Giulivo, pp. 223-229. Associazione La Venta, CONECULTA, and Tipografía Turra, Padua.

1999m    The Río La Venta Ceramics. In *Río La Venta, Treasure of Chiapas*, edited by Giovanni Badino, Alvise Belotti, Tullio Bernabei, Antonio De Vivo, and Italo Giulivo, pp. 175-178. Associazione La Venta, CONECULTA, and Tipografía Turra, Padua.

1999n    The Río La Venta and the Zoque Culture. In *Río La Venta, Treasure of Chiapas*, edited by Giovanni Badino, Alvise Belotti, Tullio Bernabei, Antonio De Vivo, and Italo Giulivo, pp. 223-229. Associazione La Venta, CONECULTA, and Tipografía Turra, Padua

2000a    El arte y la arqueología del cañón del río La Venta, Chiapas. In *Las culturas de Chiapas en el periodo prehispánico*, edited by Dúrdica Ségota, pp. 121-136. CONECULTA and CONACULTA, Tuxtla Gutiérrez.

2000b    Cuatro rutas, siete viajeros. *Fin de Siglo: Arte, Ciencia, Literatura.* Año 3, 1(8):57. Tuxtla Gutiérrez.

2000c    Il Progetto Archeologico Río La Venta (Chiapas, Messico): Risultati delle Campagne 1997-98. In *Studi Americanistici*, edited by Luciano Gallinari, pp. 209-233. Instituto sui Rapporti Italo-Iberici, Consiglio Nazionale delle Ricerche, Cagliari, Sardinia.

2000d    K'inich Janab Pakal. *Espacios* 3(16):6-7.

2000e    La importancia de la investigación del patrimonio cultural y acciones en ella para el futuro. *Fin de Siglo: Arte, Ciencia, Literatura* Año 3, 1(10):12-13. Tuxtla Gutiérrez.

2000f    Una aproximación a los problemas cuantitativas de los museos de Chiapas. *Fin de Siglo: Arte, Ciencia, Literatura* Año 3, 1(10):3-4. Tuxtla Gutiérrez.

2001    El camino real de Chiapas a Guatemala. *Arqueología Mexicana* 50(jul-ago):50-55.

2002    Historia breve de las rutas de comunicación alrededor de Comitán. *Tertulia* 3:3-9.

2003c   Informe de Investigaciones de las calas arquitectónicas en el conjunto Iglesia – Convento de Tecpatan, Chiapas. Report submitted to Instituto Nacional de Antropología e Historia, Mexico, and the Museo Arqueológico del Estado, Tuxtla Gutiérrez.

2003a   El niño florero: Una tradición chiapaneca. *Anuario 2001 CESMECA*, pp. 161-179. Tuxtla Gutiérrez.

2003b   A Preliminary Folk System: Zoque Aesthetics. In *Il Sacro e il Paesaggio nell' America Indigena*, edited by Davide Domenici, Carolina Orsini, Sofia Venturoli, pp. 171-181. Biblioteca di scienze uname 14, Attai del Colloquio Internazionale. L' Universitat di Bologna, Bologna.

2004a   *El ámbar de Chiapas: Historia, ciencia y estética*. Gobierno del estado de Chiapas, Tuxtla Gutiérrez.

2004b   Los olmecas: ¿Una tradición cultural propia o compartida? In *Acercarse y mirar: Homenaje a Beatriz de la Fuente*, edited by María Teresa Uriarte, Leticia Staines Cicero, pp. 167-185. UNAM, Mexico.

2004c   En la orilla del inframundo: El Proyecto Arqueológico Río La Venta (Chiapas) y la arqueología de la selva El Ocote. *Anuario 2002 CESMECA*, pp. 443-473. Tuxtla Gutiérrez.

2005    Chalchiuhtotolin, la gallina de piedra preciosa y la cueva de la Chumpa, Municipio de Jiquipilas, Chiapas. *Liminar: Estudios Sociales y Humanísticos* 6:142-152. Tuxtla Gutiérrez.

2006a   Las calas arquitectónicas del complejo Santo Domingo de Tecpatán, Chiapas. In *Presencia zoque: Una*

*aproximación multidisciplinaria*, edited by Dolores Aramoni C., Thomas A. Lee, and Miguel Lisbona, pp. 297-306. UNICACH, Consejo de Ciencia y Tecnología del Estado de Chiapas, UNACH, and UNAM, Mexico.

2006b   Cambios en la sanidad del pueblo Coxoh durante los siglos XIII al XVII en Chiapas. *Anuario 2005 CESMECA*, pp. 455-474. Tuxtla Gutiérrez.

2006c   *Chiapas arqueológico. (Serie: Lecturas para entender a Chiapas)*. Gobierno del estado de Chiapas, Talleres Gráficos, Tuxtla Gutiérrez. (Reprint of 3 articles, 1992c, 1992d, and 1991c)

2006d   Prólogo al libro *Monumentos de piedra del sur de México*, por Matthew W. Stirling, pp. 15-18. Biblioteca Popular de Chiapas. CONECULTA, Mexico.

2007a   Escultura en la frontera chimalapa. In *Historia, sociedad y ambiente en la cuenca del río Negro frontera Chiapas-Oaxaca*, edited by Carlos Uriel del Carpio Penagos and Thomas A. Lee Whiting, pp. 75-114. UNICACH, Tuxtla Gutiérrez.

2007b   Los olmecas en Chiapas. *Arqueología Mexicana* 87:66-70.

2007c   Prólogo. *Uninquibal ... Socoltenango: Desde San Bartolomé de los Llanos*, por Juan María Morales Avendaño, pp. 1-2. Tuxtla Gutiérrez.

2009    El papel civilizatorio de los olmecas y sus protagonistas, los mixe-zoques en Mesoamérica. In *Medioambiente, antropología e historia y poder regional en el occidente chiapaneco y frontera con Oaxaca*. edited by Thomas A. Lee, Jr., Víctor Manuel Esponda, and Carlos Uriel del Carpio, pp. 67-80. UNICACH, Tuxtla Gutiérrez.

2010a   Los coxoh de la cuenca superior del río Grijalva: ¿Quienes eran? Paper presented at the conference "Arqueología de las Tierras Altas y la Depresión Central de Chiapas,"1, 2 y 3 de diciembre de 2010. Instituto de

Investigaciones Filológicas, UNAM, Mexico.

2010b   *Exploración del cañón del Sumidero.* Segunda edición. Secretaria de Educación Pública and Gobierno del Estado de Chiapas, Tuxtla Gutiérrez.

2011a   La Venta: Un associazione pertinente. *Kur magazine*

16(junio): 23-25. Associazione La Venta, Rome. https://issuu.com/ laventaesplorazionigeografiche/docs/ kur16 (accessed 9/2016)

2011b   *New World Archaeological Foundation, 60th Anniversary*: Breve Resumen Histórico. CESMECA and Editorial Philadelphia, San Cristóbal de Las Casas.

## II. Co-authored works

ARAMONI, DOLORES, THOMAS A. LEE, AND MIGUEL LISBONA (EDITORS)
1998    *Cultura y etnicidad zoque. Nuevos enfoques en la investigación social de Chiapas.* UNICACH and UNACH, Tuxtla Gutiérrez.

2006b   *Presencia zoque: Una aproximación multidisciplinaria.* UNICACH, Consejo de Ciencia y Tecnología del Estado de Chiapas, UNACH, and UNAM, Mexico.

BLAKE, MICHAEL, DOUGLAS D. BRYANT, THOMAS A. LEE, JR., PIERRE AGRINIER, AND SUSANNA M. EKHOLM
2005    Late Classic Ceramics. In *Ceramic Sequence of the Upper Grijalva Region, Chiapas, Mexico*, Part 2, edited by Douglas D. Bryant, John E. Clark, and David Cheetham, pp. 415-547. Papers of the New World Archaeological Foundation, No. 67. BYU, Provo.

BLOM, FRANS, CLARENCE W. WEIANT, AND THOMAS A. LEE
1995    Moxquivil. Manuscript in the archives of the Museo Na Bolom, San Cristóbal de las Casas.

BRYANT, DOUGLAS, D, THOMAS A. LEE, JR., AND MICHAEL BLAKE
2005    Postclassic Ceramics. In *Ceramic Sequence of the Upper Grijalva Region, Chiapas, Mexico*, Part 2, edited by Douglas D. Bryant, John E. Clark, and David Cheetham, pp. 549-625. Papers of the New World Archaeological Foundation, No. 67. BYU, Provo.

CHEETHAM, DAVID AND THOMAS A. LEE, JR.
2005    Cerámica zoque terminal en Chiapa de Corzo: Secuencia, transición y relaciones externas. *Anuario 2004 CESMECA*, pp. 287-315. Tuxtla Gutiérrez.

CLARK, JOHN E., AND THOMAS A. LEE, JR.
1979    A Behavioral Model for the Obsidian Industry of Chiapa de Corzo. *Estudios de Cultura Maya* 12:33-51.

1980    Patrones de comercio en la cuenca del Grijalva, Chiapas. In *Rutas de Intercambio en Mesoamerica y el Norte de Mexico, XVI Reunión de Mesa Redonda, septiembre 1979*, Vol. 2: 339-344, Sociedad Mexicana de Antropología, Saltillo, Coahuila.

1984    Formative Obsidian Exchange and the Emergence of Public Economies in Chiapas, Mexico. In *Trade and Exchange in Early Mesoamerica*, pp. 235-274, edited by Kenn Hirth. University of New Mexico Press, Albuquerque.

1990    Intercambio de obsidiana y las primeras economías públicas en Chiapas, Mexico. In *Nuevos enfoques en el estudio de la lítica*, edited by D. Soto de Arechavaleta, pp. 347-404. Instituto de Investigaciones Antropologicas, UNAM, Mexico.

2007    The Changing Role of Obsidian Exchange in Central Chiapas. In *Archaeology, Art, and Ethnogenesis in Mesoamerican Prehistory: Papers in Honor of Gareth W. Lowe*, edited by Lynneth S. Lowe and Mary E. Pye, pp. 109-159. Papers of the New World Archaeological Foundation, No. 68, BYU, Provo.

2013    *Minor Excavations in Lower Izapa.* Papers of the New World Archaeological Foundation, No. 75. BYU, Provo.

CLARK, JOHN E., THOMAS A. LEE, JR., AND DOUGLAS DONNE BRYANT
2005    Introducing the Grijalva Maya Project. In *Ceramic Sequence of the Upper Grijalva Region, Chiapas, Mexico,* edited by Douglas D. Bryant, John E. Clark, and David Cheetham, pp. 1-20. Papers of the New World Archaeological Foundation, No. 67. Brigham Young University, Provo.

CLARK, JOHN E., THOMAS A. LEE, JR., AND TAMARA SALCEDO
1989    The Distribution of Obsidian. In *Ancient Economies of the Soconusco: The Prehistory and History of the Economic Development in the Coastal Lowlands of Chiapas, Mexico,* edited by Barbara Voorhies, pp. 268-284. University of Utah Press, Salt Lake City.

1991    La distribución de la obsidiana. In *La economía del antiguo Soconusco, Chiapas,* edited by Barbara Voorhies, ed., and translated by Raúl del Moral, pp. 131-331. UNAM and UNACH, Mexico.

CLARK, JOHN E., GARETH W. LOWE, AND THOMAS A. LEE, JR.
2015    The Malpaso Project and Zoque Prehistory. In *Reconnaissance and Excavations in the Malpaso Basin, Chiapas, Mexico,* edited by Thomas A. Lee, Jr., Carlos Navarrete, and John E. Clark. Papers of the New World Archaeological Foundation, No. 78, pp. 172-224. BYU, Provo.

DOMENICI, DAVIDE, AND THOMAS A. LEE
1998    Proyecto Arqueológico Río La Venta: Informe Final de la Campaña 1998. Annual report submitted to INAH, Mexico.

1999    Proyecto Arqueológico Río La Venta: Informe Final de la Campaña 1999. Annual report submitted to INAH, Mexico.

1999    Il Progetto Archeologico Río La Venta (Chiapas, Messico): Risultati delle Campangne 1997-98. In *Studi Americanistici,* pp. 223-233.

2000    Proyecto Arqueológico Río La Venta: Informe Final de la Campaña 2000. Annual report submitted to INAH, Mexico.

2001    Proyecto Arqueológico Río La Venta: Informe Final de la Campaña 2001. Annual report submitted to INAH, Mexico.

2002    Proyecto Arqueológico Río La Venta: Informe Final de la Campaña 2002. Annual report submitted to INAH, Mexico.

2003    Proyecto Arqueológico Río La Venta: Informe Final de la Campaña 2003. Annual report submitted to INAH, Mexico.

2003    El Contexto. In Proyecto Arqueológico Río La Venta: Informe Final de la Campaña 2003, edited by Davide Dominici and Thomas A. Lee, Jr., pp. 4-18. Annual report submitted to INAH, Mexico.

2004    En la orilla del inframundo: El Proyecto Arqueológico Río La Venta (Chiapas) y la arqueología de la selva El Ocote. *Anuario 2002 CESMECA,* pp. 443-474.

2009    Periodización y desarrollo cultural del área río La Venta, Chiapas. In *Cronología y periodización en Mesoamérica y el norte de México: V Coloquio Bosch-Gimpera,* edited by Annick Daneels, pp. 405-433. UNAM, Mexico.

2012    Classic and Postclassic Zoque Settlement Patterns and Ritual Practices along the Middle La Venta River (Chiapas, Mexico). In *Arqueología reciente de Chiapas: Encuentro Celebrado en el 60°*

*Aniversario de la Fundación Arqueológica Nuevo Mundo*, edited by L. Lowe and M. Pye, pp. 69-86. Papers of the New World Archaeological Foundation, No. 72. BYU, Provo.

DOMENICI, DAVIDE, THOMAS A. LEE, AND LORENZO ZURLA
2012     Baños de vapor monumentales en la cultura zoque del Clásico Tardío. Paper presented at the Symposium Arqueología, historia y ecología de Chiapas y Oaxaca: hacia un diálogo multidisciplinario, 54th International Congress of Americanists, Vienna, Austria, July 25-20.

ESPONDA, VÍCTOR MANUEL
2014     'La cueva de Monte Virgen, Chalchihuitán, Chiapas: un espacio sagrado natural de continuidad cultural prehispánica,' de Thomas Arvol Lee Whiting. *Liminar: Estudios Sociales y Humanísticos* 12(1). http://www.scielo.org.mx/scielo.php?script=sci_arttext&pid=S1665-80272014000100013, accessed 9/2016.

ESPONDA, VÍCTOR MANUEL AND THOMAS LEE W.
1996     Representaciones arquitectónicos precolombinos de Santo Ton, Chiapas, México. *Anuario 1995 CESMECA*, pp. 382-443. Tuxtla Gutiérrez.

KOLPAKOVA, ALLA, AND THOMAS A. LEE
2013     Impresiones de semillas en la cerámica Cuadros-Jocotal del Soconusco como reflejo de antiguos rituos agrícolas. In *Religión maya: Rasgos y desarollo histórico*, edited by Alejandro Sheseña. Colección Selva Negra, UNICACH, Tuxtla Gutiérrez.

LAMBERT, JOSEPH B., JAMES S. FRYE, THOMAS A. LEE, JR., CHRISTOPHER J. WELCH, AND GEORGE O. POINAR, JR.
1989     Analysis of Mexican Amber by Carbon-13 NMR Spectroscopy. In *Archaeological Chemistry IV*, edited by R. O. Allen, pp. 381-388. American Chemical Society, Washington, D. C.

LEE, THOMAS A., JR., AND DOUGLAS D. BRYANT
1977     A Preliminary Report of Archaeological Investigations at Los Encuentros, Chiapas (Tr-54). Report submitted to Instituto Nacional de Antropología e Historia, Mexico.

1988     The Colonial Coxoh Maya. In *Ethnoarchaeology Among the Highland Maya of Chiapas, Mexico*, edited by Thomas A. Lee, Jr., and Brian Hayden, pp. 5-106. Papers of the New World Archaeological Foundation, No. 56. BYU, Provo.

1996     Patrones domésticos del Posclásico Tardío en la cuenca superior del río Grijalva. *Quinto Foro de Arqueología del Estado de Chiapas*, pp. 53-68. CESMECA, Tuxtla Gutiérrez.

LEE, THOMAS A., AND DAVID CHEETHAM,
2008     Lengua y escritura olmeca. In *Olmeca, balance y perspectivas: Memoria de la Primera Mesa Redonda*, edited by M. T. Uriarte and R. B. González Lauck, Vol. 2:695-713. UNAM, INAH, Fundación Arqueológica Nuevo Mundo, Mexico.

LEE, THOMAS A., JR., AND JOHN E. CLARK
1988     Oro, tela y xute: Investigaciones arqueológicas en la región Camcum, Colonia Las Delicias, Chiapas. *Arqueología* 4:7-46.

2015     Excavations along the Totopac and Grijalva Rivers. In *Reconnaissance and Excavations in the Malpaso Basin, Chiapas, Mexico*, edited by T. A. Lee, C. Navarrete, and J. E. Clark, pp. 137-170. Papers of the New World Archaeological Foundation, No. 78. BYU, Provo.

2015     Notes on the Ceramics and Artifacts. In *Reconnaissance and Excavations in the Malpaso Basin, Chiapas, Mexico*, edited by T. A. Lee, C. Navarrete, and J. E. Clark, pp. 119-136. Papers of the New World Archaeological Foundation, No. 78. BYU, Provo.

2016     *Chiapa de Corzo, Mound 17: Comparative Analysis of a Salvage*

*Excavation.* Papers of the New World Archaeological Foundation, no. 80.

LEE, THOMAS A., JR., AND ÁLVARO DE LA CRUZ LÓPEZ BRAVO
1998    La fundación colonial de Chicomuselo, Chiapas. *Primer Congreso Nacional de Arqueología Histórica, Memoria, Oaxaca, 1997,* edited by E. Fernández Dávila and S. Gomez Serafin, pp. 317-325. CONACULTA and INAH, Mexico.

LEE, THOMAS A., AND VÍCTOR MANUEL ESPONDA JIMENO (EDITORS)
2014    *Música vernácula de Chiapas: Antología.* UNICACH and CONECULTA, Tuxtla Gutiérrez.

LEE, THOMAS A., VÍCTOR MANUEL ESPONDA, AND CARLOS URIEL DEL CARPIO (EDITORS)
2009    *Medioambiente, antropología e historia y poder regional en el occidente chiapaneco y frontera con Oaxaca.* UNICACH, Tuxtla Gutiérrez.

LEE, THOMAS A. LEE, JR., AND BRIAN HAYDEN (EDITORS)
1988    *Introduction to the Ethnoarchaeology of the Chiapas Maya.* Papers of the New World Archaeological Foundation, No. 56. BYU, Provo.

LEE, THOMAS A., JR., AND BRIAN HAYDEN
1988    *San Pablo Cave and El Cayo on the Usumacinta River, Chiapas, Mexico.* Papers of the New World Archaeological Foundation, No. 53. BYU, Provo.

1987    Preface. In *Lithic Studies among the Contemporary Highland Maya,* edited by Brian Hayden, pp. viii-xii. University of Arizona Press, Tucson.

LEE, THOMAS A., JR., FANNY LÓPEZ JIMÉNEZ, VÍCTOR M. ESPONDA, DAVIDE DOMENICI, AND CARLOS U. DEL CARPIO PENAGOS
2007    Escultura en la frontera chimalapa. In *Historia, sociedad y ambiente en la cuenca del Río Negro frontera Chiapas-Oaxaca,* edited by C. U. del Carpio Penagos and T. A. Lee, pp. 75-114. UNICACH, Tuxtla Gutiérrez.

LEE, THOMAS A., JR., AND GARETH W. LOWE
1968    La situación arqueológica de la escultura de Izapa, Chiapas, México. *Boletín* No. 14 of the Sec. 37 of S.N.T.E. Tuxtla Gutiérrez.

LEE, THOMAS A, JR., GARETH W. LOWE, AND PIERRE AGRINIER
1987    Román Piña Chán y la arqueología de Chiapas. In *Homenaje a Román Piña Chán,* edited by Barbro Dahlgren, Carlos Navarrete, Mari Carmen Serra Puche, Yoko Sugiura, pp. 121-129 UNAM, Mexico.

LEE, THOMAS A., JR., AND SIDNEY MARKMAN
1977    The Coxoh Colonial Project and Coneta, Chiapas, Mexico: A Provincial Maya Village Under the Spanish Conquest. *Historical Archaeology* 2:56-66.

1979    Coxoh Maya Acculturation in Colonial Chiapas: A Necrotic Archaeological-Ethnohistorical Model. *Actes du XLII Congrés International des Américanistes,* vol. 8:57-66. Congrés du Centenaire, Paris.

LEE, THOMAS A., JR., AND D. MENDOZA, L. TORRES, L. CARAPÍA, M. F. FRANCO, AND V. RODRÍQUEZ
2000    Analysis by SEM, EDS and XRF of Mineral and Soil Belonging to a Colonial Oven from Jolentón, Chiapas. *Antropología y Técnica* 6, Arqueometría, Nueva Época, pp. 49-58.

LEE, THOMAS A., AND AYAX MORENO
2008    Esculturas mayas del sitio de Cucalhuitz, municipio del Bosque y de San Juan de la Libertad, Chiapas. In *Estudios del patrimonio cultural de Chiapas,* edited by Alejandro Sheseña, Sophia Pincemin, and Carlos Uriel del Carpio, pp. 23-36. UNICACH, Tuxtla Gutiérrez.

LEE, THOMAS A., JR., AND CARLOS NAVARRETE (EDITORS)
1978    *Mesoamerican Communication Routes and Cultural Contacts.* Papers of the New World Archaeological Foundation, No. 40. BYU, Provo.

2015    *Reconnaissance and Excavations in the Malpaso Basin, Chiapas, Mexico.* Papers of the New World Archaeological Foundation, No.78. BYU, Provo.

LEE, THOMAS A., JR., AND CARLOS NAVARRETE
2015    Background to the Surveys. In *Reconnaissance and Excavations in the Malpaso Basin, Chiapas, Mexico.* Papers of the New World Archaeological Foundation, No. 74, edited by Thomas A. Lee, Jr., Carlos Navarrete, and John E. Clark, pp.1-4. BYU, Provo.

LEE, THOMAS A., JR., CARLOS NAVARRETE, PIERRE AGRINIER, AND SUSANNA EKHOLM
2015    Archaeological Sites of the Malpaso Basin. In *Reconnaissance and Excavations in the Malpaso Basin, Chiapas, Mexico.* Papers of the New World Archaeological Foundation, No. 74, edited by Thomas A. Lee, Jr., Carlos Navarrete, and John E. Clark, pp. 5-118. BYU, Provo.

LEE, THOMAS A., JR., KIPP VANAKEN, AND DOUGLAS DONNE BRYANT
2005    Colonial Ceramics. In *Ceramic Sequence of the Upper Grijalva Region, Chiapas, Mexico*, Part 2, edited by Douglas D. Bryant, John E. Clark, and David Cheetham, pp. 627-650. Papers of the New World Archaeological Foundation, No. 67. BYU, Provo.

LEE WHITING, THOMAS A., LUIS ALBERTO VARGAS AND ANDRÉS DEL ÁNGEL
1994    El camino real de Chiapas: Enlace entre tiempos y pueblos. *Revista de CIHMECH* 3(2): 91-102. Mexico.

LOWE, GARETH W., THOMAS A. LEE, JR., AND EDUARDO MARTINEZ ESPINOSA
1982    *Izapa: An Introduction to the Ruins and Monuments.* Papers of the New World Archaeological Foundation, No. 31. BYU, Provo.

2000    *Izapa: Una introducción a las ruinas y los monumentos.* Gobierno del Estado de Chiapas, CONECULTA, UNICACH and Fundación Arqueológica Nuevo Mundo, Tuxtla Gutiérrez.

NAVARRETE, CARLOS, AND THOMAS A. LEE, JR.
1969    Apuntes sobre el trabajo del ámbar en Simojovel, Chiapas. *Boletín del INAH* 35:13-19.

NAVARRETE, CARLOS, THOMAS A. LEE, JR., AND CARLOS SILVA
1993    *Un catálogo de frontera: Esculturas, petroglifos y pinturas de la región media del Grijalva, Chiapas.* Centro de Estudios Mayas, UNAM, Mexico.

OREFICI, GIUSEPPE, THOMAS A. LEE, AND DAVIDE DOMENICI
1999    The Archaeological Project. In *Río La Venta, Treasure of Chiapas*, edited by Giovanni Badino, Alvise Belotti, Tullio Bernabei, Antonio De Vivo, and Italo Giulivo, pp. 142-148. Associazione La Venta, CONECULTA, and Tipografía Turra, Padua.

OREFICI, GIUSEPPE, ELVINA PIERI, THOMAS A. LEE, ELISEO LINARES, AND CARLOS SILVA
1998    Proyecto Arqueológico Río La Venta: Informe Final de la Temporada 1997. Report submitted to INAH, Mexico.

PARIS, ELIZABETH H., ERIC TALADOIRE, AND THOMAS A. LEE, JR.
2013    Estatus, poder y construcción del paisaje en el centro monumental de Moxviquil, Chiapas, México. *Anuario 2011, CESMECA*, pp. 13-48. Tuxtla Gutiérrez.

2015    Return to Moxviquil: Form and Function in a Small Maya City. *Ancient Mesoamerica* 26(1): 81-112.

RIQUELME, FRANCISCO, JESÚS ALVARADO-ORTEGA, MARIO RAMOS-ARIAS, MIGUEL HERNÁNDEZ, ISABELLE LE DEZ, THOMAS A LEE-WHITING, AND JOSÉ LUIS RUVALCABA-SIL
2014    A Fossil Stemmiulid Millipede (Diplomada: Stemmiulida) from the Miocene Amber of Simojovel, Chiapas, Mexico. *Historical Biology* 26(4): 415-427.

SANTIAGO LASTRA, GLORIA DE LOS ÁNGELES, AND THOMAS A. LEE, JR.
2012    La arquitectura como aproximación a la etnicidad grupal: Los zoques

de Chiapas. *Temas Antropológicos, Revista Científica de Investigaciones Regionales* 35(1): 171-194. Merida.

SECHSEÑA, ALEJANDRO, AND THOMAS A. LEE, JR.
2004    Yugo incrustado con glifos mayas procedente de los alrededores de Chilón, Chiapas. *Mexicon* 26(6):127-132.

URIEL DEL CARPIO, CARLOS, AND THOMAS A. LEE (EDITORS)
2007    *Historia, sociedad y ambiente en la cuenca del Río Negro frontera Chiapas-Oaxaca.* UNICACH, Tuxtla Gutiérrez.

# REFERENCES CITED

AGRINIER, PIERRE

1964    *The Archaeological Burials at Chiapa de Corzo and Their Furniture.* Papers of the New World Archaeological Foundation, No. 16. BYU, Provo.

1970    *Mound 20, Mirador, Chiapas, Mexico.* Papers of the New World Archaeological Foundation, No. 28. BYU, Provo.

1975a    *Mound 1A, Chiapa de Corzo, Chiapas, Mexico.* Papers of the New World Archaeological Foundation, No. 37. BYU, Provo.

1975b    *Mounds 9 and 10 at Mirador, Chiapas, Mexico.* Papers of the New World Archaeological Foundation, No. 39. BYU, Provo.

2000    *Mound 27 and the Middle Preclassic Period at Mirador, Chiapas, Mexico.* Papers of the New World Archaeological Foundation, No. 58. BYU, Provo.

2014    *Mound 1 at Ocozocoautla, Chiapas, Mexico.* Papers of the New World Archaeological Foundation, No. 76. BYU, Provo.

AGRINIER, PIERRE, DAVID CHEETHAM, AND GARETH W. LOWE

2000    Appendix 1: Three Early Ceramic Complexes from Miramar, Chiapas, Mexico. In *Mound 27 and the Middle Preclassic Period at Mirador, Chiapas, Mexico*, by Pierre Agrinier. Papers of the New World Archaeological Foundation, No. 58. BYU, Provo.

AGRINIER, PIERRE, AND JOHN E. CLARK

2014    Mound 1 in Perspective. In *Mound 1 at Ocozocoautla, Chiapas, Mexico*, by Pierre Agrinier, pp. 81-91. Papers of the New World Archaeological Foundation, No. 76. BYU, Provo.

AGRINIER, PIERRE, AND GARETH W. LOWE

1960b    The Mound 1 Tombs and Burials. In *Mound 1, Chiapa de Corzo, Chiapas, Mexico*, by Gareth W. Lowe and Pierre Agrinier, pp. 39-54. Papers of the New World Archaeological Foundation, No. 8. BYU, Provo.

ANDREWS, E. WYLLYS, V.

1990    The Early Ceramic History of the Lowland Maya. In *Vision and Revision in Maya Studies*, edited by Flora S. Clancey and Peter D. Harrison, pp. 1-19. University of New Mexico Press, Albuquerque.

BACHAND, BRUCE R.

2013    Las fases Formativas de Chiapa de Corzo: Nueva evidencia e interpretaciones. *Estudios de Cultura Maya* XLII:11-52.

BACHAND, BRUCE R., AND LYNNETH S. LOWE

2011    Chiapa de Corzo y los olmecas. *Arqueología Mexicana* 107:74-83.

BACHAND, BRUCE R., EMILIANO GALLAGA, AND LYNNETH S. LOWE

2008    El Proyecto Arqueológico de Chiapa de Corzo: Informe de la Temporada 2008. Report submitted to INAH, Mexico.

BERLIN, HEINRICH

1946    Archaeological Excavations in Chiapas. *American Antiquity* 21:19-28.

BLAKE, MICHAEL

2013    Solar Orientations and Formative Period Site Layouts in SE Mesoamerica: Sunrise and Sunset alignments during the Equinoxes and Solstices. Paper presented at the 78th Annual Meetings of the Society for American Archaeology, Honolulu, April.

BROCKINGTON, DONALD L.

1967    *The Ceramic History of Santa Rosa,
        Chiapas, Mexico.* Papers of the New
        World Archaeological Foundation,
        No. 23. BYU, Provo.

n.d.    Fieldnotes on Chiapa de Corzo.
        Manuscript on file, NWAF, San
        Cristobál de Las Casas.

BRYANT, DOUGLAS D., AND JOHN E. CLARK

1983    Los primeros mayas precolumbinos
        de la cuenca superior del río
        Grijalva. In *Homenaje a Frans Blom:
        Anthropologia e historia de los mixe-
        zoques y mayas*, pp. 223-239, edited by
        Lorenzo Ochoa and Thomas A. Lee Jr.,
        Centro de Estudios Mayas, UNAM,
        Mexico.

2005a   Late Preclassic Ceramics. In *Ceramic
        Sequence of the Upper Grijalva Region,
        Chiapas, Mexico, Part 1*, edited by
        Douglas D. Bryant, John E. Clark, and
        David Cheetham, pp. 265-282. Papers
        of the New World Archaeological
        Foundation, No. 67. BYU, Provo.

2005b   Protoclassic Ceramics. In *Ceramic
        Sequence of the Upper Grijalva Region,
        Chiapas, Mexico, Part 1*, edited by
        Douglas D. Bryant, John E. Clark, and
        David Cheetham, pp. 283-349. Papers
        of the New World Archaeological
        Foundation, No. 67. BYU, Provo.

BRYANT, DOUGLAS D., JOHN E. CLARK, AND DAVID
CHEETHAM, (EDITORS)

2005    *Ceramic Sequence of the Upper
        Grijalva Region, Chiapas, Mexico,*
        2 vols. Papers of the New World
        Archaeological Foundation, No. 67.
        BYU, Provo.

CHASE, ARLEN F., AND DIANE Z. CHASE

1995    External Impetus, Internal Synthesis,
        and Standardization: E Group
        Assemblages and the Crystallization of
        Classic Maya Society in the Southern
        Lowlands. In *Emergence of Maya
        Civilization: The Transition from
        the Preclassic to the Early Classic,*
        edited by Nikolai Grube, pp. 87-101.
        Saurwein, Markt Schwaben, Germany.

CHEETHAM, DAVID, AND THOMAS A. LEE JR.

2005    Cerámica zoque temprana en Chiapa
        de Corzo: Secuencia, transición y
        relaciones externas. *Anuario 2004
        (Centro de Estudios Superiores de
        México y Centroamérica)*:287-315.

CLARK, JOHN E.

1983    A Preclassic Mesoamerican Society:
        Analysis of Francesa-phase Burials
        from Chiapa de Corzo. Paper for a
        Mortuary Seminar at the University
        of Michigan taught by John O'Shea.
        Manuscript on file with the NWAF.

1987    Politics, Prismatic Blades, and
        Mesoamerican Civilization. In *The
        Organization of Core Technology*, pp.
        259-284, edited by Jay K. Johnson
        and Carol A. Morrow pp. 259-284.
        Westview Press, Boulder.

1988    *The Lithic Artifacts of La Libertad,
        Chiapas, Mexico.* Papers of the New
        World Archaeological Foundation,
        No. 52. BYU, Provo.

1997    The Arts of Government in Early
        Mesoamerica. *Annual Review of
        Anthropology.* Vol. 26:211-234.

2000    Los pueblos de Chiapas en el
        Formativo. In *Las culturas de Chiapas
        en el periodo prehispánico*, edited by
        Durdica Segota, pp. 36-59. Consejo
        Estatal para la Cultura y las Artes
        de Chiapas y Consejo Nacional para
        la Cultura y las Artes, Piancoteca
        Editores, Mexico.

2001    Ciudades tempranas olmecas. In
        *Reconstruyendo la ciudad maya: El
        urbanismo en las sociedades antiguas*,
        edited by Andrés Ciudad Ruiz, María
        Josefa I. Ponce de León, and María del
        Carmen Martínez Martínez, pp. 183-
        210. Sociedad Española de Estudios
        Mayas, Madrid.

2008    Cities and Towns of the Olmec. In
        *Encyclopedia of the History of Science,*

Technology, and Medicine in Non-Western Cultures, Vol. 1., 2nd ed., edited by Helaine Selin, pp. 554-558. Springer Verlag.

2013 Some Observations on Preclassic Izapa. In *Minor Excavations in Lower Izapa*, by John E. Clark and Thomas A. Lee pp. 117-148. Papers of the New World Archaeological Foundation, No. 75. BYU, Provo.

2014 Notes on Culture History. In *A Brief Reconnaissance of Three Chiapas Municipalities*, by Fredrick A. Peterson, pp. 217-240. Papers of the New World Archaeological Foundation, No. 77. BYU, Provo.

2016 Western Kingdoms of the Middle Preclassic. In *Early Maya States*, edited by Robert J. Sharer and Loa P. Traxler, pp. 123-224. University of Pennsylvannia Museum of Arcaheology and Anthropology, Philadelphia.

CLARK, JOHN E., BARBARA ARROYO, AND DAVID CHEETHAM

2005 Early Preclassic and Early Middle Preclassic Ceramics. In *Ceramic Sequence of the Upper Grijalva Region, Chiapas, Mexico, Part 1*, edited by Douglas D. Bryant, John E. Clark, and David Cheetham, pp. 20-139. Papers of the New World Archaeological Foundation, No. 67. BYU, Provo.

CLARK, JOHN E., AND ARLENE COLMAN

2012 Structure of the Mesoamerican Universe, from Aztec to Olmec. In *Enduring Motives: The Archaeology of Tradition and Religion in Native America*, edited by Linea Sundstrom and Warren DeBoer, pp. 15-59. University of Alabama Press, Tuscaloosa.

2014 Dressed Ears as Comeliness and Godliness. In *Wearing Culture: Dress and Regalia in Early Mesoamerica and Central America*, edited by Heather Orr and Matthew G. Looper, pp. 145-205. University of Colorado Press, Boulder.

CLARK, JOHN E., AND RICHARD D. HANSEN

2001 The Architecture of Early Kingship: Comparative Perspectives on the Origins of the Maya Royal Court. In *The Maya Royal Court*, edited by Takeshi Inomata and Stephen D. Houston, pp. 1-45. Westview Press, Boulder.

CLARK, JOHN E., RICHARD D. HANSEN, AND TOMÁS PÉREZ SUÁREZ

2000 La zona maya en el Preclásico. In *Historia antigua de México, Vol 1: El México antiguo, sus áreas culturales, los orígenes y el horizonte Preclásico*, 2nd ed., edited by Linda Manzanilla and Leonardo López Luján, pp. 437-510. UNAM, Mexico.

CLARK, JOHN E., AND THOMAS A. LEE JR.

1980 Patrones de comercio en la cuenca del Grijalva, Chiapas. In *Rutas de intercambio en Mesoamérica y el norte de México*, pp. 339-344. XVI Reunión de Mesa Redonda, September 1979, Saltillo.

1984 Formative Obsidian Exchange and the Emergence of Public Economies in Chiapas, Mexico. In *Trade and Exchange in Early Mesoamerica*, pp. 235-274, edited by Kenn Hirth. University of New Mexico Press, Albuquerque.

1990 Intercambio de obsidiana y las primeras economías públicas en Chiapas, México. In *Nuevos enfoques en el estudio de la lítica*, edited by Dolores Soto de Arechavaleta, pp. 347-404. UNAM, Mexico.

2007 The Changing Role of Obsidian Exchange in Central Chiapas. In *Archaeology, Art, and Ethnogenesis in Mesoamerican Prehistory: Papers in Honor of Gareth W. Lowe*, edited by Lynneth S. Lowe and Mary E. Pye, pp., 109-159. Papers of the New World Archaeological Foundation, No. 68. BYU, Provo.

2013    *Minor Excavations in Lower Izapa*. Papers of the New World Archaeological Foundation, No. 75. BYU, Provo.

CLARK, JOHN E., AND GARETH W. LOWE
2013    Izapa History. In *Middle and Late Preclassic Izapa: Ceramic Complexes and History*, by Gareth W. Lowe, Sussana M. Ekholm, and John E. Clark. Papers of the New World Archaeological Foundation, No. 73. BYU, Provo.

CLARK, JOHN E. Y TOMÁS PÉREZ SUÁREZ
1994    Los olmecas y el primer milenio de Mesoamérica. In *Los olmecas en Mesoamérica*, edited by John E. Clark, pp. 261-275. El Equilibrista and Turner Libros, Mexico and Madrid.

CLARK, JOHN E., AND MARY E. PYE
2000    The Pacific Coast and the Olmec Problem. In *Olmec Art and Archaeology in Mesoamerica*, edited by John E. Clark and Mary E. Pye, pp. 217-251. Studies in the History of Art 58. National Gallery of Art, Washington, DC.

2011    Re-visiting the Mixe-Zoque: A Brief History of the Preclassic Peoples of Chiapas. In *The Southern Maya in the Late Preclassic: The Rise and Fall of an Early Mesoamerican Civilization*, edited by Michael Love and Jonathan Kaplan, pp. 25-45, University Press of Colorado, Boulder.

COE, MICHAEL D.
2005    *The Maya*, 7th ed. Thames and Hudson, London.

COE, WILLIAM R.
1959    *Piedras Negras Archaeology: Artifacts, Caches, and Burials*. Museum Monographs, University of Pennsylvania, Philadelphia.

COLMAN, ARLENE
2010    *The Construction of Complex A at La Venta, Tabasco, Mexico: A History of Buildings, Burials, Offerings, and Stone Monuments*. Unpublished Master's Thesis, Department of Anthropology, Brigham Young University, Provo.

CON URIBE, MARÍA JOSÉ
1976    Síntesis de los trabajos realizados en el salvamento arqueológico de la presa de la Angostura, Chiapas. *Las fronteras de Mesoamérica: XIV Mesa Redonda de la Sociedad Mexicana de Antropología*, pp. 173-180. Honduras.

CYPHERS, ANN
1984    The Possible Role of Women in Formative Exchange. In *Trade and Exchange in Early Mesoamerica*, edited by Kenn Hirth, pp. 115-123. University of New Mexico Press, Albuquerque.

DELGADO, AGUSTÍN
1965    *Excavations at Santa Rosa, Chiapas, Mexico*. Papers of the New World Archaeological Foundation, No. 17. BYU, Provo.

DÍAZ DEL CASTILLO, BERNAL
1968    *Historia verdadera de la conquista de la Nueva España*, 6th ed. Editorial Porrúa, Mexico.

DEMAREST, ARTHUR A.
2011    The Political, Economic, and Cultural Correlates of Late Preclassic Southern Highland Material Culture: Evidence, Analyses, and Controversies. In *The Southern Maya in the Late Preclassic: The Rise and Fall of an Early Mesoamerican Civilization*, edited by Michael Love and Jonathan Kaplan, pp. 345-386. University Press of Colorado, Boulder.

DIXON, KEITH A.
1959    *Ceramics from Two Preclassic Periods at Chiapa de Corzo, Chiapas, Mexico*. Papers of the New World Archaeological Foundation, No. 5. BYU, Provo.

DORN, HAROLD
1962    World Population Growth: An

International Dilemma. *Science*, Vol. 125:283-290.

DRUCKER, PHILIP
1952    *La Venta, Tabasco: A Study of Olmec Ceramics and Art.* Bureau of American Ethnology Bulletin 153, Smithsonian Institution, Washington, DC.

DRUCKER, PHILIP, ROBERT F. HEIZER, AND ROBERT J. SQUIER
1959    *Excavations at La Venta Tabasco, 1955.* Bureau of American Ethnology Bulletin 170, Smithsonian Institution, Washington, DC.

EKHOLM, SUSANNA.
1969    *Mound 30a and the Early Preclassic Sequence of Izapa, Chiapas, Mexico.* Papers of the New World Archaeological Foundation, No. 25. BYU, Provo.

1989    Las figurillas preclásicas cerámicas de Izapa, Chiapas: Tradición mixe-zoque. In *Preclasico o Formativo: Avances y perspectivas*, coordinated by Martha Carmona Macias, pp. 333-352. Museo Nacional de Antropología, Mexico.

GLASER, KAREL H.
1998    Les olmèques: L'Èlosion des chefs-d'oeuvre. In *Mexique, terre des dieux: Trésors de l'art précolombien, Musée Rath.* Département des Affaires Culturelles, Musées d'arte d'histoire Geneve, Geneva.

GLAUNER, DARLENE, SUZANNE HERMAN, AND JOHN E. CLARK
in press    *The Archaeological Salvage of Mound 15, Chiapa de Corzo, Chiapas, Mexico.* Papers of the New World Archaeological Foundation, No. 81. BYU, Provo.

GÓMEZ RUEDA, HERNANDO
1995    Exploración de sistemas hidráulicos en Izapa. In *VIII Simposio de Investigaciones Arqueológicas en Guatemala, 1994*, pp. 9-18. Ministerio de Cultura y Deportes, INAH, Asociación Tikal, Guatemala.

1996a    Izapa: organización espacial de un centro del Formativo en la costa Pacífica de Chiapas. *IX Simposio de Investigaciones Arqueológicas en Guatemala, 1995*, pp. 549-563. Asociación Tikal, Guatemala.

1996b    *Las Limas, Veracruz, y otros asentamientos prehispánicos de la región olmeca.* INAH, Mexico.

GONZÁLEZ, ARNOLDO, AND MARTHA CUEVAS
1998    *Canto versus canto: Manufactura de artefactos líticos en Chiapa de Corzo, Chiapas.* INAH, Mexico.

GONZÁLEZ LAUCK, REBECCA
1988    Proyecto arqueológico La Venta. *Arqueología* 4:121-165.

1995    La Venta: Una Gran Ciudad Olmeca. *Arqueologia Mexicana* 2(12):38-42.

1996    La Venta: an Olmec capital. In *Olmec Art of Ancient Mexico*, edited by Elizabeth P. Benson and Beatriz de la Fuente, pp. 73-81.Washington DC, National Gallery of Art.

1997    Acerca de pirámides de tierra y seres sobrenaturales: observaciones preliminares en torno al Edificio C-1, La Venta, Tabasco. *Arqueología, segunda época* 17:79-97.

2004    Observaciones en Torno a los Contextos de la Escultura Olmeca en La Venta. In *Acercarse y Mirar: Homenaje a Beatriz de la Fuente*, edited by María Teresa Uriarte and Leticia Staines Cicero, pp. 75-106. Instituto de Investigaciones Estéticas, UNAM, Mexico City.

2006    La Venta. In *Olmecas, Mayas y Otras Culturas: Tabasco y la Zona Arqueológica de Palenque.* CONACULTA, INAH, Mexico.

2010a    Pre-Olmec and Olmec Architecture. In *Pre-Columbian Architecture in Mesoamerica*, edited by M. T. Uriarte, pp. 71-82. Abbeville Press Publishers and INAH, New York.

2010b    The Architectural setting of Olmec Sculpture Clusters at La Venta,

Tabasco. In *The Place of Stone Monuments: Context, Use, and Meaning in Mesoamerica's Preclassic Transition*, edited by Julia Guernsey, John E. Clark, and Barbara Arroyo, pp. 129-148. Dumbarton Oaks, Washington DC.

GROVE, DAVID C.
1984    *Chalcatzingo: Excavations on the Olmec Frontier*. Thames and Hudson, London.

1989    Chalcatzingo and its Olmec Connection. In *Regional Perspectives on the Olmec*, edited by Robert J. Sharer and David C. Grove, pp. 122-147. Cambridge: Cambridge University Press.

1999    Public Monuments and Sacred Mountains: Observations on Three Formative Period Sacred Landscapes. In *Social Patterns in Preclassic Mesoamerica*, edited by David C. Grove and Rosemary Joyce, pp. 255-290. Dumbarton Oaks, Washington, DC.

GUSSINYER, JORDI
1972    Rescate arqueológico en la presa de la Angostura (primera temporada). *Boletín de la Instituto Nacional de Antropología e Historia*, Epoch II(1):3-14.

HATCH, MARION POPENOE DE
1971    An Hypothesis on Olmec Astronomy, with special Reference to the La Venta Site. In *Papers on Olmec and Maya Archaeology*, pp. 1-64. Contributions of the University of California Archaeological Research Facility, University of California, Berkeley.

HEIZER, ROBERT F.
1968    New Observations on La Venta. In *Dumbarton Oaks Conference on the Olmec*, edited by Elizabeth P. Benson, pp. 9-40. Dumbarton Oaks, Washington DC.

HEIZER, ROBERT F., JOHN A. GRAHAM, AND LEWIS K. NAPTON
1968    The 1968 Excavations at La Venta. *Contributions of the University of California Archaeological Research Facility* No. 5:127-154. Berkeley.

HICKS, FREDERICK, AND CHARLES E. ROZAIRE
1960    *Mound 13, Chiapa de Corzo, Chiapas, Mexico*. Papers of the New World Archaeological Foundation, No. 10. BYU, Provo.

INOMATA, TAKESHI, RAÚL ORTIZ, BARBARA ARROYO, AND EUGENIA J. ROBINSON
2014    Chronological Revision of Preclassic Kaminaljuyú, Guatemala: Implications for Social Processes in the Southern Maya Area. *Latin American Antiquity* 25:377-408.

INOMATA, TAKESHI, DANIELA TRIADAN, KAZUO AOYAMA, VICTOR CASTILLO, AND HITOSHI YONENOBU
2013    Early Ceremonial Constructions at Ceibal, Guatemala, and the Origins of Lowland Maya Civilization. *Science* 340:467-471.

KAUFMAN, TERRENCE
1994a   The Native Languages of Meso-America: General Comments. In *Atlas of the World's Languages*, edited by Christopher Moseley and R. E. Asher, pp. 31-33. Routledge, London.

1994b   The Native Languages of Meso-America. In *Atlas of the World's Languages*, edited by Christopher Moseley and R. E. Asher, pp. 34-45. Routledge, London.

KAUFMAN, TERRENCE AND JOHN JUSTESON
2007    The History of the Word for Cacao in Ancient Mesoamerica. *Ancient Mesoamerica* 18:193-237.

KILLION, THOMAS W. AND JAVIER URCID
2001    The Olmec Leagcy: Cultural Continuity and Change in Mexico's Southern Gulf Coast Lowlands. *Journal of Field Archaeology* 28:3-25.

LEE THOMAS A.

1969a    Archaeological Salvage at Chiapa de
         Corzo, Chiapas, Mexico. Preliminary
         Report submitted to the Instituto
         Nacional de Antropología y Historia,
         Mexico.

1969b    Salvamento Arqueológico en Chiapa de
         Corzo. *Boletín* INAH 38 (dic.):17-22.

1969c    *The Artifacts of Chiapa de Corzo,
         Chiapas, Mexico.* Papers of the New
         World Archaeological Foundation, No.
         26. BYU, Provo.

1974a    *Mound 4 Excavations at San Isidro,
         Chiapas, Mexico.* Papers of the New
         World Archaeological Foundation, No.
         34. BYU, Provo.

1974b    The Middle Grijalva Chronology and
         Ceramic Relationships: A Preliminary
         Report. In *Mesoamerican Archaeology:
         New Approaches*, edited by N.
         Hammond, pp. 1-20. University of
         Texas Press, Austin.

1989     Chiapas and the Olmec. In *Regional
         Perspectives on the Olmec*, edited by
         R. J. Sharer and D. C. Grove,
         pp. 198-226. Cambridge University
         Press, Cambridge.

LEE THOMAS A., JR., CARLOS NAVARRETE, AND
JOHN E. CLARK, (EDITORS)

2015     *Reconnaissance and Excavations
         in the Malpaso Basin, Chiapas,
         Mexico.* Papers of the New World
         Archaeological Foundation, No. 78.
         BYU, Provo.

LOWE, GARETH W.

1959a    *Archaeological Exploration of the
         Upper Grijalva River, Chiapas,
         Mexico.* Papers of the New World
         Archaeological Foundation No. 2,
         Orinda.

1959b    *The Chiapas Project 1955-1958.* Papers
         of the New World Archaeological
         Foundation No. 1, Orinda.

1960a    Brief Archaeological History of the
         Southwest Quadrant. In *Mound 1,
         Chiapa de Corzo, Chiapas, Mexico*, by
         Gareth W. Lowe and Pierre Agrinier,
         pp. 7-12. Papers of the New World
         Archaeological Foundation, No. 8.
         BYU Provo.

1960b    The Mound 1 Caches. In *Mound 1,
         Chiapa de Corzo, Chiapas, Mexico*, by
         Gareth W. Lowe and Pierre Agrinier,
         pp. 55-66. Papers of the New World
         Archaeological Foundation, No. 8.
         BYU, Provo.

1962a    Algunos resultados de la Temporada
         1961 en Chiapa de Corzo, Chiapas.
         *Estudios de Cultura Maya* 2:185-196.

1962b    *Mound 5 and Minor Excavations,
         Chiapa de Corzo, Chiapas,
         Mexico.* Papers of the New World
         Archaeological Foundation, No. 12.
         BYU, Provo.

1964     Burial Customs at Chiapa de Corzo. In
         *The Archaeological Burials at Chiapa
         de Corzo and Their Furniture*, by
         Pierre Agrinier, pp. 65-75. Papers of the
         New World Archaeological Foundation,
         No. 16. BYU, Provo.

1967     Current Research, Eastern
         Mesoamerica. *American Antiquity*
         32:135-141.

1972     Quarterly Report to the NWAF Board
         of Directors, November. Manuscript on
         file at the HBL Library, BYU.

1977     The Mixe-Zoque as Competing
         Neighbors of the Early Lowland Maya.
         In *The Origins of Maya Civilization*,
         edited by R. E. W. Adams, pp. 197-
         248. University of New Mexico Press,
         Albuquerque.

1978     Eastern Mesoamerica. In *Chronologies
         in New World Archaeology*, edited by
         R. E. Taylor and Clement W. Meighan,
         pp. 331-393. Academic Press, New
         York.

1981     Olmec Horizons Defined in Mound 20,
         San Isidro, Chiapas. In *The Olmec and
         Their Neighbors*, edited by Elizabeth
         Benson, pp. 231-255. Dumbarton Oaks,
         Washington, DC.

1982 Izapa Religion and Ritual. In *Izapa: An Introduction to the Ruins and Monuments*, by Gareth W. Lowe, Thomas A. Lee Jr., and Eduardo Martinez, pp. 268-305. Papers of the New World Archaeological Foundation, No. 31. BYU, Provo.

1989a Algunas aclaraciones sobre la presencia olmeca y maya en el Preclásico de Chiapas. In *Preclasico o Formativo: Avances y Perspectivas,* coordinated by Martha Carmona Macias, pp. 363-84. Museo Nacional de Antropología, Mexico.

1989b The Heartland Olmec: Evolution of Material Culture. In *Regional Perspectives on the Olmec*, edited by Robert J. Sharer and David C. Grove, pp. 33-67. Cambridge University Press, Cambridge.

1991 Buscando una cultura olmeca en Chiapas. *Primer Foro de Arqueología de Chiapas*, pp. 111-130. Gobierno del Estado de Chiapas and Instituto Chiapaneco de la Cultura, Tuxtla Gutiérrez.

1995 Presencia maya en la cerámica del Preclásico Tardío en Chiapa de Corzo. In *Memorias del Segundo Congreso Internacional de Mayistas*, pp. 321-341. UNAM, Mexico.

1998a *Los olmecas de San Isidro en Malpaso,* Chiapas. INAH, Mexico.

1998b *Mesoamérica olmeca: Diez preguntas.* INAH, Mexico.

1999 *Los zoques antiguos de San Isidro.* Consejo Estatal para la Cultura y las Artes de Chiapas, Tuxtla Gutiérrez.

2007 Early Formative Chiapas: The Beginnings of Civilization in the Central Depression of Chiapas. In *Archaeology, Art, and Ethnogenesis in Mesoamerican Prehistory: Papers in Honor of Gareth W. Lowe*, edited by Lynneth S. Lowe and Mary E. Pye, pp. 63-108. Papers of the New World Archaeological Foundation, No. 68. BYU, Provo.

LOWE, GARETH W., AND PIERRE AGRINIER
1960 *Mound 1, Chiapa de Corzo, Chiapas, Mexico.* Papers of the New World Archaeological Foundation, No. 8. BYU, Provo.

LOWE, GARETH W., SUSANNA M. EKHOM, AND JOHN E. CLARK
2013 *Middle and Late Preclassic Izapa: Ceramic Complexes and History.* Papers of the New World Archaeological Foundation, No. 73. BYU, Provo.

LOWE, GARETH W., THOMAS A. LEE JR., AND EDUARDO MARTINEZ ESPINOSA
1982 *Izapa: An Introduction to the Ruins and Monuments.* Papers of the New World Archaeological Foundation, No. 31. BYU, Provo.

LOWE, GARETH W., AND J. ALDEN MASON
1965 Archaeological Survey on the Chiapas Coast, Highlands, and Upper Grijalva Basin. In *Handbook of Middle American Indians*, Vol. 2, edited by G. R. Willey, p. 195-236. University of Texas Press, Austin.Martínez Donjuán, Guadalupe

MARTÍNEZ DONJUÁN, GUADALUPE
1994 Los olmecas en el estado de Guerrero. In *Los olmecas en Mesoamérica*, edited by John E. Clark, pp. 143-163. Citibank, Mexico.

MARTÍNEZ ESPINOSA, EDUARDO
1959 Una nueva escultura olmeca de Tonalá, Chiapas. *Instituto de Ciencias y Artes de Chiapas* 3:79-81.

MARTÍNEZ ESPINOSA, EDUARDO, AND GARETH W. LOWE
in press *Montículo 32, Chiapa de Corzo, Chiapas: Su salvamento y consolidación.* Papers of the New World Archaeological Foundation. BYU, Provo.

MARTÍNEZ MURIEL, ALEJANDRO, AND CARLOS NAVARRETE
1978 El salvamento arqueológico en el

estado de Chiapas. *Revista Mexicana de Estudios Antropológicas* 24(3):229-255.

MASON, J. ALDEN
1960a *Mound 12, Chiapa de Corzo, Chiapas, Mexico.* Papers of the New World Archaeological Foundation, No. 9. BYU, Provo.

1960b *The Terrace to North of Mound 13, Chiapa de Corzo, Chiapas, Mexico.* Papers of the New World Archaeological Foundation, No. 11. BYU, Provo.

McANANY, PATRICIA A.
1995 *Living with the Ancestors: Kinship and Kingship in Ancient Maya Society.* University of Texas Press, Austin.

McDONALD, ANDREW J.
1974 Middle Preclassic Ceremonial Centers in Southern Chiapas. Paper presented at the 41st International Congress of Americanists, Mexico.

1977 Two Middle Preclassic Engraved Monuments at Tzutzuculi on the Chiapas Coast of Mexico. *American Antiquity* 42:560-566.

1983 *Tzutzuculi: A Middle-Preclassic Site on the Pacific Coast of Chiapas, Mexico.* Papers of the New World Archaeological Foundation, No. 47. BYU, Provo.

1999 *Middle Formative Pyramidal Platform Complexes in Southern Chiapas, Mexico: Structure and Meaning.* Unpublished Ph. D. dissertation, Department of Anthropology, The University of Texas at Austin.

MILLER, DON E.
2014 *Excavations at La Libertad, A Middle Formative Ceremonial Center in Chiapas, Mexico.* Papers of the New World Archaeological Foundation, No. 64. BYU, Provo.

MILLER, DON E., DOUGLAS DONNE BRYANT, JOHN E. CLARK, AND GARETH W. LOWE
2005 Middle Preclassic Ceramics. In *Ceramic Sequence of the Upper Grijalva Region, Chiapas, Mexico, Part 1.* edited by Douglas D. Bryant, John E. Clark, and David Cheetham, pp. 141-264. Papers of the New World Archaeological Foundation, No. 67. BYU, Provo.

NAVARRETE, CARLOS
1959 *Explorations at San Agustin, Chiapas, Mexico.* Papers of the New World Archaeological Foundation, No. 3. Orinda.

1966 *The Chiapanec History and Culture.* Papers of the New World Archaeological Foundation, No. 21. BYU, Provo.

NELSON, FRED W., JR., AND JOHN E. CLARK
1998 Obsidian Production and Exchange in Eastern Mesoamerica. In *Rutas de intercambio en Mesoamérica: III Coloquio Pedro Bosch Gimpera,* edited by Evelyn C. Rattray, pp. 277-333. UNAM, Mexico.

PAILLÉS, H., MARICRUZ.
1980 *Pampa El Pajón: An Early Middle Preclassic Site on the Coast of Chiapas, Mexico.* Papers of the New World Archaeological Foundation, No. 44. BYU, Provo.

PETERSON, FREDRICK A.
1963 *Some Ceramics from Mirador, Chiapas, Mexico.* Papers of the New World Archaeological Foundation, No. 15. BYU, Provo.

POOL, CHRISTOPHER A.
2003 Centers and Peripheries: Urbanization and Political Economy at Tres Zapotes. In *Settlement Archaeology and Political Economy at Tres Zapotes, Veracruz, Mexico,* edited by Christopher A. Pool, pp. 90-98. Costen Institute of Archaeology, University of California, Los Angeles.

2007    *Olmec Archaeology and Early Mesoamerica*. Cambridge University Press, Cambridge.

2010    Stone Monuments and Earthen Mounds: Polity and Placemaking at Tres Zapotes, Veracruz, Mexico. In *The Place of Stone Monuments: Context, Use, and Meaning in Mesoamerica's Preclassic Transition*, edited by Julia Guernsey, John E. Clark, and Barbara Arroyo, pp. 97-127. Dumbarton Oaks, Washington, DC.

PYE, MARY E., AND JOHN E. CLARK
2006    Los olmecas son mixe-zoques: Contribuciones de Gareth W. Lowe a la arqueología del Formativo. *Presencia zoque: Una aproximación multidisciplinaria*, edited by Dolores Aramoni, Thomas A. Lee and Miguel Lisbona, pp. 207-222. UNICACH, Tuxtla Gutiérrez.

REILLY, F. KENT, III
1990    Cosmos and Rulership: The Function of Olmec-Style Symbols in Formative Period Mesoamerica. *Visible Language* 24(1):12-37.

RICKETSON, OLIVER G., JR.
1928a   Astronomical Observations in the Maya area. *Geographic Review* 18(2):215-225.

1928b   Notes on Two Maya Astronomic Observatories. *American Anthropologist* 30:425-445.

1930    The Excavations at Uaxactun. *Proceedings of the Twenty-third International Congress of Americanists*, September 17-22, 1928, New York.

ROMERO, JAVIER
1970    Dental Mutilation, Trephination and Cranial Deformation. In *Handbook of Middle American Indians*, Vol. 9. University of Texas Press, Austin.

ROSENSWIG, ROBERT M., RICARDO LÓPEZ-TORRIJOS, CAROLINE E. ANTONELLI, AND REBECCA R. MENDELSOHN
2013    LIDAR Mapping and Surface Survey of the Izapa State on the Tropical Piedmont of Chiapas, Mexico. *Journal of Archaeological Science* 40:1493-1507.

RUPPERT, KARL
1940    A Special Assemblage of Maya Structures. In *The Maya and Their Neighbors: Essays on Middle American Anthropology and Archaeology*, edited by Clarence L. Hay, Ralph Linton, Samuel Lothrop, Harry L. Shapiro, and George C. Vaillant, pp. 222-231. Dover Publications, Inc., New York.

SHAFER, W., M. HINE AND B. LEVY
1974    *A Textbook on Oral Pathology*, Third Edition. W. B. Saunders, Philadelphia.

SMITH, A. LEDYARD
1950    *Uaxactun, Guatemala: Excavations of 1931-1937*. Publication 588. Carnegie Institution of Washington, Washington DC.

STIRLING, MATTHEW W.
1943    *Stone Monuments of Southern Mexico*. Bureau of American Ethnology Bulletin 138, Smithsonian Institution, Washington, DC.

1968    Three Sandstone Monuments from La Venta Island. *Contributions of the University of California Archaeological Research Facility*, Studies in Mesoamerican Archaeology 5:35-39.

SULLIVAN, TIMOTHY
2009    *The Social and Political Evolution of Chiapa de Corzo: A Regional Analysis of the Development of a Middle Formative through Early Classic Mesoamerican Political Center*. Unpublished Ph. D. dissertation, Department of Anthropology, University of Pittsburgh, Pittsburgh.

2015 Shifting Strategies of Political Authority in the Middle through Terminal Formative Polity of Chiapa de Corzo, Chiapas, Mexico. *Latin American Antiquity* 26(4): 452-472.

TUCKER, TIM M.
1970 *Excavations in Mound III, Chiapa de Corzo, Mexico.* Unpublished MA thesis, Department of Anthropology, Brigham Young University. Provo.

VON NAGY, CHRISTOPHER L.
2003 *Of Meandering Rivers and Shifting Towns: Landscape Evolution and Communities with the Grijalva Delta.* Unpublished Ph. D. dissertation, Department of Anthropology, Tulane University, New Orleans.

WARREN, BRUCE W.
1959 New Discoveries in Chiapas, Southern Mexico. *Archaeology* 12:98-105.

1961a A Chiapa de Corzo Sherd Report. *Katunob* 2(1):14-17. Fayetteville.

1961b The Archaeological Sequence at Chiapa de Corzo. In *Los mayas del sur y sus relaciones con los nahuas meridionales*, VIII Mesa Redonda de la Sociedad Mexicana de Antropología, pp. 75-83. San Cristóbal de las Casas.

1978 *The Sociocultural Development of the Central Depression of Chiapas, Mexico: Preliminary Considerations.* Unpublished Ph. D. dissertation, Department of Anthropology, University of Arizona.

WEDEL, WALDO R.
1952 Structural Investigations in 1943. In *La Venta, Tabasco: A Study of Olmec Ceramics and Art,* edited by Philip Drucker, pp. 34-79. Bureau of American Ethnology Bulletin 153. Smithsonian Institution, Washington, DC.

WEIANT, C. W.
1943 *An Introduction to the Ceramics of Tres Zapotes, Veracruz, Mexico.* Bureau of American Ethnology, Bulletin 139, Smithsonian Institution, Washington DC.

WILLEY, GORDON R., GORDON F. EKHOM, AND RENE MILLON.
1964 The Patterns of Farming Life and Civilization. In *Handbook of Middle American Indians*, edited by Robert Wauchope, vol. 1, pp. 446-498. University of Texas Press, Austin.